Heidegger, Morality and Politics

Heidegger has often been seen as having no moral philosophy, and a political philosophy that can only support fascism. Sonia Sikka's book challenges this view, arguing instead that Heidegger should be considered a qualified moral realist, and that his insights on cultural identity and cross-cultural interaction are not invalidated by his support for Nazism. Sikka explores the ramifications of Heidegger's moral and political thought for topics including free will and responsibility, the status of humanity within the design of nature, the relationship between the individual and culture, the rights of peoples to political self-determination, the idea of race and the problem of racism, historical relativism, the subjectivity of values, and the nature of justice. Her discussion highlights aspects of Heidegger's thought that are still relevant for modern debates, while also addressing its limitations as reflected in his political affiliations and sympathies.

SONIA SIKKA is Professor of Philosophy at the University of Ottawa. Her publications include *Herder on Humanity and Cultural Difference* (Cambridge, 2011), *Multiculturalism and Religious Identity: Canada and India* (2014), and *Living with Religious Diversity* (2015).

Heidegger, Morality and Politics

Questioning the Shepherd of Being

Sonia Sikka
University of Ottawa

CAMBRIDGE
UNIVERSITY PRESS

University Printing House, Cambridge CB2 8BS, United Kingdom

One Liberty Plaza, 20th Floor, New York, NY 10006, USA

477 Williamstown Road, Port Melbourne, VIC 3207, Australia

314–321, 3rd Floor, Plot 3, Splendor Forum, Jasola District Centre, New Delhi – 110025, India

79 Anson Road, #06-04/06, Singapore 079906

Cambridge University Press is part of the University of Cambridge.

It furthers the University's mission by disseminating knowledge in the pursuit of education, learning, and research at the highest international levels of excellence.

www.cambridge.org
Information on this title: www.cambridge.org/9781108419796
DOI: 10.1017/9781108304207

First published 2018

Printed in the United Kingdom by Clays, St Ives plc

A catalogue record for this publication is available from the British Library.

ISBN 978-1-108-41979-6 Hardback

Contents

Acknowledgments

I thank the Indiana University Press for permission to include in this book a revised version of my essay, "Heidegger and Race," which previously appeared in *Race and Racism in Continental Philosophy*, ed. Robert Bernasconi (Bloomington: Indiana University Press, 2003), 74–97.

Portions of the book also incorporate material from the following articles:

"The Philosophical Bases of Heidegger's Politics," *Journal of the British Society for Phenomenology*, 25 (1994), 241–62.

"Heidegger's Concept of *Volk*," *Philosophical Forum*, 26 (1994), 101–26.

"Heidegger's Appropriation of Schelling," *Southern Journal of Philosophy*, 32 (1994), 421–48.

"Kantian Ethics in *Being and Time*," with response by Tom Rockmore, and reply by author. *Journal of Philosophical Research*, 31 (2006), 309–34.

Note on Citations

For Heidegger's works, references are generally given to both the original German texts and English translations. I have quoted from the indicated English translations, making minor changes occasionally. When no English translation is cited, the translation is my own. Page references for *Being and Time* are to the German edition, which is cross-referenced with the Macquarrie and Robinson translation. In the case of primary texts by other authors, references are usually to English translations alone where these exist, with the exception of Kant's works, cited extensively in Chapter 2, for which both German and English page references are given.

Abbreviations

Works by Heidegger

BPP	*Basic Problems of Phenomenology* (Heidegger 1982)
BT	*Being and Time* (Heidegger 1962c)
BTr	*Being and Truth* (Heidegger 2010)
BW	*Basic Writings* (Heidegger 1993)
CP	*Contributions to Philosophy* (Heidegger 1989)
DT	*Discourse on Thinking* (Heidegger 1966)
EB	*Existence and Being* (Heidegger 1968a)
EGT	*Early Greek Thinking* (1984b)
EHF	*The Essence of Human Freedom* (Heidegger 2002a)
EP	*The End of Philosophy* (Heidegger 1973)
ET	*The Essence of Truth* (Heidegger 2002b)
FCM	*Fundamental Concepts of Metaphysics* (Heidegger 1995)
G	*Gelassenheit* (Heidegger 1959)
GA	*Gesamtausgabe* (Heidegger 1975–)
H	*Hölderlin's Hymnen 'Germanian' und 'Der Rhein'* (GA39)
H:J	*Martin Heidegger/Karl Jaspers: Briefwechsel, 1920–1963* (Heidegger 1990)
IM	*Introduction to Metaphysics* (Heidegger 1987)
L	*Logik: Als die Frage nach dem Wesen der Sprache* (GA 38)
MFL	*Metaphysical Foundations of Logic* (1984a)
NH	*Nachlese zu Heidegger* (Heidegger 1962b)
NHS	*Nature, History, State* (Heidegger 2013)
NI, NII	*Nietzsche: Volumes One and Two* (Heidegger 1996)
OWL	*On the Way to Language* (1971b)
P	*Pathmarks* (Heidegger 1998)
PLT	*Poetry, Language, Thought* (1971a)
QCT	*The Question Concerning Technology and Other Essays* (Heideger 1977)
STF	*Schelling's Treatise on the Essence of Human Freedom* (Heidegger 1985)

SU *Die Selbstbehauptung der Deutschen Universität* (Heidegger 1983b)
TK *Die Technik und die Kehre* (Heidegger 1962a)
VA *Vorträge und Aufsätze* (Heidegger 1954b)
WCT *What is Called Thinking*? (Heidegger 1968)
WhD *Was heißt Denken?* (Heidegger 1984)

Works by Other Authors

Karl Jaspers

FM *The Future of Mankind* (Jaspers 1961)

Immanuel Kant

AA *Kants Werke*, Akademie Ausgabe (Kant 1902-)
CPrR *Critique of Practical Reason* (Kant 1997)
GMM *Groundwork of the Metaphysics of Morals* (Kant 1998)
MM *Metaphysics of Morals* (Kant 1996)
MPV *Metaphysical Principles of Virtue* (Kant 1983a)
PP *Perpetual Peace and Other Essays* (1983b)

Emmanuel Levinas

TI *Totality and Infinity* (Levinas 1969)

Friedrich Nietzsche

GM *The Genealogy of Morals* (Nietzsche 1989)
WP *The Will to Power* (Nietzsche 1967)

F. W. J. Schelling

F *Philosophische Untersuchungen über das Wesen der menschlichen Freiheit* (Schelling 1860)
SW *Friedrich Wilhelm Joseph vom Schellings sämmtliche Werke* (Schelling 1856–61)

Introduction

This book offers an exegesis and friendly critique of Martin Heidegger's moral and political philosophy, interpreted on the basis of his metaphysics. Most scholars, I realize, view Heidegger as a thinker who proposed no moral or political philosophy, and who held no metaphysical position on which any such philosophy could be grounded. Support can be found for this view in Heidegger's writings, where he problematizes such concepts as "morality" and "politics," and claims to be attempting an "overcoming" of metaphysics in favor of a different mode of thinking. Nonetheless, I believe and will seek to demonstrate that Heidegger's relation to the philosophical tradition he allegedly overcomes involves less of a radical break than is often supposed, and that he is still grappling with recognizable issues within moral and political philosophy.

These issues include: free will and responsibility; the place of humanity within the design of nature; the subjectivity of values and the nature of justice; cultural, national, and racial identity; historical relativism; and the status of reason, public and private. Certainly, Heidegger's engagement with such issues does not result in his developing a moral and political philosophy of the sort one finds in the writings of thinkers such as Aristotle or Kant, and it would seem that his primary focus is on ontology rather than ethics. Heidegger's reflections are not explicitly normative, and his guiding question concerns the meaning of being rather than what is good or right. Richard Velkley therefore claims that, for Heidegger, furthering the renewal of this question "takes precedence over any considerations of the good, the moral, and the just, as these have been understood in the philosophic tradition as having some universal articulation, reflecting ends (happiness, perfection, virtue) inherent in human nature or reason" (Velkley 2011, 93). I will suggest in the following pages, however, that such judgments about Heidegger's privileging of ontology over ethics misconstrue his attempt to retrieve an original understanding of being that precedes its bifurcation into the "is" and the "ought," into fact and value. An implication of my analysis is that, for Heidegger, questions of truth are not separate from questions of right and wrong, in the normative sense of these terms, since being and goodness are intimately intertwined. Heidegger's descriptions *are* normative, for on his analysis an appropriate understanding of how things "are" necessarily includes reference to the good.

At the same time, an essential element in Heidegger's understanding of how things are is that they are constantly changing. Heidegger's critique of substance ontology and his insistence on the temporality of being carry the consequence that there are no eternal forms to be grasped, and that all thinking is in time. If "metaphysics" is defined as the quest for a permanent and stable rational foundation for knowing and acting, then Heidegger not only has no metaphysics himself but undermines its possibility. This consideration has led interpreters to label his thinking as postmodern or postmetaphysical, and some to worry that it entails historicism, relativism, or irrationalism. Appropriating Heidegger positively, Leslie Thiele writes that for Heidegger "thinking is necessarily open-ended" (Thiele 1995a, 96), and "philosophy is a decidedly lawless endeavor" (101). Thiele supports this judgment by citing Heidegger's remark, made in a posthumously published interview, that "in the domain of thinking, there are no authoritative statements ... The only measure for thought comes from the thing itself to be thought."[1] Similar observations lead to Reiner Schürmann's description of Heidegger's thinking as "anarchic," in the literal sense of lacking an *arche* or fundamental principle on which being and acting are grounded (Schürmann 1987, 1), and to Werner Marx's searching in Heidegger's thought for a "measure on earth" that could serve as a foundation for a "nonmetaphysical ethics" (Marx 1987, 4).

Against these and other readings of Heidegger as a "postmetaphysical" thinker, I contend that he is so only in a highly particular sense involving a narrow understanding of "metaphysics." In a broader sense, where the term indicates judgments about the relation between humanity and being (what the Western philosophical tradition has sometimes termed "reality," though this is a term Heidegger questions), Heidegger is better understood as espousing and providing cogent arguments to support a particular metaphysical position. This is a qualified realist position, and my analysis will challenge readings of Heidegger as an anti-realist (Braver 2007, 2014). Getting this issue right is essential to understanding Heidegger's positions on moral and political subjects, which constitute a "philosophy" not in a postmodern but remarkably ancient sense: a conception of the nature of things and of humanity's place among them. Determining the sense in which Heidegger is a realist is crucial to assessing whether he counts as a cultural or historical relativist, a judgment with serious repercussions for his position on goodness and justice. Likewise, Heidegger's understanding of the status of humanity within nature affects the normative implications of his thought for our treatment of both human and

[1] The remark is from Heidegger's interview in *Der Spiegel*; cited Thiele 1995a, 101.

nonhuman individuals. I argue that Heidegger's recognition of the limitations on what is in fact thinkable in a particular age and culture does not commit him to historical or cultural relativism, if that means we have no access to truth. This argument requires some clarification of his metaphysical – or if one prefers, ontological – standpoint, which might be best described as a form of dynamic monism.[2]

It also requires attention to the thought of Heidegger's philosophical antecedents. There exists a wealth of scholarly literature on Heidegger's readings of past philosophers as evidenced in his explicit engagement with their thought in lectures and published writings (e.g. Schalow 1992, 2013; Pöggeler 1993; Kisiel 1993; van Buren 1994; Boer 2000; Brogan 2005; Gonzalez 2009). Less thoroughly recognized and examined are Heidegger's largely unacknowledged adaptations of his sources of influence in the formulation of his own positions, particularly in relation to his moral and political thought. There are, for example, strong similarities between Heidegger's and Herder's understandings of culture, although he rarely discusses Herder except in a rather uninspired lecture course (GA 85). There are also intriguing parallels between Heidegger's dismantling of the fact/value distinction, and Plato's conception of the idea of the good. And Heidegger's sense of what we owe to others creatively adapts ideas of justice as inscribed within nature among pre-Socratic thinkers. From a modern perspective, the latter are likely to be judged as involving an anthropomorphization of nature, but Heidegger challenges precisely this genre of judgment. In light of such parallels, I would question Fred Dallmayr's reading of Heidegger "chiefly as a nontraditional or postmetaphysical philosopher of 'freedom,' including political freedom" as well as "a philosopher of human solidarity," and thus "as the oblique heir of at least two enlightenment maxims: liberty and fraternity" (Dallmayr 1984, 207). In my view, Heidegger is better understood as a counter-Enlightenment thinker, where this does not mean, however, that he is an irrationalist or dogmatic traditionalist, as some of his critics have alleged (Wolin 1990; Philipse 1998).

I do, on the other hand, agree strongly with Dallmayr's contention that "the episode of 1933 holds the key neither to Heidegger's philosophical opus nor to 'the problem of the political' in his thought," and that "the latter problem really can be decoded only via a close interpretation of the general philosophical work" (Dallmayr 1984, 3). Heidegger's commitment to Nazism has cast a long and very dark shadow over the entirety of his corpus, especially in relation to moral and political matters. Yet it is odd that, although the basic facts of

[2] I prefer this term to John Cooper's description of Heidegger as a "dynamic panentheist," which assumes, without having demonstrated, an identity between "being" and "God" (Cooper 2006, 216). I explore the relation between these terms in "Heidegger's Argument for the Existence of God?" (Sikka 2016).

Heidegger's membership in the Nazi party and his public support of Hitler in 1933 have never been hidden, these same facts have repeatedly been presented over the past few decades as if they were a new discovery warranting a complete reappraisal of his thought. The first episode in this repetitive tale occurred in the 1980s with the publication of Victor Farias's *Heidegger et le nazisme* (1987). Already at that time, Gadamer expressed surprise at the uproar provoked in France by Farias's book, pointing out that "almost all of what Farias reveals has long been known" (Gadamer 1988, 176). Still, Farias's book, along with Hugo Ott's *Heidegger: Unterwegs zu seiner Biographie* (1987), claimed to provide evidence that Heidegger's commitment to National Socialism was stronger and deeper than those who had judged his thought in a positive light and incorporated it into their own had realized. In line with such findings, Lacoue-Labarthe argued in *La fiction du politique: Heidegger, l'art et la politique* (1987) that is was no longer possible to dismiss the issue by assuming that Heidegger's political commitment had been accidental.[3] Analyses like Richard Wolin's *The Politics of Being* (1990) addressed the relation between Heidegger's politics and his philosophy, claiming to establish an intrinsic connection between these on a number of significant points.

Given the flurry of debate generated by Farias's and Ott's books, one might have expected that the issue would be resolved one way or the other in the few years that followed. Peculiarly, though, the publication in 2005 of Emmanuel Faye's *Heidegger, l'introduction du nazisme dans la philosophie: autour des séminaires inédits de 1933–1935* employed the same gesture of purportedly offering shocking new revelations that would demonstrate once and for all the extent of Heidegger's agreement with Nazism and its deep roots within his philosophy. Again the evidence turned out to be not so decisive after all, generating arguments and counterarguments much like those occasioned by Farias's work. In the latest episode, at the time of writing in 2016, the publication of the so-called "Black Notebooks" has turned out to be déjà vu all over again. A 2014 item in *Slate* magazine can stand for many others. Titled "Heidegger's Hitler Problem Is Worse Than We Thought," its first sentence runs: "The upcoming publication of the Black Notebooks – three never-before-seen volumes by the legendary German philosopher Martin Heidegger – may reveal a direct link between Heidegger's lengthy dalliance with Nazism and his landmark treatise *Being and Time*" (Schuman 2014). Yet since then more than one Heidegger scholar has pointed out how little there is in these notebooks that we did not know before (Farin 2016, 307; Harries 2016, 207).

No doubt there are a number of factors behind the recurrence of this highly polarized debate, but one explanation for its repeated semblance of

[3] See English translation of this work (Lacoue-Labarthe 1990), pp. 17–29.

novelty, I suspect, is that Heidegger's Nazism easily gets forgotten, because the vast majority of his published philosophical works contain no overt sign of fascism or anti-Semitism. It does not follow that the works are unproblematic, or that in interpreting them there is no hermeneutic advantage to knowing about Heidegger's political actions and remarks. Heidegger had serious faults in both his character and his philosophy, and there is certainly a link between the man and his works. There is also considerable room for informed disagreement about the interpretation, as well as the value, of his central claims. However, in assessing Heidegger's contribution to *philosophy*, it is not helpful that the launch of each new Heidegger exposé seems to proceed in ignorance of the substantial existing scholarship on the issue, or dismisses it as apologetics, even though many of its authors are not Heidegger acolytes and do not maintain that his association with Nazism is inconsequential to understanding his philosophical corpus. The rhetoric of Heidegger's most hostile detractors often implies that there is an attempt at cover-up on the part of Heidegger scholars as a whole, or that those who take his philosophy seriously are dangerously unaware of the Nazi ideas hidden within his writings, by which they may become unconsciously infected as by some latent virus.

My aim is to build on existing scholarship in order to highlight what is of continuing value in Heidegger's moral and political philosophy, while addressing at the same time the limitations of his thinking as reflected in his political affiliations and sympathies. With this aim in mind, I have chosen to organize my inquiry according to topics rather than works or chronological periods. In each chapter, I offer a critical explication of Heidegger's position on the topic in question, challenging misinterpretations while acknowledging what is genuinely problematic in his account. As a further step, I also seek to isolate those aspects of Heidegger's thought on a given issue that survive critical analysis, including awareness of the objectionable moral and political implications that he himself drew, and to highlight their positive significance. Heidegger's political acts and sympathies were foolish, as well as morally culpable, but that should not lead us to overlook what is interesting and insightful in, for instance, the phenomenological grounding he provides for the Kantian idea of human beings as ends in themselves, or his subsequent critique of the modern sense of alienation that this very idea entails, and his proposed alternative. Similarly, the blind spots in Heidegger's thinking and personality that made possible his support for Nazism in its early days do not render invalid the resources offered by his rich account of the significance of culture and place in the lives of individuals, and the consequences for a just form of politics. Thus, my approach to Heidegger's thought in this book is itself Heideggerian in its method of engagement with the philosopher I am questioning. It includes critical confrontation and transformative appropriation, relating what is being said in the text to what is being talked about (BT 168), led by an orientation toward what needs to be thought at the moment.

Because this was Heidegger's own approach to thinking, appreciating his revisionary adaptations of philosophical antecedents – the pre-Socratics, Plato, Eckhart, Schelling, Hegel, Kierkegaard, Nietzsche, to name a few – is essential for understanding his initial enthusiasm for National Socialism, as well as the philosophical aftermath of his disillusionment, for it reveals the way he connected philosophical ideas with contemporary events. Much of the scholarship on "Heidegger's Nazism" has been oriented toward his proximate social and political context. Such research enriches our knowledge of Heidegger's milieu, which is naturally relevant to understanding his decisions, personal as well intellectual. It can also be misleading and superficial, however, yielding a one-sided and ultimately false portrait of the movement and foundations of Heidegger's moral and political ideas, while losing what is of lasting philosophical significance in them.[4]

Heidegger actually inhabited two realms, I will suggest, the one a realm of deep reflection in dialogue with his philosophical and theological heritage, the other the realm of concrete events and circumstances. His way of bringing these together was at times prescient, and at other times demonstrated a stunning lack of the *phronesis* he valued in Aristotle and partially emulated in some of his own writings (Bernasconi 1990). In the latter respect, Heidegger's case provides an object lesson in how not to be an engaged philosopher. But his philosophical reflections on the current age also contain an unusual depth, isolating and interrogating fundamental assumptions about knowledge and reality that shape the modern worldview and its way of negotiating questions about how we should be, and how we know how we should be.

I begin this book with an examination of Heidegger's position on human freedom, assessing the twin, and on the face of it contradictory, characterizations of his thought as endorsing decisionism or voluntarism on the one hand, and determinism or fatalism on the other. I argue that Heidegger actually embraces neither. Rather, we find in his writings a consistent and complex analysis of the situated character of human freedom, affirming its existence while exposing its limits, which are at the same time the conditions for its possibility.

While Chapter 1 focuses on the "how" of being moral, I argue in Chapter 2 that the early Heidegger is also committed to a general moral principle, as *Being and Time* provides a phenomenological and ontological basis for one

[4] A case in point is the otherwise highly informative work of Charles Bambach (2003, 2013). Alexander Duff also misses Heidegger's transformative appropriations of authors such as Kant and Hegel, as well as his retrieval of ancient modes of ethical realism (to use an anachronistic descriptor). This leads Duff to conclude, in my view wrongly, that "Heidegger's thought forecloses ethics and in doing so articulates an understanding of human existence that entails profound ethical and political consequences" (Duff 2015, 26).

version of Kant's categorical imperative, namely the formula of humanity stating that a rational being should never be treated merely as a means but always also as an end in itself. Heidegger's later works seem to reverse this judgment, with humanity standing in the service of something that transcends it, a view that also finds some surprising parallels within Kant's moral philosophy and philosophy of history. Although it has some troubling aspects, this idea of humanity as "for" something is proposed as an antidote to a nihilistic vision of our place within the scheme of things. On that vision, which Heidegger thinks forms the dominant worldview of the present age, being has no meaning except in relation to subjective judgments of value, and nature is nothing but raw material for the satisfaction of collective wants in light of these values. Heidegger offers and defends an alternative interpretation of ourselves, one that preserves and may even enhance human dignity.

The next chapter takes up the problem that Heidegger's analytic of Dasein – the entity that I myself am (BT 53) – in *Being and Time* leaves uncertain the status of animals. They neither conform to the structure of "care," the term Heidegger uses to describe Dasein's self-interested but also necessarily self-reflexive character, nor are they merely tools or objects. Heidegger's later works seem to stress a greater continuity of human beings with the rest of nature in some respects, and have therefore been taken up in a positive way within environmental ethics. Humanity retains a special status in these later writings, though, and the question of where animals and nonliving entities stand in relation to this status needs further examination. I argue that one of the implications of the very Kantian account of Dasein in *Being and Time* could be the exclusion of nonhuman sentient beings from moral concern altogether, but that Heidegger's explicit uncertainty about the character of animals – which we understand, he suggests, through modifying our understanding of our own being – also leaves room for reaching a different conclusion. Animals may not possess the full structure of Dasein as "care," to which "liberating solicitude," Heidegger's version of the Kantian notion of respect, is the appropriate response. But there is nonetheless a sense in which their being is an issue for them, too, and in which they also "project" themselves forward into the future while registering what may befall them. These features of the being of animals mean that they cannot appropriately be treated as tools or objects. Furthermore, Heidegger's later works, in which the special status of humanity consists in its being able to discern the design of things, and to take up an appropriate place within that design, can be developed as a form of environmental philosophy that sees human beings as privileged *precisely because* they are able to take care of other beings, whether sentient or nonsentient, in their relations to one another, and are responsible for doing so.

Chapter 4 examines Heidegger's adaptation of Plato's idea of the good, and of pre-Socratic writings that speak of justice, arguing that ideas gleaned from these sources inform Heidegger's historically dynamic but nonetheless ultimately realist conception of goodness and justice. To some, this will seem an unexpected reading of Heidegger, who does not propose a theory of "objective values" or of "justice." Yet a close analysis of a number of Heidegger's works reveals a repeated attempt to retrieve an ancient manner of understanding the way of things that can form the basis for a theory of natural justice. Such a retrieval might strike modern sensibilities as naïve and unscientific in its understanding of the world, but again Heidegger questions fundamental modern assumptions about the nature of nature, according to which it could not possibly contain ends, purposes, or prescriptions.

In the first part of Chapter 5, I examine the view of nations and peoples expressed in Heidegger's directly political speeches and lectures, against the background of the German line of thinking about *Volk* that includes Herder, Fichte, and Schleiermacher, among others. Because this line of thought emphasizes cultural particularity and played a role in the development of National Socialist ideology, it is often contrasted with Enlightenment universalism. Its emphasis on *Volk*, however, was generally accompanied by a species of cosmopolitanism influenced by Kant's conception of the proper relation between peoples. This type of cosmopolitanism is preserved in Heidegger's validation of a form of interaction between peoples that would be based on national autonomy and mutual respect.

I go on to suggest in this chapter that *Being and Time* offers resources for thinking about the constitution and political significance of cultural identity that have remained underutilized due to an understandable suspicion of such themes in the writings of a philosopher who supported fascism. There are certainly shortcomings in Heidegger's understanding of culture as grounding the unity and identity of peoples and nations, in particular the cultural essentialism Heidegger shares with the Herderian tradition, along with its positioning of Jews as perpetual outsiders to European nations. While Heidegger's conception of being a "people" is guilty of essentialism, and his views about different peoples are contaminated by self-preference and bigotry, his writings are nonetheless helpful for analyzing the role of language, place, and history in the constitution of cultural identity; the possibilities and pitfalls of cross-cultural dialogue; and the narrative structure of cultural identity that conditions who we imagine ourselves to be. Some of these ideas have been taken up by contemporary philosophers such as Charles Taylor, who apply them to support multiculturalism, rather than cultural nationalism. I maintain that this type of application is not invalidated by Heidegger's own political conclusions, and may be fruitfully extended through a closer consideration of Heidegger's phenomenological reflections on culture, space and time.

Heidegger's concept of *Volk*, nation or people, is based primarily on cultural characteristics, but he also seems to have thought that cultural membership was decided by birth. For a time, moreover, he did support a political regime whose ideology was heavily based on the idea of race, and he has been accused of being a racist of some sort – cultural, metaphysical, or "ontohistorical" (Trawny 2014, 11). Approaching the question of race and racism in Chapter 6, I emphasize that Heidegger was clearly not a biological racist, and that biological racism was central to Nazi ideology, as Heidegger came to understand. He consequently criticized biologism and the idea of race itself as based on ideas inappropriate to an understanding of human beings, and typical of modern scientism. Biological racism is not the only kind there is, though, and descent does play a role in Heidegger's understanding of what identifies a people, whom he always imagines as belonging to a common stock. But I contend that, in spite of his own bigotries, Heidegger is in a way right on this point, albeit for reasons he does not make explicit, because descent, in the form of self-identification through lineage, does play an important role in people's own understanding of the community or communities to which they belong. Only it does not follow that states should be monoethnic, even if Heidegger himself inclined to that view. On the contrary, recognizing the role of lineage in self-identification can lend support to multiculturalist policies, leading to an acknowledgment that narratives of descent play a legitimate role in people's self-location among communities and that their self-interpretations on this point should be respected.

The final chapter in this book takes up Heidegger's critique of "reason" and the accusations of irrationalism elicited by it, as well as by the style and methodology of his thinking. It has been charged that Heidegger's suspicion of reason abandons science and objectivity in favor of a historically relative and ultimately confused notion of truth, leaving us with no sure grounds for assessing existing social structures and relations, or producing normative prescriptions. In response to such charges, I ask whether Heidegger's diagnosis of modernity as the triumph of calculative rationality works with a one-sided conception of reason, as Jaspers and Habermas claim. Granting that there are problems with the insular manner of Heidegger's thinking, moreover, I argue that models of communicative reason aiming for clarity and consensus are also problematic, as they disallow novel forms of critique, ones that challenge what are taken to be the self-evident truths of a universal reason, but may in fact only be a set of hardened cultural assumptions. In addition, Heidegger's understanding of truth as historical "disclosure" suggests that poetry, art, and myth can never be permanently superseded by reason. They are instead much-needed participants in an ongoing and never completed historical process of responding to distress, while envisioning salutary change.

The position Heidegger develops does not undermine the use of reason understood in a more humble and flexible manner, nor does it leave us with historical relativism. Recognition of the temporality of being, and thus of the fact that all thinking is timely, is compatible with commitment to revealing the truth about how things are, and how we are to comport ourselves toward them if we genuinely hold ourselves to that truth. Belief in the possibility of such revelation is a condition for commitment to it, and Heidegger argues for a way of understanding our relation to being that legitimates such belief. That argument forms the core of Heidegger's revisioning of human thinking, including our thinking about moral and political issues. It could be described as a "realism about values," were it not for the queer metaphysical pictures on which such assertions rest and the pseudo-problems they consequently generate.

I end this introduction with a note on style. Heidegger's texts are notoriously difficult, a fact that likely explains the ever-increasing number of introductory books on his philosophy.[5] It is also a factor in efforts at translating Heidegger's idiom into terms that would be more readily familiar to analytic philosophers, although these efforts are equally motivated by a sense that the division between "analytic" and "continental" philosophy is unhelpful, serving as a barrier to potentially fruitful lines of philosophical investigation (Thomson 2012). This book is not meant to be an introduction, and I will not attempt to assimilate Heidegger's thought to the style of analytic philosophy, whose methodology and assumptions are, in my view, at odds with Heidegger's own, and apt to be distorting. That said, I do seek to elucidate rather than merely channel Heidegger's own language. This is a complex task, since Heidegger's vocabulary is essential to his meaning and to the critical thrust of his thinking. The multiple solutions I adopt include avoiding Heideggerese as much as possible (and admittedly it is not always possible), explaining why Heidegger uses the terms he does while rejecting more readily comprehensible ones, and highlighting Heidegger's critiques as well as his revisionary appropriations of contemporaries and predecessors, to show why he wants to speak differently about what may appear to be the same matter. I hope thereby to clarify and evaluate Heidegger's moral and political ideas in a manner that will be comprehensible to more than a small circle of Heidegger experts, but that still retains what is original in his thinking.

[5] Examples include Richardson 2012, Wisnewski 2013, and Braver 2014.

1 Freedom and Necessity

Karl Jaspers once wrote that "Heidegger doesn't know what freedom is" (Jaspers 1978, 77, n.50). If true, Heidegger would hardly be the only philosopher to have struggled with the meaning of this concept. Within modern Western philosophy, the question of human freedom is often posed as "the problem of free will," and seen as presenting both conceptual and metaphysical difficulties. At the conceptual level, the problem is of how to understand decision as the determining ground for an action that is neither forced nor arbitrary. At the metaphysical level, the problem is that of finding room for a ground of this sort within a causally closed natural world. That Heidegger understood such difficulties well enough is clear from these lines in one of his lecture courses on Schelling:

> … if one takes undecidedness in a purely negative sense, according to which no possibilities at all are prefigured and oriented in the inclination of a path, and if one understands self-determination also only in a negative sense – according to which there is no determining ground at all, but pure arbitrariness – the essence of freedom dissolves into empty chance. The will remains without direction and origin; it is no longer a will at all. On the other hand, if one understands the determining ground for the decision as a cause which itself must again be the effect of a preceding cause, the decision is forced into a purely mechanical causal context and loses the character of decision. Pure arbitrariness does not give a determining ground for decision. Mechanical force does not give a determining ground for what it is supposed to, for decision. (STF 154/ GA 42, 266–77)

Many of Heidegger's writings are centrally preoccupied with human freedom, addressing puzzles about the relation between individual choice and historical or contextual determinacy, and about the peculiar character of ethical decision in particular, which involves a type of demand that obligates without compelling. In the present chapter, I trace Heidegger's treatment of these puzzles over the course of his writings, from his phenomenological account of authenticity and resolve in *Being and Time*, through his reflections on the metaphysics of freedom in essays and lecture courses composed over the 1930s, which reflect a turn in his thinking about the relation between humanity and being.

The Phenomenology of Freedom in *Being and Time*

While Heidegger does not provide an explicit account of human freedom, so-described, in *Being and Time*, the analyses in that work of phenomena such as potentiality, conscience, authenticity, resoluteness, decision, and responsibility clearly present the capacity to project ends, choose between them, and assume ownership of one's life as essential to the character of Dasein, Heidegger's term for the structure of the entity that I myself am. Moreover, the ideal of authenticity Heidegger outlines is decidedly an ethical one,[1] as it involves a readiness to follow conscience and contains implications for appropriate being with others. In light of his political acts and speeches a few years later, though, many of Heidegger's most prominent critics and opponents have suspected that precisely this aspect of his thinking paved the way for his decision to support Hitler and National Socialism, both by allowing him to accept the content of an illiberal and undemocratic ideology and by encouraging him to make an aggressive commitment without adequate grounds.

Central to these concerns is the charge of "decisionism," which interprets *Being and Time*'s analysis of "resoluteness" and "resolve" as valorizing arbitrary assertions of will, in line with the *Zeitgeist* of European nihilism resulting from loss of faith in traditional sources of meaning.[2] Heidegger's decision to support Nazism is, on this reading, a reflection of the historical process Nietzsche named in pronouncing the death of God, where the undermining of absolutes leaves a void in which the individual subject is the sole source of willing and may affirm anything as long as he does so with gusto. Strangely, in the case of Heidegger, this alleged valorization of unconstrained willing is sometimes said to be accompanied by determinism, eliminating genuine choice between options, and disburdening individuals of responsibility for the outcomes of the decisions they make. Richard Wolin, for instance, contends that Heidegger's analysis of resolve and decision is paradoxically both a "contentless voluntarism" and a form of fatalism, a tension that is never resolved in *Being and Time*" (Wolin 1990, 60).[3]

Wolin's conclusion is based on placing *Being and Time* as an "existentialist" work, reflecting the condition of humanity in a specific historical and cultural

[1] Heidegger's account of authenticity and inauthenticity in *Being and Time* is inescapably normative, in spite of his insistence that he is only describing the phenomena (BT 68, 210–11). As Robert Bernasconi points out, languages are already shaped by ethical meanings, which cannot be eradicated by simple edict (Bernasconi 1985b, 49).

[2] Examples of critics who level some version of this charge against Heidegger include: Löwith 1986, 132–35; Löwith 1995, 159–68; Jonas 1990, 197–203; Habermas 1993b, 155; Bourdieu 1991, 69; Wolin 1990, 51–53.

[3] Other critics who accuse Heidegger of fatalism include Hans Jonas (Jonas 1964, 214–17) and Richard Feenbeerg (Feenberg 2005, 11–17, 100–105).

place, and proposing a way of being that accords with this condition. *Being and Time* is, however, a work of *phenomenology*. Its aim is to lay out the fundamental characteristics of being in the world at *any* time and not, in contrast with Heidegger's later works, to diagnose the state of humanity and being at the present time. Heidegger's own findings in *Being and Time* may cast doubt on the full realizability of the work's phenomenological ambitions, since they point to the time-bound character of all understanding. The author's own partialities and cultural circumstances are also evident in this philosophical text, as in any other. Yet the intention of *Being and Time* is to isolate the structures of human existence that make possible a variety of interpretations across cultures and ages. While this project includes bringing to light what is commonly hidden and therefore may be critical, its identification of the formal structures of being-in-the-world has to enable us to make sense of these varying interpretations. The principle of charity would then seem to rule out interpreting Heidegger as offering in *Being and Time* a decisionistic response to nihilism. It is surely obvious that not all people at all times confront an intrinsically meaningless world onto which they must, if truthful, project their arbitrarily self-chosen values and ends, and it is hard to imagine a phenomenologist supposing otherwise.

Why, then, has Heidegger been interpreted, or misinterpreted, as a moral nihilist who espoused decisionism? One reason is the language of "nothing" within some of his descriptions. Authenticity is said to be achieved when an individual faces the anxiety from which, when inauthentic, he or she seeks to flee. In such moments, Heidegger writes, the significance of the everyday world, constituted by the complex of things and tasks in which people are usually absorbed, slips away (BT 186), and Dasein is brought before the "nothing" of this world (BT 187). This condition of anxious suspension in the face of nothingness, moreover, is said to reveal Dasein's own being "as a naked 'that it is and has to be' " (BT 134).

However, in such passages, Heidegger is making a phenomenological point about the awareness of freedom that lies at the heart of Dasein as a "potentiality-for-being" and is covered over when we are taken up with our usual pragmatic concerns. "Anxiety discloses Dasein *as being-possible*" (BT 188) by making it aware of itself as projected toward that future in which it may become what it is called upon to be. It therefore discloses to Dasein that it is never a "present-at-hand" substance, an object whose being just stands there as a finished thing. Since this "being-possible" is realized only in the world, "that in the face of which one has anxiety is being-in-the-world as such" (BT 186). The anticipation of death is an important element in the realization of freedom that anxiety delivers, for in this mood "Dasein finds itself *face to face* with the 'nothing' of the possible impossibility of its existence" (BT 266). In confronting my own death, that is, I anticipate the possibility of the end of my possibilities, and this anticipation brings me more clearly before the concrete possibilities of my own existence that lie before the end.

The possible way of being that Heidegger calls "resoluteness" (*Entschlossenheit*) consists in choosing to be this self in its fundamental freedom, within the world into which I am thrown as an individual being. On Heidegger's description of this choice, it is a kind of willing*ness*, to hear the call of conscience:

To the call of conscience there corresponds a possible hearing. Our understanding of the appeal unveils itself as our *wanting to have a conscience* [*Gewissenhabenwollen*]. But in this phenomenon lies that existentiell choosing which we seek – the choosing to choose a kind of being-one's-self which, in accordance with its existential structure, we call 'resoluteness'." (BT 270)

Studies of Heidegger's early development have demonstrated the extent of his debt to Christian authors such as St. Paul, Augustine, Luther, Kierkegaard, and Pascal (Kisiel 1993, van Buren 1994). These figures are not modern nihilists. They stress the "nothingness" of the world in another sense, emphasizing the triviality and ephemerality of the things to which we are inclined to attach ourselves, whose projected significance is threatened by the fact of death. They also point to the possibility of being in the world in a different manner, which involves an acceptance of guilt and responsibility. Heidegger's analysis finds in these accounts a specific historical interpretation of a universal phenomenon whose basis in the structure of Dasein he seeks to make explicit. That is the phenomenon of conscience, and the possibility of choosing to hear it.

On its own, Heidegger's account of conscience provides no moral norms to guide action, and this has been another major reason for the worry that *Being and Time* promotes decisionism against a background of nihilism.[4] Posing the question of *what* the call of conscience communicates to Dasein, Heidegger answers:

Taken strictly, nothing. The call asserts nothing, gives no information about world-events, has nothing to tell. Least of all does it try to set going a 'soliloquy' in the self to which it has appealed. 'Nothing' gets called *to* [*zu*-gerufen] this self, but it has been *summoned* [*aufgerufen*] to itself – that is, to its ownmost potentiality-for-being. (BT 273)

[4] This concern cannot be addressed merely by demonstrating that Dasein is able to follow, and therefore potentially also to violate, norms of some sort. Mark Tanzer argues that Heidegger's analysis of tool-use presents Dasein as able to use tools appropriately or not and thereby as capable of observing or refusing restrictions, which it can also do in the case of the social prescriptions of the "they" (Tanzer 2001). But that does not answer worries about the lack of any universally binding content in Heidegger's description of moral obligation. I take up this subject in the next chapter.

But Heidegger is not talking about the *content* of moral principles here. He is talking about the *act* of deciding to follow or evade conscience. This act is "groundless" in the sense that, phenomenologically – that is, staying with the phenomena as they present themselves to us – *nothing* compels an individual to follow his or her conscience. If it did, the decision would not be a free one.

In this respect, Heidegger's analysis accepts a fundamental tenet of Christian anthropology, shorn of its theological commitments. *Being and Time* makes no positive assertion about whether or not there is a God who speaks within the conscience of individuals, and whose voice a person can choose to hear or not, but it does attempt to uncover the sources within the character of human existence that could evoke such a thesis.[5] In so doing, *Being and Time* affirms a conception of moral freedom found in Christianity as well as in the strands of Western secular morality that are continuous with Christian anthropology. On this conception, moral choice centrally involves an act, the deed of a moral agent, deciding for the right path or the wrong one. Knowledge and deliberation may play a role in determining what is the right path, and ignorance and external influences may interfere with such determination. Nonetheless, individuals are capable of knowing the good and yet refusing to heed it, and this act of refusal constitutes the wrong for which they are responsible. Heidegger's description of conscience thematizes this act, in all its strangeness and inexplicability, where conscience calls me but I may refuse to listen. It makes no claims about the content of conscience because it is not about content at all.

Being and Time also *cannot* in principle answer the question about the precise content of an individual's ownmost "calling" because, on its analysis, there is no general answer to be given. The answer depends on who a particular individual is, with his or her unique history and circumstances. I discuss elsewhere the striking resemblance between Heidegger's dissection of the components of the voice of conscience – what is talked about in the call, what it calls toward, what is said, and who does the calling (¶56, "The Character of Conscience as a Call," BT 273–74) – and a similarly structured account of the call of God to the soul in a sermon by the 14th century German theologian, Johannes Tauler.[6]

[5] This can be construed as a "demythologization" of Christianity, interpreting Christian doctrines as metaphorical or storytelling expressions of the truth of the human condition, as it was by Rudolf Bultmann when he drew on Heidegger's existential categories to interpret the narratives of the New Testament (Bultmann 1984). However, Heidegger's phenomenological account in *Being and Time* purports to be neutral rather than reductive toward all the positive "sciences," and so toward all accounts, including theological ones, that would explain the phenomena within the framework of an inherited body of knowledge rather than laying them out as they show themselves to us.

[6] See *Forms of Transcendence*, Chapter 6 (Sikka 1997, 201–24). Max Weber notes that Tauler's sermon on Ephesians iv, which I discuss (Sikka 1997, 187–200), is the first occurrence in German of this particular use of the term *Ruf*, "call" or "calling" in the sense of "vocation" (Weber, 1976, 208 n. 3).

Tauler was a significant influence on Luther, and in this sermon he maintains the direct communication of God to the soul through an inner voice that directs a person to his or her proper calling in the world. In addition to the structure of their analysis of this inner voice, Tauler's and Heidegger's accounts have in common an affirmation of the experienced character of the call as a kind of command, and the idea that what it calls toward is specific to the individual. Heidegger says that the potentiality for being that is communicated by the voice is not "ideal and universal," but disclosed "as that which has been currently individualized and which belongs to that particular Dasein" (BT 280).

I am suggesting that Heidegger's description of conscience as issuing a commanding appeal to a particular individual, whom it calls to a particular task, offers a phenomenological account of the sense of having an individual "calling" found in Christian discourses like that of Tauler, though not only there. The term *Ruf*, which Heidegger uses in speaking of the "call" of conscience, is the root of the German word *Beruf*, occupation or profession, and *Beruf* literally means "calling," as does the Latin-derived term "vocation." These literal meanings reflect the perception of deciding upon a possible path – whether an action, a social role, or a profession – as involving discovery and response rather than fabrication and assertion. They express the sense of having a "mission" in life, as we sometimes say, which gives our lives meaning and which we seek to find rather than invent. The finding is often experienced as an insight into what a person is "meant" to be or to do, as we also sometimes say. Heidegger's account tries to capture this experience of decision as intertwined with insight, where the freedom of the act lies in the willingness to follow a direction rather than in performing an act of will.

Heidegger does not identify the caller of the call of conscience with God, of course, nor does his analysis either maintain or require the existence of a supernatural agent who has literally appointed each one of us to a task. In accordance with the aims and constraints of the phenomenological method, he refrains from any speculative explanation that would construe the voice of conscience as "an alien power by which Dasein is dominated." But he also refuses any reductive biological account of conscience, maintaining that "both these explanations pass over the phenomenal findings too hastily" (BT 275). The caller of the call turns out to be, on Heidegger's interpretation of the phenomenal findings, Dasein itself as an individualized, thrown potentiality for being in the world (BT 277). Heidegger is attempting to express the peculiar nature of moral autonomy here, where the relation of command and obedience is not a relation between two independent agents but a relation of the agent to himself. Conscience does issue a commanding imperative, which a person can choose to hear and submit to (Heidegger uses the term *hörig*, which connotes both [BT 288]), and yet this basic decision constitutes the essence of freedom, since the command comes from Dasein itself. Conscience is an essential feature of this entity that has the potentiality to be, in that it is called upon to perfect itself by taking over its own becoming, and is therefore answerable or responsible (*verantwortlich*) for that becoming. Standing beyond itself toward the future of its possible (never fully actual) perfection, Dasein can "speak," as it were, to the self that is absorbed in the world of its ordinary concerns.

What makes conscience possible, therefore, on Heidegger's description, is the "doubleness" of Dasein, the reflexive relation to being through which it projects beyond the actual, beyond what it is and what is currently around it, toward the possible, the "may be" of the future. Nietzsche's injunction to "become what you are," which Heidegger quotes (BT 145), positing a better and higher possible self to which I aspire, is rooted in this same structure. The self-reflexive division between what I am and what I may be is the source of the capacity to envision and bind myself to a better possibility of myself, and therefore to any form of "should." It is then also the source of the capacity to make promises, to oneself and others, and to have power over oneself. In the *Genealogy of Morals*, Nietzsche claims that consciousness of this capacity is what "the sovereign man" calls his conscience (GM 60), but the character of Heidegger's account in *Being and Time* gives no warrant for the peculiarly Nietzschean features of this interpretation: a sense of pride in oneself, superiority over others, and the right to give those who are lesser a kick (GM 60). It also rejects the reductive explanation of conscience given by Nietzsche, where conscience and morality in general are functions of the same will to power that informs all living beings.[7]

Additionally, while for Heidegger the free decision to follow conscience is more than a mere following of established conventions and may break with them, this decision is not a stronger assertion of one's own needs and drives, nor is the capacity for it given only to "higher" types. As a constitutive feature of existence, conscience is a universal phenomenon, imposing an obligation on every entity having the structure of Dasein. The call, Heidegger writes, "reaches him who wants to be brought back" (BT 271). It is necessarily there, but the willingness to hear it, to bind oneself to its directive and thus place oneself under its obligation, is not. The division between authentic and inauthentic is not a division between two innately different types of people but between two ways in which any person may be. It involves a fundamental decision between two possible "selves," an "owned" and an "unowned" one, where selfhood means "a way of existing" (BT 267). These possible ways of existing

[7] Later, in the first of his lecture courses on Nietzsche, *The Will to Power as Art*, Heidegger says that by "will," Nietzsche actually means "resoluteness," interpreting this as a "resolute openness to oneself" that "is always a willing out beyond oneself" (NI 41/GA 43, 48). This claim, however, is based on a rather violent reading of Nietzsche, which insists that in his writings, words such as "biological" and "life" do not have a reductive biological meaning, in spite of appearances to the contrary (NI 114/GA 44, 133).

are open to any entity whose own being is an issue for it and who is capable of projecting possibilities and choosing between them. Heidegger's analysis seeks to ground the capacity for such projection in the structure of Dasein's temporality, stressing the primacy of Dasein's always being "ahead of itself," its existing self-reflexively toward the future, into which it is able to project possible designs. There is then a certain sense in which Dasein "is" nothing, since its existence is always a being underway.

Authenticity does involve a self-distinguishing from the "they," in that it contrasts with being herdlike, a way of being in which one drifts along in accord with convention and in response to what is immediately attractive or distracting. If "morality" is understood as following conventional rules, then authenticity contrasts with it, although the capacity to be responsible – and therefore guilty – is also the condition for the possibility of morality in another sense (BT 286). Drifting along with the crowd, of which mere rule-following is an example, means, for Heidegger, refusing to take hold of oneself in a responsible manner in accord with the call of conscience, and in this sense not "choosing to be oneself." The idea of "choosing oneself" as choosing a mode of being in which I accept to be responsible for myself – what Heidegger describes as "choosing to choose a kind of being one's self" (BT 280) – is adapted from Kierkegaard.[8] It is paradoxical, in that it suggests choosing to be what an individual already "is" (Kierkegaard 1971, 218–19). Nietzsche's injunction to "become what you are" touches upon the same phenomenon, where the possible self to which I aspire is already given to me in a fashion, such that I may even take it to be my "true" self, but is at the same time the goal of a task that I may freely choose to undertake or not. When envisioned in a genuine manner, moreover, with transparency and responsibility, this self is not a fantastic ideal remote from reality, but a definitely realizable possibility for the person I am. Heidegger writes in *The Metaphysical Foundations of Logic* that "in the express self-choice there is essentially the complete self-commitment, not to where it might not yet be, but to where and how it already always is, qua Dasein, insofar as it already exists" (GA 26, 245/MFL 190). Likewise, in *Being and Time*, while authenticity requires a breaking free of the crowd in one sense, resoluteness also in its own way accepts a place and role that are in large measure given. The call of conscience is *per se* empty of determinate content, but it summons an individual toward readiness to accept the demands of his or her situation, which is in turn determined by the very particular conjunction of that individual's capacities and historical location. The terms of Heidegger's description affirm the possibility, therefore, of finding an appropriate fit between who and where I am, and what I ought to do and

[8] Heidegger acknowledges having learned from Kierkegaard on this point, in *The Metaphysical Foundations of Logic* (GA 26, 246/MFL 190–91). See Han-Pile 2013, 298–302.

be. They also affirm that something "in" me (to speak metaphorically) directs me to be responsible and follow the direction to this fitting place, although I may be inclined instead to take an easier path, or to drift along on no clear path at all.

While these features of his description obviate the charge that Heidegger is endorsing arbitrary assertions of will, they might also seem to limit the scope of human freedom. And indeed they do; but Heidegger's analysis of this point seeks to reflect the reality of human thought and action. We do not determine our being from the ground up, and we do find ourselves already in a situation where our capabilities and historical location are "predetermined" insofar as they are not our own creation. This predetermination includes limits on understanding, since we require resources in order to think, and those resources are given by the traditions we inherit. Heidegger's account suggests that, far from eliminating freedom, these limitations actually give freedom its sense, as the idea of an unbounded freedom is incoherent. The given dimensions of a person's being in the world provide the meaningful context in which a possible path may be charted, upon which an individual may resolve in response to conscience, and the materials provided by tradition are essential to reflection and imagination. The definiteness, and consequent finitude, of these elements of existence should not be perceived merely as negative restrictions on human freedom; they are rather the enabling conditions for its meaningful exercise.

That exercise includes the creative envisioning of new possibilities, since what is required of an individual by his or situation cannot be discerned through an inventory of facts alone, even if it is nonetheless a kind of discovery. In "On the Essence of Truth" (1930), Heidegger writes:

> Freedom is not what common sense is content to let pass under that name: the random ability to do as we please, to go this way or that in our choice. Freedom is not licence in what we do or do not do. Nor, on the other hand, is freedom a mere readiness to do something requisite and necessary (and thus in a sense "actual" [*Seiendes*]). Over and above all this ("negative" and "positive" freedom) freedom is a participation in the revealment of what-is-as-such (*das Seiende als ein solches*). (GA 9, 189/EB 334)

Being and Time does describe the act of freedom that chooses to follow conscience precisely in terms of readiness, as a resolve to do what is required by the situation, but the event of understanding what is required does not occur through an engagement only with what is actual. It cannot be produced by knowledge of circumstances, no matter how profound, or by applying a formula. Freedom requires the projection of a good, a "for-the-sake-of," that transcends being as actuality and gives it the kind of meaningful shape that moral action requires. This creative envisioning of an end is what turns a concatenation of circumstances into a "situation" calling for resolute and conscientious action (BT 338, 384). Yet it emerges out of responsiveness to the needs of the time and place at which an individual stands, in her being in the world with others. Frank Schalow notes that, for Heidegger, freedom cannot be defined through a clash between activity and passivity, but arises through a mode of configuration that "balances activity and passivity, spontaneity and receptivity, and thereby charts a new landscape for ethical action" (Schalow 2002, 36).

The spontaneity of the projection that "discovers" the truth of what is required of a person by a situation is still dependent on the resources of tradition. There is scope for imagining the new, but imagination must have models with which to work. Thus, Heidegger's idea that authentic historical repetition may involve choosing a hero and "loyally following in the footsteps of that which can be repeated" (BT 385) is a component of his understanding of autonomy rather than compromising it. Both Kierkegaard and Nietzsche view the value of history, for instance in its records of remarkable individual lives, as resting in the repeatable possibilities for existence it offers.[9] Heidegger adopts this idea, whereby choosing a hero means patterning my life upon a model, fictional or actual, handed down by the tradition in which I stand. What counts as a hero or a remarkable individual is deliberately left open, as Heidegger's objective at this juncture is not to propose a specific ethical model but to describe the structures of human existence that make it possible to follow one. The point is that, in struggling to perfect themselves, individuals may and do follow the lives of figures they take to be exemplary, holding these up as ideals for themselves and criticizing the way a past ideal is working itself out in the present (BT 386).

This element in Heidegger's analysis of freedom, focusing on the act of binding oneself to an ideal, is compatible with a variety of actual historical ideals reflecting different values and judgments about what constitutes human greatness. Different individuals and cultures may value glory, or self-sacrifice, or humility. Individuals may admire the historical examples of Akbar, or Napoleon, or Wu Zetian, or seek to imitate Christ, or to follow in the footsteps of Confucius, or Buddha, or Mahatma Gandhi. Heidegger's description of the free decision by which an individual binds oneself to a particular ideal is neutral toward all of these ideals. Its formal emptiness, however, provides no positive affirmation of either nihilism or relativism. The indeterminacy of Heidegger's account of resolve is, rather, a function of the phenomenological aim of describing the act of decision whereby an individual chooses to follow his or her conscience and strive toward an ideal, in the measure permitted by the clear-sighted recognition of both freedom and finitude.

[9] See, for example, Kierkegaard's remarks in *Concluding Unscientific Postscript* (Kierkegaard 1941, 320–21). Nietzsche's definitive statement on the point is "On the Advantages and Disadvantages of History for Life," which Heidegger refers to directly in *Being and Time* (BT 396–97).

There is also in Heidegger's account an implicit description of the possibility of *being* a hero, of knowing and seizing the opportune moment for a fateful act. At various points in *Being and Time*, the tenor of Heidegger's account of fate and destiny points to the possibility of individuals who have a "clear vision for the accidents of the situation that has been disclosed" (BT 385) and who may therefore be especially suited to lead a people into its "destiny," or to be the voice of conscience for their generation. Heidegger does not talk explicitly of being a hero, but his rather lofty description of the possibility of Dasein's standing in "the moment of vision for 'its time' " and thereby taking up its fate (BT 385) suggests a pattern of life that is not quite that of the average person, especially when these passages are read retrospectively, in view of the speeches Heidegger made in support of Nazism and its leader in 1933–34.

Heidegger's description of such a possibility is reminiscent of Hegel's remarks on "world-historical individuals," precisely those who "may be called heroes," in the *Philosophy of History*. These are men (and on Hegel's account they are all *men*) such as Alexander, Napoleon, and Caesar, who were governed, Hegel says, by "an unconscious impulse that occasioned the accomplishment of that for which the time was ripe" (Hegel 1956, 30). The "vocation" of these "world-historical persons" was "to be the agents of the world-spirit," although they were not conscious of fulfilling this mission. They were rather "practical, political men," but at the same time "thinking men, who had an insight into the requirements of the time – what was ripe for development," and "they are great men, because they willed and accomplished something great; not a mere fancy, a mere intention, but that which met the case and fell in with the needs of the age" (Hegel 1956, 29–31).

Portions of Heidegger's account of authentic historicality could easily be read as a phenomenological description of being such a person. This is admittedly ominous, in light of Hegel's further remarks that "so mighty a form must trample down many an innocent flower – crush to pieces many an object in its path" and "the particular is for the most part of too trifling value as compared with the general: individuals are sacrificed and abandoned" (Hegel 1956, 32–33). I will argue in the next chapter that in fact no such sacrifice of individuals is morally permissible, given Heidegger's analysis of Dasein; however, it should also be underlined that the resolute individual is described as following the call of conscience. In the case of the heroic individual, this may be a call to assume a grand "fate," inseparable from the shared "destiny" of the people to whom this person belongs, but responding to it is not supposed to involve an assertion of self-interested desire or the will to dominate others.

Of course, in practice, it is not always easy to distinguish between these two modes – egoistic assertion, and the readiness to follow conscience – even for an individual himself, let alone for others. The essentially private character of the call of conscience exacerbates this problem. For Heidegger, the incommunicability of the call follows in part from the particularity of the task to which an individual is called. Conscience does in a way direct an individual beyond "morality," interpreted as a matter of following rules and conventions that are supposed to be universally applicable. The result is a highly situationist ethics, and it is open to the various criticisms that might be directed against such a position. It is not, however, nihilistic, decisionist, or voluntarist. Heidegger's description maintains not that Dasein, in being resolute, asserts whatever it wants in a licentious manner, but that it freely binds itself to the categorical voice of its own conscience. Both binding oneself freely to conscience and doing what one likes can be described as acting according to one's "own" law,[10] but they are antithetical ways of being.

Heidegger's familiarity with radical German theologians such as Meister Eckhart and Johannes Tauler is instructive in this context, as the kind of freedom they describe involves a transcending of self-will rather than an assertion of it. Reiner Schürmann's interpretation in *Heidegger on Being and Acting: From Principles to Anarchy* (1987), draws on the medieval theological tradition initiated by Eckhart, but without adequately emphasizing the fact that, for Eckhart, perfect freedom involves an elimination of self-centered desire.[11] That is also Eckhart's model of perfectly just action, where a person acts for the sake of the good alone, all egoistic inclinations having ceased to operate as motives. Eckhart's description of this state anticipates Kant's notion of the "holy will," in which duty and desire entirely coincide, except that the action flowing from this condition is situational and in *this* sense "unprincipled." But it is not therefore licentious; it is supposed to be the opposite.

One reason for the Church's accusation of heresy against Eckhart, however, was fear of antinomianism of the sort attributed to the Brethren of the Free Spirit, which posed a serious threat to the established ecclesiastical order by implying that its intermediation was unnecessary for salvation, and its rules and regulations not binding. Jan van Ruusbroec, a Flemish mystic influenced by Eckhart, tried to ward off a similar interpretation of his thought, which also promoted a form of radical freedom. Differentiating his own teaching from that of followers of the Free Spirit, he writes: "They are self-willed and subject to none, and this is what they call spiritual liberty ... They practice the freedom of the flesh by giving the body what it lusts after; and they consider that to be nobility of nature" (Ruusbroec 1989, 118). Ruusbroec means to advocate the opposite of this kind of liberty, as do Eckhart and Tauler, who, as I noted, influenced Martin Luther.

[10] Cf. Mark Tanzer's discussion of Heidegger's relation to Kant on this issue (Tanzer 2002, 55–58).
[11] See Meister Eckhart's Sermon 39 (Eckhart 1986, 296–300).

Heidegger's brand of moral "anarchy" parallels these kinds of analyses, with their orientation toward the still small voice of conscience, rather than Nietzsche's opposing valorization of an individual will to power that places itself "beyond good and evil." He was influenced by Nietzsche, and powerfully so during the years leading up to his endorsement of Nazism, but his debt to such thinkers as Eckhart, Pascal, and Kierkegaard helps to make sense of his later interpretations of *Being and Time* as never having promoted voluntarism. This issue of voluntarism links with the question of what exactly "resoluteness" means in *Being and Time*. In "The Origin of the Work of Art" (1935), Heidegger claims that "the resoluteness intended in *Being and Time* is not the deliberate action of a subject," but a kind of openness on the part of Dasein (PLT 67/GA 5, 53). The term is actually ambiguous in *Being and Time*, and this later interpretation of it may be one-sided but is not merely a retroactive revision. In fact, the interpretation of resoluteness as decision requiring an act of will, or as openness requiring a letting go of will, are not mutually exclusive alternatives (Schalow 2001, 261). Resoluteness, as Heidegger presents it in *Being and Time*, consists in a decision to let go of self-seeking absorption in the daily business of meeting one's wants and needs, and an openness – *Entschlossenheit*, literally, "unclosedness" – to the possibility of a different way of being.

That said, there are certainly objections to the idea of conscience as the authentic individual's guide to action. What guarantee does an individual have that what he perceives as a deep insight into the need of the times and his own duty in response to that need is accurate and not instead an error or delusion? And how do those confronted with the decision of supporting or rejecting a leader know whether he is even acting out of a sense of duty, misguided or not, rather than a self-interested will to power? Heidegger's own actions in supporting Nazism make this an especially pertinent question (although, for what it's worth, he did write in his notebook in 1932: "Pressed into accepting the Rectorate, I am acting for the first time *against* the innermost voice" [GA 94, 110]). We may well worry that conscience, even when followed with a pure heart, is not a reliable guide to what ought to be done in all situations, and that general rules, along with a reliable method for arriving at them, are needed. Hegel was suspicious of conscience for precisely these reasons, limiting its role in ethical life out of concerns about its arbitrariness, and the danger of an individual's relying on subjective certainty rather than on objective social duties and the moral rules connected with them.[12]

Acknowledging these risks, though, the sense of having a capacity to stand beyond one's times in response to conscience has its virtues, as well. M. K.

12 Yet Hegel did not reject the positive role of individual conscience altogether; for a detailed critical analysis of this topic, see Wood 1990, 174–94.

Gandhi once wrote, "The only tyrant I accept in this world is the 'still small voice' within me … And even though I have to face the prospect of being a minority of one, I humbly believe I have the courage to be in such a hopeless minority" (Gandhi 2002, 160). There are times when this "hopeless minority" is right, after all, and when the majority is wrong, even though it has all good sense and reason (or what counts at the time as such) on its side. There are also times when situations call for exceptions to legitimate moral rules, or when the application of those rules does not sufficiently determine what ought to be done, or leads to conflicting conclusions. Furthermore, for Heidegger, the summons of conscience never provides absolute certainty about what is to be done, a certainty that is simply not there to be had for a finite being thrown into a constantly changing world. It provides only the possibility of making a free decision between conscience and falling, for a being who has been released from causes.

The Metaphysics of Freedom: Heidegger and Schelling

This brings us to the subject of Heidegger's position on the metaphysical question about human freedom, its status within a nature whose movements appear to be, if not entirely determined by causes, at least not affected by the acts of a conscious agent who may go one way or another. That *Being and Time* is ostensibly a phenomenological work means that its methodology is supposed to bracket such questions in favor of close attention to the phenomena as they present themselves to us. By contrast, a number of lectures and treatises composed in the years following the publication of *Being and Time* shift from a purely phenomenological account of freedom to an analysis of the metaphysical picture behind the modern framing of the topic as a problem. These include *On the Essence of Ground* (1929), *The Essence of Freedom: An Introduction to Philosophy* (1930), *On the Essence of Truth* (1930), and *Plato's Doctrine of Truth* (1930/31). In relation to the possibility of freedom, these works offer a historical and deconstructive analysis of the idea of "cause," and more broadly a critique of the interpretation of being as a reality consisting of present objects standing in causal connections with one another, with movement and change being the result of one such object affecting or bringing about the presence of another.

Heidegger's most sustained and explicit engagement with the metaphysical puzzle about freedom, though, takes place through his reflections on Schelling. Heidegger taught two complete lecture courses on Schelling, one in 1936, and one in 1941, both of which deal with only one of Schelling's works, the *Philosophical Investigations on the Essence of Human Freedom and Related Matters*, first published in1809. He had also given a seminar on this text in 1927/28, shortly after *Being and Time* was published (Kisiel 2000, 293), and an adapted appropriation of Schelling's position on freedom is already evident in *Being and Time*, as well as in works written over the 1930s, in spite of Heidegger's explicitly negative appraisals of Schelling's place in the history of metaphysics.[13] To be sure, Schelling's philosophy does exemplify attributes centrally targeted within Heidegger's critique of metaphysics. It is distinctly ontotheological, asking about beings as such and as a whole, and tracing their existence to a primal ground conceived as the highest being, God (STF 51/GA 42, 88). It describes the essence of reality as "will" (STF 95f/GA 42, 164f), helping to prepare the way for the subjectivist nihilism that finds its fullest expression in Nietzsche (see STF 172–73). It attempts to formulate a system comprehending the entire order of being, a project of absolute mastery that is doomed to catastrophe and failure. But there are also positive parallels between Heidegger's and Schelling's positions on freedom, and respects in which the shift in Heidegger's thinking over the early 1930s was shaped by his engagement with Schelling's metaphysics.

The explicit question raised by Schelling in the *Philosophical Investigations on the Essence of Human Freedom* concerns the place of human freedom not within nature but within a system of philosophy. For Schelling, though, a genuine "system" of philosophy, as Heidegger writes in his commentary, is a sketch or projection (*Entwurf*) that discovers and makes visible the "jointure" (*Gefüge*) of being, the basic structure of the way entities are put together (STF 25–28/GA 42, 45). Glossing Heidegger's interpretation of the idea of a system within German idealism, Parvis Emad explains:

> Seen in this light the concept with which Schelling operates is not to be confused with a frame designed for the purpose of transmitting an organized body of knowledge. It *is* Being's pattern of arrangement as mirrored in thought. As knowledge of the absolute system, thought appears to be identical with Being's arrangement. (Emad 1975, 173)

Prima facie, it would appear that freedom and system in this sense are incompatible (F 336). For if human beings can genuinely choose between different possibilities, the unfolding of reality is indeterminate and therefore incapable of being organized within a complete system of thought. But if reality does conform to some comprehensive logical and causal pattern, there is no freedom. The prime example of the latter option is the pantheistic system of Spinoza.

Schelling argues, however, that Spinoza's system excludes freedom not because it is pantheistic but because it is mechanistic. Its error lies in conceiving all entities as *things*, and correspondingly conceiving the relations between

[13] I mean not only in the lectures on Schelling, but also in other works where there are occasional brief references to Schelling, such as *The Basic Problems of Phenomenology* (1927), BPP 152–53/GA 24, 216–18; *Contributions to Philosophy* (1936–39), GA 65, 199–204; "What is Called Thinking?" (1952), WCT 98, 102, 109/ WhD 42, 47, 77; "Who is Nietzsche's Zarathustra?" (1953), NII 222–23/VA 109–10.

them as mechanical (F 359–50). Spinoza's system is in this sense one-sidedly "realistic," opposing the principle of idealism that all reality is activity, life and freedom, which for Schelling means that all reality is "will." "In the last and highest instance," Schelling writes, "there is no other being (*Seyn*) but will (*Wollen*)," and a pantheism understanding primordial being (*Ursein*) as will rather than substance need not be fatalistic (F 350). There remains the theological problem that if God is responsible for all that is and all that occurs, then God would seem to be the source of evil, as well (F 353). Schelling's proposed solution is that the source of evil resides in a principle within God, which is yet not God.

To arrive at this solution, Schelling employs a distinction between "ground" and "existence." "By ground," Ryan Hellmers explains, "Schelling means the foundation for a thing; by existence he means not only what is, but what is *generated* into being," so that the relation between the two terms describes "the process by which a particular existing being is generated from its foundation" (Hellmers 2008, 144). Glossing Schelling, Heidegger calls the distinction between ground and existence the "jointure of being" (*Seynsfuge*) (STF 106). It is not a distinction between two entities, or kinds of entities, but between two aspects of being that each entity displays (GA 49, 12). Ground is being as primal will, a blind striving or longing (*Sehnsucht*), uninformed and unordered by understanding. In a sense, it is not "being," or at least not actual being, but names the possibility or power of being. Existence is this same power as determinate and actual. Every entity is structured according to this distinction, since the distinction is a feature of the immanent source of all, the primal being (*Urwesen*) that Schelling's pantheism identifies with God.[14]

Human beings reflect this source in a special way within Schelling's account. Among all other beings, the relation between ground and existence is determined and mastered by the universal will of God which, as "love," maintains a harmonious accord that keeps every entity within the bounds of its nature. Human freedom, by contrast, reflects the freedom of God, in that human beings are conscious unities of ground and existence in whom the will, the dark striving of the ground, is raised to the level of understanding. Human beings are also different from God, however, in that the proper relation between ground and existence is indissoluble in God but not in humanity. This identity and difference are necessary for the self-revelation of God, but mean that human beings are able to choose the relation between ground and existence within

[14] Werner Marx points out that "God" or the "absolute" can have a number of possible referents in Schelling's writings: "Taken as the absolute purely for itself before the separation of the principles ... the absolute appears as 'that which is above beings,' as the 'primal ground,' the 'non-ground,' or 'indifference'. After this separation, it appears as a being (existence) in opposition to the ground (its Being). Furthermore, from the vantage point of the first absolute, it appears as the ground itself" (Marx 1984, 83–84).

themselves, and this ability is the source of evil (F 363–64). For Schelling, evil is not a mere negation or lack. It is positive discord, arising when a particular will opposes itself to the universal will by perversely asserting its own existence in opposition to, rather than in harmony with, other entities. On this theological picture, evil is the refusal to accept limitation, on the part of a finite being. Although Schelling describes freedom as the decision for good *or* evil (F 382), Heidegger observes that it is actually the possibility of good *and* evil since, with the being of humanity, these come to presence together (STF 97/ GA 42, 271).

Freedom is also not, for Schelling, opposed to every understanding of "necessity." He argues that "true freedom is in accord with a holy necessity, of a sort which we feel in essential knowledge when heart and spirit, bound only by their own law, freely affirm that which is necessary" (F 391–92). Freedom *is* necessity in this sense, because it is the accordance of a free being with its own nature, which is in turn self-determined: "Man's being is essentially *his own deed*" (F 385). Heidegger describes this "deed" as an individual's free decision for the necessity of his own essence. It is said to occur in the moment (*Augenblick*) where past and future blend together in the present, and the whole essence of a person flashes before him, so that he feels he has always had to be what he is, and it was he himself who determined this (STF 155/GA 42, 268). According to Schelling, this act of self-determination does not contradict the omnipotence of God, since what a person sees and wills in the moment of eternity is the same as what God sees and wills when he glimpses the image of himself in a kind of internal imagination (*Ein-bildung*) that is simultaneously an act of creation. Heidegger comments that humanity, as this image, originates from and "is" the glance of light and life (*Lichtblick, Lebensblick*) constituting the highest self-vision of God (STF, 152–3/GA 42, 266).

Near the end of his first lecture course on Schelling, Heidegger points out that Schelling equates "system" with understanding, and opposes it to the other aspect of being, the irrational will of the ground. It follows that the irrational, which also "is" in some way, remains outside the system, so that the system is actually no longer a system. Here lies the essential difficulty, Heidegger contends, upon which Schelling's thought eventually founders (STF 160–61/ GA 42, 278–79).

Being and Time predates the lectures courses on Schelling by many years, but at points shows evidence of an engagement with Schelling, as a number of scholars have noticed.[15] Heidegger was acquainted with Schelling's

[15] In addition to Hellmers (2008), comparisons between Schelling and the early Heidegger have been drawn by Walter Schulz (Schulz 1953/54, 71; Schulz 1975, 287–96), Xavier Tillete (Tillette 1970, 598–99), and Otto Pöggeler (Pöggeler 1987, 45; Pöggeler 1993). While these authors make rather different points than the ones I will take up, they do focus on the same sections and passages.

thought by time the text was written,[16] and reading certain passages with an eye to Schelling's *Treatise* draws attention to a curious ambiguity. In ¶58 of *Being and Time*, for example, Heidegger raises the question of the nature of guilt, and the form of negativity associated with it (BT 284). Like Schelling in the *Treatise*, he is concerned with the possibility and ontological status of the kind of fault of which only a free being is capable. His analysis also rests on a distinction between "ground" and "existence," but the meaning of both is delimited by Heidegger's application of them to describe only one kind of entity, Dasein. On Heidegger's analysis, this entity is distinguished from all others by the fact that it, as "existing" – in the peculiar sense Heidegger assigns to this term where it indicates Dasein's always surpassing the actual toward the possible – is called upon to take over being the ground of itself (BT 284).

One way to look at the parallel between Heidegger and Schelling on the "jointure" of being is to see Heidegger as providing a phenomenological account of this distinction in relation to the being of Dasein, examining the difference we experience between potentiality and actuality within our own being. Through this examination, Dasein is revealed as a special kind of being-possible, which apprehends itself as standing before possibilities that it is responsible for actualizing, even though it is thrown into its situation and never determines its being from the ground up (BT 285). On this reading, Heidegger is performing a phenomenological deconstruction of Schelling's metaphysics, not engaging in any flights of speculation but seeking to unearth the roots, within Dasein's experience of its own being, of the ontotheological story Schelling constructs. In that case, the distinction between ground and existence, as well as the possibility of a dis-jointure in which a finite being like Dasein might run away from its responsibility for itself or refuse to accept its proper limits, describes the existence of Dasein, and nothing "more."

[16] In his inaugural address at Heidelberg in 1957, Heidegger reports: "What the exciting years between 1910 and 1914 mean for me cannot be adequately expressed: I can only indicate it by a selective enumeration: the second, significantly enlarged edition of Nietzsche's *The Will to Power*, the words of Kierkegaard and Dosteoevsky in translation, the awakening interest in Hegel and Schelling . . ." ("A Recollection," trans. Hans Siegfried, Sheehan 2009, 22). Although he had apparently been dismissive of Schelling earlier (see Pöggeler 1993, 361), in a letter to Jaspers dated April 24, 1926, Heidegger writes that Schelling is philosophically more venturesome, if conceptually less orderly, than Hegel. In the same letter, he also says that he has only begun reading the *Freedom* treatise (H:J 62), yet we know that Heidegger was familiar enough with this text to give a seminar on it in 1927/28. Of this seminar, Gadamer – who, however, misremembers the year – reports:

> In 1925, in a seminar on Schelling, I had already heard Heidegger read this sentence from the *Freiheitsschrift*: "The dread (*Angst*) of life drives the creature from its center," and he added: "Gentlemen, show me a single sentence of such depth in Hegel." Behind Kierkegaard and later even behind Nietzsche, the late Schelling was always visible for Heidegger. He repeatedly brought the work on the essence of human freedom into his lessons. (Gadamer 1987, 306).

But there is an ambiguity in certain passages, brought into focus in the following lines:

In being *itself*, Dasein, as a self, is the thrown being (*Seiende*). It has been released (*entlassen*) from the ground, *not through* itself, but *to* itself, in order to be *as this ground*. Dasein is not the ground of its being, inasmuch as this ground first arises from its own projection; rather, as being-itself it is the *being (Sein)* of the ground. (BT 284–85)

The closeness of the language here to Schelling's account, and especially to Heidegger's own gloss in his lectures on the *Freedom* treatise (STF 159–60/GA 42, 277–78), is striking. The passage can be read as saying only that Dasein experiences itself as released from "ground," understood as "cause," and as having to actualize its own being by realizing the possibilities granted to it in virtue of its character and situation. This reading would be in accord with the existentialist and anthropological reading of *Being and Time* – which, however, Heidegger later rejects (see, for example, *Contributions to Philosophy*, GA 65, 69, 87, 296).

Or the passage can be read as saying that Dasein is released from *the* ground, of itself and of what-is as a whole, in order to realize *it*, the ground. Heidegger echoes these sentences in the second of his lecture courses on Schelling when he says that, for Schelling, the essence of humanity "is determined from the essence of what is created, i.e. from the independence which has been released (*entlassen*) from the ground to which it thus belongs and which it does not master (GA 49, 131). On the second possible reading I am identifying, Heidegger is suggesting that what Dasein realizes is not "only" itself, but *being* – the existence or coming to presence of the ground as an ontological principle. It can never get that ground into its power (BT 284), but its own powers are enabled by it and in a certain sense "are" it. This would make Dasein the locus of the determinate self-realization of the ground of what is as a whole, the potentiality of being itself.

Yet Heidegger is not a metaphysician and does not want to tell an ontotheological story. *Being and Time* is engaged in a this-worldly analytic of Dasein, not in otherworldly speculation about a divine being or transcendent ground. What then should we make of this other possible reading? Let me suspend this question for a moment to examine another point at which there is a telling ambiguity in Heidegger's wording in *Being and Time*, again inviting an interpretation that would bring him close to Schelling's metaphysics. This is Heidegger's account of the "moment of vision" (*Augenblick*) (BT 328, 338). Here, too, Heidegger's description can be read as a deconstruction of previous metaphysical formulations, and an attempt locate the existential bases of theological concepts, such as predestination and eternity. In *Being and Time*, the "moment of vision" is the "authentic present" that belongs to "anticipatory resoluteness," a possible way of being for Dasein, where it decides to take responsibility for being "the entity which it already is" (BT 339). This "moment," Heidegger insists, must *not* be clarified in terms of the "now" (*Jetzt*) in which something occurs. It is instead the "waiting-towards" of resoluteness, wherein the present "gets held in the future and in having been" (BT 338).

There are echoes of this analysis as well in Heidegger's lectures on Schelling, when he analyzes the idea of eternity at play within Schelling's understanding of the becoming of God. "In this becoming everything 'is' simultaneous," Heidegger remarks, but:

> Simultaneous does not mean here that past and future give up their nature and turn 'into' the pure present. On the contrary, original simul-taneity consists in the fact that being past and being present assert themselves and mingle with each other together with being present as the essential fullness of time itself. And this mingling of *true temporality*, this Moment (*Augenblick*), 'is' the essence of eternity, but not the present which has merely stopped and remains that way, the *nunc stans*. (STF 113/GA 42, 197).

This is the "moment" of decision in which an individual decides for "the necessity of his essence." Heidegger offers the following gloss on the relation between such decision and the idea of predestination:

> This decision was not made at some time, at a point of time in the series of time, but falls as a decision to temporality. Thus where temporality truly presences, in the moment, where past and future come together in the present, where man's essence flashes before him as his own, man experiences the fact that he must always already have been who he is, as he who has determined himself for this. (STF 155/GA 42, 268)

There is no compulsion in such an experience of one's own being, Heidegger adds; "rather necessity is freedom here and freedom is necessity" (STF 155/GA 42, 268).

If Heidegger is engaged here in a phenomenological deconstruction of onto-theological ideas, he is pointing to an immanent feature of human existence as the ultimate source for notions of eternity and predestination. This feature is pointed out by Schelling himself, when he writes that "there is indeed in each man a feeling … as if he had been what he is already from all eternity and had by no means become so first in time" (F 386). Schelling connects this feeling with the sense that a person is responsible for his actions, even if they are also necessary (F 386). One dimension of this phenomenon that Heidegger's account seeks to describe is the peculiar kind of necessity that characterizes moral obligation, of the sort imposed by conscience, as opposed to the necessity pertaining to the causal interaction between present things. Another dimension is the perception of moral choice as the decision to do what is "necessary" in the sense of needed. This element of Heidegger's and Schelling's accounts helps to make sense of moral acts being judged as free, even in cases where no deliberation occurred, as when a person wants to say "I did what I had to do" or "I cannot do otherwise." Statements like these do point to a kind of necessity, but not of a sort that removes moral freedom. Quite the reverse, we often judge courageous moral acts in which a person submits herself to this kind of necessity as exemplifying moral freedom.

This analysis remains oriented toward human existence alone, but read in conjunction with Schelling, Heidegger's account of the "moment" points to another possibility. For if the existence of Dasein is a realization of the ground of being – is itself the "be-ing," the coming to definite existence, of the ground of what is as a whole – the import of the "moment" is different. It can then be construed as a moment in which Dasein comes into accord with being, a moment when the decidedness of its being corresponds to the decision in which the possibility of that being is determined and granted. The decision is in a way made "before" being and outside time, given that it is a decision about what is to be realized *in* time. Heidegger's later understanding of decision as a characteristic of *being* rather than of humanity follows this second interpretation (*Contributions to Philosophy*, GA 65, 83–84), suggesting that fundamental characteristics of humanity, such as freedom, indicate something about being itself. Heidegger is not telling an ontotheological story, and he does not mean there is a transcendent entity in whose image Dasein is made, or whose commands it is supposed to follow. But he does mean that we should not suppose that the features of Dasein are merely "subjective," whereas concepts and categories derived from and applied to "objects" delineate true being.

In a letter to William Richardson, Heidegger wrote that, in the thinking that characterizes the "turn" between his earlier and later works, the formulation of the question posed in *Being and Time* is completed because, given various features of the analysis in *Being and Time*, "being" cannot remain something posited by the human subject (Richardson 1974, xix). Heidegger's revisions of *Being and Time*, for instance in his marginal notations,[17] look back to what is unthought in the text from the perspective gained by following further the question of being that he had raised there. According to Heidegger's self-interpretation, this does not involve a change of standpoint (Richardson 1974, xvii), but a thinking through of the implications of what is already stated in *Being and Time*. Relating Heidegger's "turn" to the issue of "ground" and "existence," Alfred Jäger, in his analysis of Heidegger's confrontation with Schelling, writes that "the relation of human existence to the ground of being (*Seins-Grund*) and vice versa was also [Heidegger's] problem immediately after *Being and Time*" (Jäger 1978, 298). Gadamer points out that "in Schelling Heidegger recognized his very own problem, the problem of facticity, of the indissoluble darkness of the ground – in God as in all that is actually and not merely logically" (Gadamer 1987, 306). In fact, this problem is already

[17] Printed in the Appendix to *Sein und Zeit*, 439–45.

raised in *Being and Time*, in passages influenced by Schelling. The passages are ambiguous, because *Being and Time* already maintains that it is oriented toward the question of being, that its analytic of Dasein is not mere anthropology, and that Dasein is not a self-enclosed sphere cut off from the truth of what is. Heidegger's efforts to remain true to these anti-subjectivist elements of his position and methodology in the account he produces in *Being and Time* leave many opportunities for interpreting Dasein as a site for the unconcealment of being, and for supposing that its structure reveals rather than projects the structure of being, as Heidegger's subsequent marginal notations attest.[18]

The movement of thought that "completes" *Being and Time* so as to allow this manner of returning to it is a gradual one. Central to this movement is the question of truth. Charles Guignon draws attention to two meanings of the word "freedom" in Heidegger's writings of the late 1920s and early 1930s, the first connected with the modern problem of free will, and the second – which Guignon describes as "a very idiosyncratic use of the word" – with truth (Guignon 2011, 80). Explicating the second meaning, and its connection with what we ordinarily understand by freedom, he suggests that for Heidegger, "freeing things up involves stepping back, gaining some distance from the demands of the concrete and particular case, so that things can 'reveal themselves with respect to what and how they are' " (Guignon 2011, 95). This second meaning also connects with free will, though, because *genuinely* disclosing the truth of what and how things are requires, Heidegger suggests, a restrained self-binding to what shows itself, as opposed to obfuscation, self-delusion, cowardice, or egoism – in short, all the dispositions that may stand in the way of honest appraisal.

Within Heidegger's analysis, Dasein is distinguished by its understanding of being, and the free "projections" of being through which the world is lit up for it are not, when appropriate, subjective fabrications. They are themselves modes of being through which the being of entities, the truth of the way things are, is revealed. While there is never a guarantee of having gotten something right, and no possibility in principle of having gotten everything absolutely right (Dasein's being finite and all), being *in* the truth, as a way of being, means *holding* myself to the truth of being, and is therefore connected with freedom. At its most fundamental level, this still requires, even in scientific inquiry, a decision to follow the summons of conscience. Given the possibility of appropriateness to being through such a following, and the idea that being reflects itself "in" human being and doing, genuine realism and idealism coincide for Heidegger, as they do for Schelling, and human freedom is no illusion but an event within being itself.

[18] See, for example: 12a, 38b, 39a, 42a, 87a, 87b, 133a, 133b, 133c, 134a, 143a, 147c, 165a, 183a, 191a, 207c, 223a, 322a, 436a (BT 440–45).

That is why Heidegger can refuse the charge of subjectivization in works that seem to reduce the categories of being to human projection. For instance, in the 1931/32 lecture course on Plato, *On the Essence of Truth: Of Plato's Allegory of the Cave and Theaetetus,* Heidegger considers the equation between seeing in the light and becoming free, in Plato's account of exit from the cave. In this process, he says, the look or glance (*Blick*) becomes a glance of light (*Lichtblick*) (ET 44/GA 34, 59), which is the essence of freedom. It is simultaneously a becoming free *for* what is, and a freeing *of* what is, where the freeing process is a "projection of being" (*Seinsentwurf*) (ET 44/GA 34, 60–61). Through such projection, the outline of what appears is formed in advance, so that within the pre-figuring envisioning (*vor-bildende Erblicken*) of being, entities are lit up (ET 52/GA 34, 71). The projection occurs through *eros*, moreover, which Heidegger describes as an "aspiration of being" (*Seinserstrebnis*). At one point he also calls this aspiration "longing," *Sehnsucht.*[19]

To the possible objection that the account he gives in these lectures involves an anthropomorphization (*Vermenschlichung*) of the essence of truth, Heidegger responds: "Does one know then without further ado what humanity is, so that one is in a position to decide that truth cannot be something human?" (ET 55/GA 34, 74). Heidegger will make precisely the same point about "anthropomorphism" in the concluding remarks to his first lecture course on Schelling. Addressing the charge that Schelling "humanizes" God and things in general, he remarks that behind this charge "stands the conviction which it doesn't explain further that everyone, of course, generally knows what man is" (STF 163/GA 42, 283). The "turn" in Heidegger's thought consists, above all, in questioning this conviction. The question is: If humanity, arising in the midst of nature as an entity that understands being, belongs to the unfolding of being – of which it is itself an instance of a particular kind – what should one make of its faculties and characteristics? Are freedom and longing then still "only" human, or do they point to aspects of the character of being as much as do the properties of what we take to be the "objective" world? To see freedom, for instance, not as a property of humanity, but as a feature of being itself, as Schelling does, so that in a way humanity is actually the property of freedom (STF 9/GA 42, 15), does involve a kind of "humanizing" of the being of beings – an anthropomorphization of nature, the objection runs. But whether such humanization equals subjective falsification, the projection of a purely human property onto reality, or the apprehension of a true facet of being that gets revealed in the nature of this entity, remains undecided.

[19] Cf. also ¶76 of *The Fundamental Concepts of Metaphysics* (1929/30), on "Projection as the Fundamental Structure … of world-formation," where Heidegger refers to Schelling by name (FCM 364/GA 29/30, 529–30).

The decision depends upon a judgment about the character of the relation between humanity and being itself. Heidegger points out repeatedly in his works over the 1930s that, within the modern Western worldview, an unrecognized presupposition about this relation has been made in favor of subjectivism. In the essay, "On the Essence of Truth," published in 1943 but first given as a lecture in 1930, he remarks ironically, in relation to the question of freedom, that "everyone knows what the human being is" (P 143/ GA 9, 187). This essay is especially significant because Heidegger says in the "Letter of Humanism" that it "provides a certain insight into the thinking of the turning from 'Being and Time' to 'Time and Being'" (BW 231/ GA 9, 328). In it, Heidegger describes freedom as the "ground of the inner possibility" of truth (P 142/ GA 9, 185), because truth requires a form of engagement with entities that holds itself back from them in order to "let" them be what they are:

> To engage oneself with the disclosedness of beings is not to lose oneself in them; rather, such engagement withdraws in the face of beings in order that they might reveal themselves with respect to what and how they are, and in order that presentative correspondence (*vorstellende Angleichung*) might take its standard from them. (P 144/ GA 9, 188–89)

Being "true" to entities, that is, requires a withdrawal from everyday immersion in them and, at the same time, an attentive paying heed to how they are. That is possible only on the basis of the structure of Dasein as free.

After *Being and Time*, Heidegger emphasizes more and more both that human beings do not determine this structure and that they are too quick to interpret it as merely "subjective." Consequently, when Heidegger says that, for Schelling, freedom is not a property of humanity but vice versa (STF 9/ GA 42, 15), this is a claim he wants to endorse. Indeed, he advances it himself in "On the Essence of Truth," where freedom is interpreted as letting-be, a process human beings do not initiate, but into which they are appropriated. In the *Contributions to Philosophy*, the same process is described as an event of appropriation (*Ereignis*) that forms the basis of human capacities for unconcealment and discovery. In part, Heidegger is oriented in these discussions of truth toward a phenomenon that he argues is more basic than correctness: the openness of what-is, a fundamental disclosure occurring prior to, and being the necessary condition for, assertions that could be correct or incorrect. However, he is also analyzing the capacity to hold ourselves to what discloses itself within this openness, where that is an ethical decision. Before we can engage in circumspective deliberation about a practical affair, for example, the world of human concerns in the context of which this affair has its significance must already be disclosed to us. We must then have the capacity to disclose that world, which we do through our shared projecting of ends, but *being* in the truth also requires a self-binding to what the situation genuinely reveals.

Before we can make statements within physics, to give another example, we must disclose nature as a field of mathematically describable objects and relations, which we have the capacity to do by divesting things of significance and noticing properties of them that are independent of our practical ends (BT 69); but, science as an authentic mode of being also requires honest observation and revision in light of what the evidence shows. In each case, there is a struggle to *be* appropriate to the matter that commands our attention, and an understanding of being that makes it possible for us to be appropriate in that manner so as to bring the nature of what-is to light. This, for Heidegger, is the essence of truth.

Heidegger's discussion of "un-truth" (*Un-wahrheit*), "dis-essence" (*Un-wesen*), and "error" (*Irre*) in "On the Essence of Truth" needs to be read in the context of this understanding of truth. Untruth is "the hiddenness of beings" that is "older" than every revelation of this or that being (P 148/ GA 9, 193–94). The hiddenness is the "mystery" and dis-essence of truth, where disessence means pre-essence, a form of non-being or not yet being that precedes all essence (*das vor-wesende Wesen*) (P 148/GA 9, 194). This is the potentiality for being that is the enabling source of unconcealment and of the possibility of error. Error arises through Dasein's tendency toward measureless persistence in securing itself, rooted in the fact that "as eksistent, Dasein is insistent" (P 150/GA 9, 196). "Error" in this case does not mean the incorrectness of a particular statement or judgment, whether on a practical or a theoretical matter. It refers, rather, to a kind of self-forgetting that turns toward things while overlooking limitations, and that may be described as moral because it is rooted not in mere ignorance but in a simultaneous assertion and disregard for which we are responsible.

The correspondence with Schelling consists in the relations drawn between potentiality, actuality, revelation, and error ("evil," in Schelling's account). Schelling tells an ontotheological story according to which there is a distinction between potentiality and actuality in the nature of God, reproduced in all beings, where the being of these beings (i.e. their coming to be) is necessary, within this pantheistic system, for the revelation or "existing" of God. The potentiality of being is reflected in living beings in the form of the drive to be, a blind and egotistical striving. In the case of non-human nature, God's "love," interpreted not as an emotion but as a metaphysical principle of unity, heals strife by keeping each being in its place as a matter of causal necessity. But human beings are special in reflecting the freedom of the divine essence itself. They are released from causal necessity, and with that release arises the possibility of evil, for only human beings can pervert the proper order of things by raising their individual striving above the harmony of the whole in which each entity remains within its assigned limits.

Heidegger does not tell an ontotheological story in which some eternally present cosmic source is supposed to express itself in a created world, but he gives an account that agrees with Schelling's in its analysis of modalities of being and the perverse human striving to be master of all things. While this account can be read as a deconstruction of Schelling's metaphysics to uncover its sources in human experience, if humanity is the site of the unconcealing of being, made possible by being itself, then "human experience" may also point to the truth of being as such. When Heidegger speaks in his later works of the "forgetting of being," he means forgetting the truth of this relation to being, a position involving both ignorance and egoistic assertion. The fault is then both cognitive and dispositional. It fails to recognize, because it refuses to accept, either the finitude of human existence or its relatedness to being, resulting in an overstepping of limits through a drive for total power that leads instead to devastation.

This is the central message of the *Contributions to Philosophy*, in which Heidegger's ontological theses are tied together with his appraisal of the historical moment in which he stands. As in the works that follow it, the forgetting of being is associated in the *Contributions* with the grounding of reality in the subject, who is taken as the ground of being. This, for Heidegger, is a perversion (*Verkehrung*) that can be overcome only through a conversion (*Kehre*) restoring the right relation between being and humanity. Unlike *Being and Time*, the *Contributions* conceives of Dasein not as the being of humanity in general, but as a possible and future way of being for humanity (CP 396/GA 65, 300–301). It is the way of being in which humanity fulfills its essence by recognizing itself as the site of the *Wesung*, the coming to presence, of being, a process that is also the historical happening of "truth," the coming to light of what-is through the medium of human understanding and building. Being needs and uses (*braucht*) humanity for this process (CP 337/GA 65, 251), and the act in which humanity is appropriated by being for the sake of truth is simultaneously the act in which humanity achieves its essence and becomes what it is. This is the "event" referred to in the subtitle of the *Contributions*.

Like Schelling, Heidegger describes the formation of humanity within this event as a sort of internal imaging – *Einbuldung* (CP 410/GA 65, 312). Through it, humanity comes to reflect being, not as if being were there first and humanity created as an image of it, but in that the understanding of being first emerges *as* this reflection. The envisioning of humanity is then simultaneously the self-envisioning of being. It requires the relation between ground and existence, potentiality and actuality, that structures human freedom, but this relation brings with it the possibility of extreme disorder (CP 343/GA 65, 257). In the present age, according to the *Contributions*, the terrible "disessence" (*Unwesen*) of being is manifest in "machination"(CP 184–88/GA 65, 126–28), the point of absolute subjectivism, where human thought, conceived as representation but powered by the drive for mastery, is posited as the ground and measure of all being. Primary to this conception of thought is the notion of "making," and machination implicitly takes making as its lead in determining the nature of entities. It is then related to *techne* (CP 192/GA 65, 132). Both suggest a way of being involved with entities that seeks to make them over according to an idea, where the idea is a representation of the being of the maker, an expressed desire. Machination is this way of being, raised to a power that acknowledges no boundaries or limits (*Grenze*) (CP 191/GA 65, 131). The refusal of boundaries gives machination its peculiar sense of a quantity that becomes a quality (CP 195–99/GA 135–37).

To have *experienced* the age in this way, however, Heidegger suggests, is the first stage of the reversal in which the true relation between being and humanity might be restored. The reversal is prepared through a resoluteness that turns toward the need or distress (*Not*) of the age, and registers a sense of abandonment. Turning toward this need means holding oneself open for what is necessary, *das Notwendige* (CP 516/GA 65, 398). Since this is the highest decision, freedom turns out to be nothing other than turning toward what needs to be done, in a given age, with its specific forms of distress. Genuine freedom is therefore also necessity, *Not-wendigkeit*, a turning toward the distress of the times that enables the envisioning of the new that is needed. The moment in which this decision happens is now described as "the time of being" (CP 647/GA 65, 508), when humanity comes into accord with being, echoing the "moment" of decision in *Being and Time* wherein an individual both discerns and resolves upon her "fate."

There is much to question in Heidegger's ontological reading of the political and cultural movements surrounding him in mid-1930s Germany, as presented in the *Contributions to Philosophy*. But its positive appropriation of Schelling does help to clarify Heidegger's understanding of freedom as well as his critique of subjectivism. It illustrates how genuine freedom can plausibly be seen as coinciding with a form of "necessity" – not the necessity of causal determination but of placing oneself under the obligation to do what needs to be done at a given time, where the decision to accept this obligation is a kind of responsiveness rather than self-centered choosing or assertion of will.

This is not to say that Heidegger merely reproduces Schelling's metaphysics in a different guise. The history of being that ends in "machination" is also the history of the metaphysical tradition Heidegger seeks to leave behind, and an important aspect of the "other beginning" for which Heidegger attempts to prepare is that it renounces all and every attempt at a "system" (CP 112/GA 65, 65). It also bears repeating that Heidegger is *not* engaging in ontotheology. Being is not *a* being; Heidegger's account is oriented toward the origin and character of the coming to be and passing away of what is, not toward an entity that is supposed to underlie this process.

Still, for Heidegger as for Schelling, the distinction between ground and existence that we experience in our own being points to the structure of being itself, revealed in human freedom. As to evil, it is a positive force consisting in measureless self-assertion, an egoism not mastered by recognition of the proper limits of an individual being, where only human beings are capable of this recognition. Such perversion reveals something, too, though: it reveals the dark power of the ground of being, in the form of a blind striving to *be*. Because striving is not by itself evil, it cannot be said that its source is evil. It becomes evil only if not mastered by the respect for boundaries that establishes harmony, a perversion possible only for those free natures that reflect most fully the "jointure" at the heart of being.

I will have more to say about this "jointure" and its implications for morality and politics in my discussion of Heidegger's notion of justice, in Chapter 4. First, however, I want to explore the implications of Heidegger's ontology of Dasein for what is owed to entities like ourselves (Chapter 2), and to ask where this leaves those entities we encounter within the world that are not like ourselves (Chapter 3).

2 Is Humanity an End in Itself?

I have argued for the coherence of Heidegger's understanding of human freedom, against charges that he embraces either voluntarism or determinism. What, though, of the worry, expressed by many of his critics, that Heidegger's highly situated conception of knowing and acting provides no foundation for the formulation of any universal moral principles that could guide and restrict the scope of human freedom? Authenticity may consist in following conscience, but without any objective, universally binding norms determining the content of what we may and may not do to others, we are still left with too high a degree of subjective judgment and too little protection against its errors.

This concern is especially pertinent given Heidegger's engagement with Nazism. Although his active participation in the Nazi party was short-lived and based on an inaccurate interpretation of what it stood for, it is fair to wonder whether this choice demonstrates not only Heidegger's personal flaws but also the limitations of his situationist ethic. It seems that an individual is "authentic" when he or she resolutely decides upon a course of action appropriate to a radically particular historical moment. Supposing this is a response to the call of conscience and the perceived need of the times, if the implication is that there is no way of deciding what is right and wrong except in the moment, the result would appear to be moral subjectivism, even if the text does not authorize egoistic self-assertion.

In addition, *Being and Time* does insist that all choice is enabled, and therefore limited, by inherited traditions, which would seem to imply that there are no standards to guide judgment except those internal to a specific tradition. I argued that Heidegger leaves room for creative adaptation of what is inherited; but, in the absence of universal principles for moral judgment, is this not a species of historical relativism about morality?[1] To make matters worse, because the sections of *Being and Time* dealing with historicality stress the embeddedness of individual action within the collective history or "destiny" of a people (*Volk*), critics have also claimed that the work is inherently predisposed to

[1] Löwith 1995, 72. See also Julian Young's defense of Heidegger against this kind of charge in Young 1997, 96–98.

favor extreme nationalist forms of politics in general, and National Socialism in particular,[2] by legitimizing an individual's commitment to furthering the aims of his or her own community, without regard for the interests of others.[3] All of these criticisms have in common the view that *Being and Time* utterly rejects universalism, proposing no transcultural and transhistorical norms for moral conduct, and no theory of humanity upon which those norms could be grounded.

One obvious contrast with such a position is Kant's moral philosophy, and yet, among the many defenses of *Being and Time* against accusations of relativism, a number have sought to highlight commonalities with Kant. A claim made repeatedly in these defenses is that Heidegger's phenomenological account in *Being and Time* reaffirms the version of Kant's categorical imperative stating that humanity should never be treated merely as a means, but always also as an end in itself.[4] Charles Sherover, among others, suggests precisely this in "Founding an Existential Ethic":

> Heidegger's road to the centrality of responsibility and the resoluteness it engenders first comes to solicitous concern, a mode of responsible involvement with other persons. Building on the fundamental Kantian distinction between persons and things, Heidegger has differentiated that circumspective concern we display to the things about us from our solicitous comportment toward other persons. Only through solicitous behaviour do other persons enter into our experience *qua* persons (instead of things). It is toward them that we are able to exhibit moral responsibility. Reminiscent of Kant's injunction that the prime moral responsibility is to treat them *qua* persons and to enhance *their* own free self-development, Heidegger abjured the domination of others because it infringes on their own sovereignty of care. (Sherover 1981, 227)

Similarly, Lawrence Vogel proposes that Heidegger's fundamental ontology can be interpreted "as providing an existential basis for the second version of Kant's categorical imperative" (Vogel 1994, 9). Julian Young makes the same claim, arguing that Heidegger's conception of "authentic solicitude" is "a *moral* relationship … for what it amounts to is the fundamental Kantian principle of respect: never treat humanity either in your own person or that of another as a mere means, but always as an end-in-itself" (Young 1997, 104).[5]

[2] Rockmore 1992, 47–48; cf. Farias 1992, 345.

[3] Lawrence Vogel raises, but does not support, this suspicion in *The Fragile "We"* (Vogel 1994, 65–66).

[4] One statement of this principle runs: "So act that you use humanity, whether in your own person or in the person of any other, always at the same time as an end, never merely as a means" (GMM 38).

[5] Cf. Michael Zimmerman, who, however, broadens the claim, in light of Heidegger's later works: "According to Heidegger, *authentic* human existence discloses things and people in ways appropriate to their own possibilities, while *inauthentic* human existence discloses people and things inappropriately, for example, merely as objects or as raw material" (Zimmerman 1992, 62).

These interpretations support my general thesis that Heidegger is a moral realist who grounds appropriate conduct toward entities in recognition and respect for the being – in a sense that encompasses essence and existence – of those entities. The nature of humanity is defined by freedom, and by the possession of a kind of self that has the capacity to let go of its everyday self-concern and follow the call of conscience. In this chapter, I examine what that entails for appropriate conduct toward human beings, focusing on Heidegger's relation to the Kantian thesis that human beings are ends in themselves and may never be treated purely as means.

Dasein as the Final "For-the-sake-of"

We have seen that major portions of Heidegger's analysis of Dasein in *Being and Time* are concerned with phenomena related to morality, as an aspect of being in the world, and that the terms he uses to describe these phenomena are inescapably evaluative in nature. That is certainly true of Heidegger's analysis of conscience and guilt in Division Two of *Being and Time* (BT ¶54–60), which describes the possibility of authenticity. Prior to this point, Heidegger has outlined a condition where Dasein is absorbed in its daily concerns. It is busy achieving its practical ends, and the world it encounters, as well as its understanding of itself, is determined by this manner of existence (BT ¶12–18). The subject of this kind of everyday concerned activity, Heidegger eventually claims, is not really the "I myself" (BT 115, 267), but the "they" (BT 126), everyone and no one, the force of anonymous public opinions and conventions that no in particular can be said to have authored. Heidegger calls this manner of existence *uneigentlich*, a term usually translated as "inauthentic," but also carrying connotations of being "unowned." The suggestion is that individuals are not genuinely themselves here, for they do not have a hold on their own lives. Heidegger describes the social interactions belonging to this way of being in exclusively negative terms. They are deceitful and competitive, characterized by idle talk and evasion (BT ¶27, ¶35–38).

It is difficult to accept Heidegger's own statement that such a negatively charged interpretation of everyday sociality "is purely ontological in its aims, and is far removed from any moralizing critique of everyday Dasein" (BT 167). If he means that his descriptions of inauthenticity are not intended to be disparaging, the statement might have some plausibility in relation to the sections of *Being and Time* dealing with concerned pragmatic activity. When Heidegger first introduces the terms "authenticity" and "inauthenticity," he remarks that Dasein is inauthentic "when busy, when excited, when interested, when ready for enjoyment" (BT 43), and these states are not judged negatively. But the same cannot be said of Heidegger's account of Dasein's submission to the "they," a state he describes as "seductive," "tranquillizing," and "alienating," where Dasein becomes "entangled in itself" and caught in a "downward plunge" (BT 176–78). The word "inauthenticity" is intrinsically evaluative, suggesting deception, a case of something lesser being passed off as the real thing, which is always something better. No one speaks of rhinestones not being genuine diamonds.

One might take issue with the contempt for ordinary social relations expressed in Heidegger's account of the "they" in *Being and Time*, and with the implication that everyday being with others is mainly either competitive or absorbed in joint projects of distraction and irresponsibility. The fundamental point Heidegger is making, though, about the condition of inauthenticity is that, in this way of being, an individual is not decisively in charge of her own existence, and is even running away from its truth. The possibility of a shift to responsibility and transparency is granted by the phenomenon of conscience, whose appeal breaks through Dasein's immersion in the world of its concerns, challenging the status of the dispossessed public self with whom Dasein exclusively identifies most of the time. Conscience shows me another possible form of being, if I am willing to listen and to accept responsibility for being myself.

That also means accepting "being guilty," an expression Heidegger uses to refer not primarily to an individual's having committed a fault in the past, but to her capacity for determining who and what she may be in the future, in an always definite and limited context. As noted in the previous chapter, Heidegger claims that being guilty, thus understood, is "the existential condition … for morality in general and for the possible forms which this may take factically" (BT 286). A willingness to be guilty, therefore, is a condition for being moral. It involves hearing and submitting to the voice of conscience, where such submission is, at the same time, a genuine choosing of oneself (BT 287). There is, then, a sense in which the fundamental question guiding this account *is* ontological rather than prescriptive, in that Heidegger's analysis of conscience and guilt does not identify moral norms, but the conditions for the possibility of following them. It asks, with respect to Dasein, what kind of entity is this that it *can* be moral, that it can ever bind itself to the appeal of a "should" in the first place? But the description is at the same time normative, for it is hard to see how anyone could judge self-deception, evasion, and irresponsibility as no "lesser" than self-transparency, freedom, and a willingness to answer for oneself.

The account of authenticity in *Being and Time* draws on many sources that do have normative content,[6] and its analysis of conscience includes an attempt

[6] A number of these are detailed by Kisiel in *The Genesis of Heidegger's "Being and Time,"* where Kisiel traces Heidegger's early engagement with medieval mysticism, Kierkegaard, Jaspers, Augustine, Aristotle, and St. Paul (Kisiel 1993, 77–84, 108–11, 137–46, 172–92, 221–300).

to uncover the roots of a number of specifically Kantian formulations.[7] One of these is the distinction Kant draws, within his practical philosophy, between the phenomenal and the noumenal aspects of the self. For Kant, the former is the self as it appears in the sensible world, driven by its natural inclinations and therefore, like the rest of nature, subject to the determination of causal laws. The noumenal self, on the other hand, is not an object apprehended in the world.[8] It is the source of freedom, the capacity for "unconditioned causality" (CPrR 88/AA 5, 105). This is the aspect of the self that can resist inclinations by submitting to the moral law discerned by its own reason (CPrR 68–9/AA 5, 80). This self, the subject of an autonomous will, and the ground of all the actions that follow from that will, cannot itself be *known*, Kant claims (CPrR 44/AA 5, 50). No explanation can be given of its spontaneous activity (CPrR 83/AA 5, 99), and yet its existence is undeniable, as is attested by "the judicial sentences of that wonderful capacity in us which we call conscience" (CPrR 82/AA 5, 98).

Although Heidegger takes issue with Kant's representation of conscience as a court of justice (BT 271), he is attempting to discover what he considers to be the existential origins of Kant's account of morality, its foundation in our experience of being ourselves in the world. Dasein is also described as having two "selves," two possible ways of being. One of these consists in an unsteady being driven about by daily concerns, while the other is a self-possessed choosing to be responsible. The voice of conscience resists any possibility of being made familiar to the self-understanding of Dasein when it is fleeing from anxiety and turning toward the "world." It is therefore alien to the everyday self of absorbed activity, but it is nonetheless only the call of Dasein to itself and does not issue from a foreign power (BT 275).[9] *Entschlossenheit*, resoluteness, names the decision to heed the voice of this

[7] Kisiel does note the influence of Kant, but mainly addresses the epistemological issues that are the focus of the first critique (Kisiel 1993, 408–15).

[8] Julian Young misses the agreement with Kant in Heidegger's account of conscience and authentic decision when he writes: "'One is what one does' (BT 239), says Heidegger bluntly, placing himself in the same camp as Schopenhauer, Wittgenstein and Ryle, and the opposite one to Descartes and Kant" (Young 1997, 58). What Heidegger actually says is: "But proximally and for the most part everyday Dasein understands itself in terms of that with *which* it is customarily concerned. 'One *is*' what one does" (B 239). It is the "they" who think this way, not Heidegger, and not authentic Dasein.

[9] Richard Wolin misreads the text when he claims that Heidegger characterizes conscience as "an alien power by which Dasein is dominated," thereby revealing an "abandonment of modern philosophical doctrines (in this case, the Kantian category of human autonomy)" (Wolin 1990, 42). Heidegger does not affirm that conscience is "an alien power." He says that this has been one way of interpreting the phenomenal findings he has just presented, which when carried further leads in the direction of theological explanations. His own claim is that both the theological and the biological explanations "pass over the phenomenal findings too hastily" (BT 320). He is actually *rejecting* the view that the appeal of conscience involves heteronomy.

other self that calls upon Dasein to be responsible or answerable (*verantwortlich*) for itself (BT 288).

There is no specific content in such a decision, just as there is no specific content in the "duty" to which Kant alludes when he speaks of the duty "to cultivate our conscience, to sharpen our attention to the voice of the internal judge and to use every means to get it a hearing (*Gehör*)" (MPV 60/AA 6, 401). Kant claims here that "unconscientiousness is not a lack of conscience but the propensity not to heed its judgement" (MPV 60/AA 6, 401). Likewise, Heidegger writes that "understanding the call is choosing; but it is not a choosing of conscience, which as such cannot be chosen ... what is chosen is *having-a-conscience* as being-free for one's ownmost being-guilty," i.e. "*wanting to have a conscience*" (BT 322). Both describe this decidedness as constituting a radical break, resulting in a steadiness or constancy on the part of the self. Kant speaks of a "revolution," "rebirth," or "explosion" through which a person first acquires the moral character to follow fixed principles against the shifting pull of inclinations and instincts.[10] Heidegger claims that "*the constancy of the self*, in the double sense of steadiness and steadfastness is the *authentic* counter-possibility to the non-self-constancy which is characteristic of irresolute falling" (BT 322).

Thus, as Sherover notes, Heidegger's analysis of guilt is primarily oriented toward understanding the "fundamental capacity to make oneself responsible – facing Kant's question of how morality's possibility may be established" (Sherover 1981, 226). Kant understands this possibility in terms of a capacity for self-legislation that situates the self between two "realms": the phenomenal or sensible realm, in which it is an object driven by inclinations that are in the final analysis causally determined, and the noumenal or intelligible realm, in which it is a rational will, unconditioned and free. In *Being and Time*, Heidegger is not directly staking out a position within the metaphysical debate about determinism and free will, and his phenomenological account rejects in principle the distinction between the phenomenal and the noumenal. He is attempting, though, to produce an account of the experiences of being in the world that give rise to such distinctions, and to lay out accurately the phenomena that any explanatory account will need to preserve.

Now, having a capacity to resist proximate inclinations, and to impose order upon oneself, does not on its own entail having any form of obligation toward others, let alone the precise form proposed by Kant. Nietzsche's explanation of conscience in *The Genealogy of Morals* also acknowledges the existence of this capacity but does not draw Kantian moral conclusions, to put it mildly

[10] *Die Religion innerhalb der Grenzen der bloßen Vernunft* (*Religion within the Limits of Reason Alone*), AA 6, 47; *Anthropologie in pragmatischer Hinsicht (Anthropology from a Pragmatic Point of View)*, AA 7, 294.

(GM 57–67). Belief in a capacity for self-legislation is compatible with rejection of any principle that would be equally binding on all persons, or that would require treating all persons in an equal manner. Indeed, Heidegger alludes to Nietzsche's interpretation of conscience, along with that of Kant and others, in a footnote to *Being and Time* (SZ 272), and his account is trying to present the phenomena on the basis of which these varying interpretations are constructed. I noted in Chapter 1 that Heidegger does not reduce conscience to will to power, but I also acknowledged the hazards of taking individual conscience as a guide to moral action.

There is, however, a further dimension to Heidegger's analysis that brings him into greater proximity with Kant. Moral philosophies proposing universally valid norms are usually based on theories about the nature of the entity to which moral concern or obligation is owed. For Kant, the category comprising such entities includes all "rational natures," where rationality, at the practical level oriented toward action, is defined in terms of autonomy, the capacity freely to choose one's own ends and to discipline one's pursuit of them through respect for the moral law. This is in turn a respect for autonomy itself. In spite of the absence of any reliance on "rationality" as a foundation for respect, Heidegger's account of Dasein is fundamentally the same. *Being and Time* is anti-universalist in many ways, claiming that all understanding proceeds on the basis of a "fore-structure," a pattern of conceptions and expectations held in advance, shaping all interpretation (BT ¶32). Nonetheless, Heidegger is trying to isolate and define the formal structures or properties of human existence, which he names "existentials" to distinguish them from "categories." The term "category," he argues, should be reserved for what we come across as lying before us in the world rather than what we ourselves are, given that our experience of dealing with objects is radically different from our experience of *being* ourselves when we make decisions and act (BT 44–45). The existence of Dasein is not like that of objects; it is fundamentally a potentiality-for-being (*Seinkönnen*) (BT 144), since Dasein is an entity that relates to itself and cares about itself, and does so primarily through a grasp of what it might be able to do or be. The ability to project possible goals or ends and choose between them therefore belongs to the very nature of the entity that I myself am. The world I share with others is organized according to these projected ends, but in my everyday mode of existence, I am not reflectively aware of this fact, and so of myself as a *capacity* for such projection. People even have a tendency to interpret themselves in terms of the "world" (BT 15–16), thereby modeling their understanding of themselves on their understanding of the things they encounter within the world.

Heidegger's description tries to correct a self-misinterpretation to which, he thinks, we are generally prone, by laying out the activity of projecting that is invisible within our day-to-day, concerned engagement with things within the world, and yet underlies it. *Being and Time* proposes that, without this activity, the "world" would not *be* at all. Entities of some sort would continue to be; Heidegger is not saying that the bare factuality of these entities depends upon our awareness of them.[11] The world we inhabit, however, the human life-world, is not made up of indifferent entities or of mathematically describable spatio-temporal objects. It is made up of things apprehended within patterns of meaning or significance, and those patterns are constructed, ultimately, by reference to human ends. The stuff of *this* world, which we encounter most of the time, consists of things that are ready-to-hand, or available for use. These things – hammers and nails, pens and paper, sewing needles, doorknobs, and brooms – are grasped with a view to accomplishing something, and they are measured in terms of that view so as to be found suitable or faulty. Heidegger labels this kind of view *Umsicht*, a word ordinarily meaning "circumspection" or "prudence." In the way of "seeing" that belongs to everyday prudential activity, that is, the things we seize upon are understood and evaluated in terms of an "in-order-to"; they are assigned or referred toward some end, so that their intelligibility and goodness rest upon their involvement in purposive projects.

The final end of these projects is human existence itself. At one point in his analysis of the "world," conceived as a component in the structure of Dasein, Heidegger writes:

> But the totality of involvements itself goes back ultimately to a 'towards-which' in which there is *no* further involvement; this 'towards-which' is not an entity with the kind of being that belongs to what is ready-to-hand within a world; it is rather an entity whose being is defined as being-in-the-world, and to whose state of being, worldhood itself belongs. This primary 'towards-which' is not just another 'towards-this' as something in which an involvement is possible. The primary 'towards-which' is a 'for-the-sake-of-which'. But the 'for-the-sake-of' always pertains to the being of Dasein, for which, in its being, that very being is essentially an *issue*. We have thus indicated the interconnection by which the structure of an involvement leads to Dasein's very being as the sole authentic 'for-the-sake-of-which': for the present, however, we shall pursue this no further. (BT 84)

When Heidegger does pursue this further, he asserts that "those entities towards which Dasein as being-with comports itself do not have the kind of being which belongs to equipment ready-to-hand; they are themselves Dasein," and "these entities are not objects of concern, but rather of *solicitude*" (BT 121). In other words, the end of all the ends, according to which the practical world is ordered and measured, is Dasein's own being, and to understand this is also to understand that Dasein's being is not constituted through an "in-order-to," but

[11] BT 212: "Being (not entities) is dependent upon the understanding of being; that is to say reality (not the real) is dependent upon care"; and BT 230: "Being (not entities) is something which 'there is' only in so far as truth is. And truth *is* only in so far as and as long as Dasein is."

is a "for-the-sake-of." The "seeing" appropriate to being with others, therefore, can never be the prudential looking around characteristic of instrumental "concern" (*Besorgen*). The appropriate form of comportment toward the other – the comportment that recognizes and respects the genuine being of the other – is, rather, solicitude or "care for" (*Fürsorge*), which, in its authentic form, "helps the other to become transparent to himself *in* his care and to become *free for* it" (BT 159).

In *Being and Time, Sorge* or "care," a word that ordinarily means "worry," describes the basic character of human existence. It is through care, Heidegger says, glossing Seneca, that "man's *perfectio* – his transformation into that which he can be in being-free for his ownmost possibilities ... is 'accomplished'" (BT 199). To care *for* others in a way that acknowledges their being *as* care, and thus as it genuinely is, means helping them to accomplish their ends, but not in a way that would "leap in" for them and disburden them of responsibility. Authentic solicitude, recognizing the true character of other persons as Dasein, wants them to be clear about that character as well. It then helps the other to become transparent to him- or herself as a free being, and to be responsive to the appeal of conscience that reveals and directs this freedom (see BT 344). That is equivalent to helping the other to be authentic.

Lawrence Vogel is therefore right to claim that "in authentic *Mitsein* ['being-with'] as 'liberating solicitude' we find the ultimate sense in which fundamental ontology is a fundamental ethics" (Vogel 1994, 68), although liberating solicitude must be distinguished from a concern for the other's "welfare" (78). On this reading, Heidegger's phenomenological sketches of authentic Dasein in *Being and Time* do not depict an isolated individual acting on the arbitrariness of its own self-seeking and self-projected resolutions. Rather, they involve "an attunement to the particularity of others, to the other *as* truly other, stemming from an awareness of the singularity of one's own existence (71). Vogel argues that, unlike the "impersonal" stance that attempts to subsume both situations and persons under general categories and rules, this attunement manifests itself as "an *interpersonal* orientation motivated by one's desire not to incorporate others into 'the universal' but, rather, to 'let others be' in their freedom for their own possibilities and to allow one's own self-understanding to be informed by theirs" (71). I have tried to demonstrate in greater detail how this "authentic being-with" is grounded in the central features of Heidegger's account of Dasein. There *is* a "universal" orientation here, in that the analysis leads to conclusions about the proper treatment of all entities having the character of Dasein.

In short, *Being and Time* attempts to uncover the phenomenological basis for Kant's view that the property of persons in virtue of which they are worthy of respect is freedom. Its interpretation of the relation between Dasein and "world" also reveals the roots of the idea that freedom has absolute "value" (though Heidegger will subject this term to critical phenomenological scrutiny), and is the ultimate source of the relative value of things. "Authenticity" is Heidegger's version of autonomy. Like Kant, he presents its possibility as the result of a decision whose motivating source appeals without compelling and is identified as the self rather than any alien authority. The result is a description of self-regulation that is supposed to represent a realization of autonomy, and to be a necessary condition for any form of morality.[12] Given that we do not find ourselves to be alone in the world, but encounter others who are there with us, we cannot consistently recognize those others as being like ourselves, while treating them as if they were not. As Sherover observes, authentic resoluteness "holds itself responsible for the freedom of others as well as for its own" (Sherover 1981, 234).

Being and Time therefore presents a phenomenological justification of a crucial element in Kant's moral theory, which Frank Schalow summarizes as follows:

> Persons have worth independently of any use they may serve to fulfill a given desire. The worth of things, on the other hand, derives from the use we assign them. Kant believes that it is possible to formulate a maxim that expresses the necessity inherent in the above contrast, so that we can stipulate a priori how we are permitted to treat persons. (Schalow 1986, 41)

Heidegger formulates no such maxim; but, it follows from his phenomenological analysis that there are ways of being toward others that accord with a recognition of the genuine character of their existence as Dasein, and ones that do not. This is a prime example of my thesis, in agreement with Schalow as well as with Julian Young (Schalow 2001, 260; Young 1997, 209), that Heidegger's moral realism (for lack of a better term) involves a rejection of the modern distinction between fact and value, which entails that the latter cannot be derived from the former. The analysis in *Being and Time* sees appropriate being with – i.e. liberating solicitude – as a necessary consequence of the genuine recognition of the being of Dasein, and of others as entities having the character of Dasein. On this understanding, it would be impossible to give a true description of what Dasein *is* while claiming that it is appropriate to use entities of this sort as tools. Genuinely *being* in the truth on this matter then means behaving in accordance with the truth of being. It means being "true" to the being of this entity, Dasein, whose structure is as has been described, while grasping that truth at a more than merely intellectual level. Thus, while Heidegger describes a way of being rather than stating a prescription, he

[12] Cf. *Metaphysical Principles of Virtue*: "For I cannot recognize myself as bound to others except insofar as I bind myself at the same time: the law by virtue of which I regard myself as bound arises in all cases from my own practical reason, through which I am constrained while being at the same time the one who constrains" (MPV 78/AA 6, 417).

is providing a justification for Kant's formula of humanity, rooted in a true understanding of how Dasein is.

Further evidence for this reading of *Being and Time* can be found in some of Heidegger's own interpretations of Kant in works composed during the period following the publication of *Being and Time*. *The Basic Problems of Phenomenology* (1927), for instance, contains the following remarks on the Kantian notion of "respect," regarded highly by Heidegger:[13]

> Respect for the law is the active ego's respect for itself as the self which is not understood by means of self conceit and self-love. (BPP 135/ GA 21, 191)

> Respect is the mode of the ego's being-with-itself according to which it does not disparage the hero in its soul. The moral feeling, as respect for the law, is nothing but the self's being responsible to itself and for itself. This moral feeling is a distinctive way in which the ego understands itself as ego directly, purely, and free of all sensuous determination. (BPP 135–36/GA 21, 192)

> Respect reveals the dignity before which and for which the self knows itself to be responsible. Only in responsibility does the self first reveal itself – the self not in a general sense as knowledge of an ego in general but as in each case mine, the ego as in each case the individual factical ego. (BPP 137/GA 21, 194)

In answer to the question, "What is the *ontological meaning of the person thus made manifest in respect?*" Heidegger says: "persons are 'objective' ends, that is, things (*res* in the broadest sense) whose existence is an end in itself," and he cites the categorical imperative that follows from this ontological determination (BPP, 138–39/GA 21, 196; EHF 198/GA 67, 291). The only criticism Heidegger makes of Kant's account of the moral personality concerns his failure to interrogate the meaning of the term "exists," in the claim that the person exists as an end in itself (BPP 147/GA 21, 209). There is then something basic left unanalyzed in Kant's understanding of the nature of persons, as distinguished from things, but that does not undermine Heidegger's agreement with what Kant's analysis has managed to uncover about this distinction.

The complaint that Heidegger's account, unlike Kant's, offers no foundation for universal moral principles and therefore falls into relativism misunderstands the conclusions of *Being and Time*. Olafson claims that "[Heidegger's] version of autonomous moral agency ... is conceived in isolation from anything like the moral law that was its essential counterpart in Kant's ethical theory" (Olafson 1998, 47), but this is true in only a limited sense. Given the stress *Being and Time* places on history and situation, Heidegger could not accept,

[13] "Kant's interpretation of the phenomenon of respect is probably the most brilliant phenomenological analysis of the phenomenon of morality that we have from him" (BPP 133/GA 21, 189).

and certainly does not advance, a set of rules that all individuals should follow in all circumstances. He also would not want to derive moral obligations from formal principles of reason, a procedure utterly alien to his philosophical methodology and assumptions. But he does propose that a proper understanding of my own being entails an appropriate manner of conduct toward any entity that, like myself, counts as a person (BT 42). To cite Vogel: "That the other is one who is free because his possibilities are his own to appropriate means that it is a violation of his 'existence' to treat him as a pawn of one's own freedom" (Vogel 1994, 91). It also follows that any other who has the structure of Dasein is appropriately held to be responsible for his or her actions.

If a great deal of indeterminacy remains as to what particular rules of conduct follow from such a general recognition of the character of Dasein as free and responsible, this does not mean that the author of *Being and Time* was a moral relativist or nihilist. As Julian Young points out:

> To claim that the procedure Heidegger offers for determining contentful ethical value is *inadequate* to that task is clearly different from claiming that Heidegger offers no procedure at all, that he does not care about values other than those of style. It is often argued that Kant's 'categorical imperative' fails to generate any of the particular duties he wants it to generate. Yet no one is tempted to call Kant a 'moral nihilist'. (Young 1997, 84)

It might be objected that Heidegger's existential rewriting of Kant's formula of humanity, stipulating that persons may not be treated purely as means, is not accompanied by a similar retrieval of Kant's formula of universality, which requires asking myself whether I could rationally will that anyone should act according to the maxim I would be following in a contemplated action. It is true that the radically situated and irreducibly unique character of being-in-the-world described in *Being and Time* carries the consequence that no universally applicable rules of moral conduct can be formulated. A problem with Kant's test of universalizability, on the other hand, is that if the maxims to be tested are fomulated as general rules, they admit of obvious exceptions, while too specific a formulation generates no moral rules at all. It is not hard to imagine situations in which lying or stealing is the right thing to do, for a particular person in a given set of circumstances. But if the question posed to test the morality of that action is only whether one could will that anyone who is *precisely* that person in that situation should lie or steal, the test is useless for the purpose of producing moral rules. Heidegger follows Tauler and Kierkegaard in conceiving of conscience as calling me to a particular task in a particular situation, while recognizing the character of others as similarly called and equally responsible. This revision preserves a revised version of Kant's respect for autonomy but abandons the aim, central to Kant's project, of formulating universal moral rules that could serve as guarantees of right action. Indeed,

Heidegger's account excludes the possibility of any such formulation, and the certainty it would bring. That is not, however, because he is a moral nihilist. It is because, on Heidegger's analysis of the fundamental character of being in the world, the search for this kind of security is mistaken about the being of Dasein.

The charge of nihilism against Heidegger often also rests on the claim that *Being and Time* offers a descriptive ontology but no normative ethics. One expects such an ethics to speak directly of values, to make judgments about good and bad and right and wrong, and to use the language of "should" and "ought," none of which is to be found in Heidegger's account. But that account points to a deeper kind of realism that does not rest on "values" and "judgments," notions Heidegger regarded as highly subjectivistic. Again, it is a matter of *truth*, of what is true about entities but also of *being* true, where this is a moral question concerning the way of being that is required to "correspond" to how things are revealed to be. Heidegger is a moral realist partly because he maintains there is a truth of the matter about what different ranges of entities are like, and this truth obligates us to treat them in a manner appropriate to their being. He is at the same time sensitive both to the historicity of our understanding and to the multiple ways that understanding is occluded by factors that are products of decisions for which we are responsible. Being *in* the truth is a mode of comportment, a way of holding myself before the truth of "things" (meant broadly as all that is), and it may be refused through other modes of comportment that are possible for a free being, such as self-conceit and self-love. These are refusals to hear the silent speaking of being, which is not a mystical voice calling from the heavens but the familiar phenomenon of a person's being able to know what is true, while refusing to heed that truth. If there remains something mysterious about the very idea of such a phenomenon, it is nonetheless a necessary condition for moral responsibility, at least for conceptions of moral wrongdoing that see it as involving not only ignorance but an act of will.

It might be, though, that some of the criticisms leveled at *Being and Time* over the years are not obviated by drawing parallels with Kant, because they point to shortcomings Heidegger shares with Kant. Furthermore, when Heidegger criticizes the subject-centeredness of Western metaphysics in his later works, his formulations risk seeing humanity as being for the sake of something other than itself after all. Obviously, it is also pertinent that, in the intervening years, Heidegger for a time supported a regime that has become in emblematic of failure to respect the humanity of all persons, and that was entirely willing to treat some as means to the ends of others, even to the point of killing them. Heidegger never supported genocide, but his embrace of Nazism in the early 1930s has to raise questions about the moral status of humanity in his thought during this period. If the analytic of

Dasein in *Being and Time* entails liberating solicitude toward all persons, how could Heidegger have set this moral constraint aside in his political actions?

According to Habermas, Heidegger's refusal to acknowledge the Christian origins of his thought in *Being and Time* lifts an important control, "the idea of the equality of all before God and of the freedom of each individual – an idea that was still central to Hegel" (Habermas 1993a, 196). But in fact, nothing in the philosophical content of *Being and Time* is disconsonant with this idea, and much reinforces it. As Nikolas Kompridis writes, "there is no evidence that the ideal of freedom as self-determination at issue in *Being and Time* is incompatible with the principle of equal respect for all; indeed, it must suppose equal respect for all" (Kompridis 1999, 130). Kompridis draws the conclusion that, "for all its deficiencies, Heidegger's ethics none the less expresses an ideal of freedom as self-determination which can be realized (once again, contrary to Heidegger's own self-understanding) only under conditions of liberal democracy" (Kompridis 1999, 130). Part of the reason Heidegger did not himself draw this conclusion has to do with his understanding of culture and ethnicity, subjects I discuss in later chapters. But in the next part of the present chapter, I suggest that some of Heidegger's failings actually arise precisely from problematic features of the Kantian conception of freedom as the basis of worth that *Being and Time* supports, and its partial continuation in Heidegger's later thought.

Humanity as a Vehicle for the Disclosure of Being

In the case of both Kant and Heidegger, the "liberating solicitude," to use Heidegger's formulation, that respects the autonomy of the other is appropriate to persons in virtue of their possession of certain capacities. These capacities *make* Dasein a person, a self properly described as a "who" rather than a "what." For Heidegger, liberating solicitude is the authentic mode of being with those others who have the structure of Dasein defined as care. That means any other for whom his own being is an issue, who is capable of projecting possibilities, and whose grasp of what there is in the moment is shaped by the anticipation of a future that has not forgotten the past. Dasein is, in other words, a narrative entity, who can tell and construct stories and histories. What makes solicitude the appropriate form of comportment toward Dasein, then, for an entity capable of such comportment, is the relation to possibility that allows Dasein to make of itself a story of which it is at least a co-author. I reserve for the next chapter the question of where this leaves other sentient beings who do not have this structure, who may live and feel, and in some sense care about their own being, but who do not transcend the actual toward the possible in quite the way Dasein does.

Another, and related, question about Heidegger's analysis concerns the status of bodily suffering and well-being among human beings. These features of human life are not, we should notice, a focus of either Heidegger's or Kant's attention. The body and its needs barely register in *Being and Time*, as Hans Jonas notes: "But is the body ever mentioned? Is 'care' ever traced back to it, to concern about nourishment, for instance – indeed, to *physical* needs at all?" (Jonas 1996, 47). In spite of Heidegger's close attention to practical activity in Division I of *Being and Time*, the networks of involvements in which tools are situated are never shown to be grounded in the needs and vulnerabilities of the body, nor is the body ever thematized as such. Rather, its needs and desires are volatilized into a system of ends. Authentic existence, moreover, is opposed to the everyday, absorbed activity of dealing with one's concerns. It consists in a self-aware and self-controlled *choosing* of ends, and this is what liberating solicitude respects. Even Heidegger's emphasis on death does not lead to a focus on the deficiencies and afflictions of the lived body. The result is a level of abstraction, where the need and fragility of the body seem to disappear altogether, drawing Levinas' complaint that "Dasein in Heidegger is never hungry" (TI 134). The want, suffering, and violence to which bodies are subject may not be the only concerns of ethics, but they are basic, as Levinas insists, and the absence of any reference to them in a description of being in the world means that an important dimension of existence to which ethics responds is missing. It also seems to demonstrate an underlying insensitivity.[14]

Vogel acknowledges that "liberating solicitude" is different from concern for another's welfare (Vogel 199, 78), but does not notice that Heidegger's lack of engagement with the latter theme poses a problem for Vogel's own description of authenticity as a posture in which one feels both an obligation to respect the dignity of other persons *and* compassion for their suffering (Vogel 1994, 9). Compassion for suffering is not represented in *Being and Time*. While the term "solicitude" (*Fürsorge*) does ordinarily mean care for the other's welfare, Heidegger's account of "liberating solicitude" emphasizes regard for the other's authentic potentiality-for-being rather than compassion for his or her afflictions. It is revealing that *Being and Time* never explores the possibility that dispositions such as love, compassion, or empathy disclose the being of

[14] In *Heidegger's Neglect of the Body*, Kevin Aho claims:

> the core motivation of Heidegger's project is not to offer phenomenological investigations into everyday life but to inquire into the meaning of being itself. And this inquiry ultimately leads us beyond the question of embodied agency to the structures of meaning itself. For Heidegger, it is only on the basis of these structures that we can begin to make sense of things – such as bodies – in the first place. (Aho 2009, 6)

This may be true, but embodiment is an important aspect of Dasein's being-in-the-world, and its absence from Heidegger's analytic of Dasein has serious consequences for his interpretation of human existence.

the other, even though it does understand affective dispositions as potentially disclosive, and its analysis of *Angst* is grounded in this understanding of moods and emotions.

Heidegger argues against the view that empathy (*Einfühlung*) provides the first bridge from my own subjectivity to that of the other, enabling understanding of the other, pointing out that we are already disclosed to one another through inhabiting a shared world (BT 124–26).[15] This is a fair point; feeling compassion or love for others requires first recognizing them *as* others, who exist as I do, rather than seeing them as present-at-hand, like a rock, or ready-to-hand, like a hammer. However, the authentic anticipation of death given in *Angst* likewise presupposes knowledge that my life has an end, yet *Being and Time* describes a condition where I do not genuinely understand this fact, even though in a sense we all "know" it. Heidegger might have considered that compassion and love can be disclosive in a similar manner, offering a *genuine* grasp of the being of the other as a person like myself, capable of suffering and pain as well as pleasure and joy. Yet Heidegger's phenomenological analysis of being with others barely mentions dispositions of this sort, and does not pause to reflect on their possible significance.

Heidegger's political involvement during the 1930s, his near-silence about the Holocaust after the war, and the tenor of his later works, which sometimes seem more concerned about assaults upon things than upon people, combine to deepen the suspicion that he is more than a little tone-deaf to the stark realities of human want and pain. At the level of philosophy, part of the problem stems from Heidegger's analysis of what it is about Dasein that makes liberating solicitude the appropriate form of comportment toward it. In *Being and Time*, it is the structure of "existence," a term Heidegger reserves for Dasein, involving Dasein's capacity for envisioning and accomplishing possibilities of being. That is the special character of this entity, as distinct from every other, which conscience regards.

Here too there is a correspondence with Kant, who says that "rational nature is distinguished from the rest of nature by this, that it sets itself an end" (GMM 44/AA 4, 437). Only such a nature, capable of resisting inclinations and freely determining itself according to universal principles, is an end in itself, possessing inherent dignity or worth rather than merely relative value: "Hence morality, and humanity insofar as it is capable of morality, is that which alone has

[15] Cf. *The Fundamental Concepts of Metaphysics*, where Heidegger says of the term "empathy" that it "suggests that we must first 'feel our way into' the other being in order to reach it," which "implies that we are 'outside' in the first place." Because, on Heidegger's phenomenological analysis, we are already among others in our being in the world, he argues that "the term 'empathy' has provided a guiding thread for a whole range of fundamentally mistaken theories concerning man's relationship to other human beings and to other beings in general, theories that we are only gradually beginning to overcome today" (FCM, 203/GA 29/30, 298).

dignity" (GMM 42/AA 4, 435). Kant opposes monkish mortification of the body (MPV 155/AA 6, 485) and acknowledges that "the natural end that all human beings have is their own happiness" (GMM 39/AA 4, 430), so that a person has a duty to promote the happiness of others insofar as he has a duty to promote their chosen ends (MPV 43, 46/AA 6, 385, 389). Neither physical comfort, though, nor happiness understood as the satisfaction of inclinations (GMM 12/AA 4, 399), have intrinsic or independent worth. In the *Critique of Judgement*, Kant writes,

> ... reason will never let itself be convinced that the existence of a human being who merely lives for *enjoyment* (no matter how industrious he is in pursuing this goal) has any worth in itself ... Only through what he does without regard to enjoyment, in complete freedom and independently of whatever nature could passively provide for him, does he give his existence, as the existence of a person, an absolute worth; and happiness, with the full abundance of its agreeableness, is far from being an unconditioned good. (AA5, 208–9)

Kant is not merely denying here that the satisfaction of inclinations is the *only* good, or that it is, on its own, the *highest* good. He is making the more radical claim that such satisfaction has *no* worth, by itself, unless conjoined with freedom. Otherwise, he could not say that "if the will of all creatures were bound to sensuous drives, the world would have no worth," and "freedom is thus the inner worth of the world" (*Moral Mrongovius*, AA 27, 1482).[16]

Nor could he ask, in his review of Johann Gottfried Herder's *Ideas for a Philosophy of the History of Mankind*,

> Does the author actually mean, that if the happy inhabitants of Tahiti were never visited by more civilized nations, and were destined to live for thousands of years in their quiet indolence, one could receive a satisfactory answer to the question of why they exist at all, and whether it would not have been just as good if this island had been inhabited by happy sheep and pigs as with these people happy in mere enjoyment? (AA8, 65)

The principle that all persons are ends in themselves does not mean, for Kant, that the happiness of individual members of the human species can be an end in itself, requiring no further justification. That is the position adopted by Herder, which Kant is opposing here.[17] Kant's contention, by contrast, is that only free

[16] Cf. *Metaphysical Principles of Virtue*:

> Man in the system of nature (*homo phaenomenon, animal rationale*) is a being of little significance and, along with the other animals, considered as products of the earth, he has an ordinary value (*pretium vulgare*). Even the fact that he excels these in having understanding and can set up ends for himself still gives him only an external value for his usefulness (*pretium usus*), namely, the value of a man in preference to another animal. This is to say that he has a price as a commodity in the exchange of these animals as things, in which he still has a lower value than the general medium of exchange, money, whose value is therefore called distinctive (*pretium eminens*). (MPV 96–97/AA 6, 434)

[17] For a discussion of the debate between Kant and Herder on this issue, see my analysis in Sikka 2011, 44–83.

self-development, in which he supposes Tahitians did not engage until they were blessed with European visitors, justifies the existence of human beings.[18] Freedom, the capacity to determine oneself according to a self-imposed obligation or law, is therefore the ground of the value of any other aspect of life.

At times, human beings even seem to be, for Kant, vehicles of a nature that it is their duty to realize, but that cannot be identified with themselves as individuals seeking their own well-being. In his *Idea for a Universal History with a Cosmopolitan Intent*, he claims that "in man (as the sole rational creature on earth) those natural capacities directed toward the use of his reason are to be completely developed only in the species, not in the individual" (PP 30/AA 8, 18), an idea pointing forward to Hegel. Here, the existence of human beings finds its purpose not in the happiness of the individual but in the historical unfolding of the highest capacities with which the species has been endowed by nature. Kant does not think, moreover, that this "nature," to which he attributes a teleological direction, should be considered as immoral if it inflicts hardships on people or favors later generations over earlier ones. He claims, rather:

> But it appears that nature is utterly unconcerned that man live well, only that he bring himself to the point where his conduct makes him worthy of life and well-being. What will always seem strange about this is that earlier generations appear to carry out their laborious tasks only for the sake of later ones, to prepare for later generations a step from which they in turn can raise still higher the building that nature had in view … (PP 31/AA 8, 20)

It is then possible to ask, within a Kantian moral framework, what human lives are good *for*. The categorical imperative does not rule out this question *a priori*, because what ultimately matters is not the happiness of individuals but their capacity for self-perfection, through which, if they apply themselves industriously, they may raise "the building that nature had in view." At his most extreme, Kant dismisses the worth of "inclinations" – whose satisfaction constitutes happiness – altogether, judging that "it must be the universal wish of every rational being to be altogether free of them" (GMM 37/AA 4:428).[19]

[18] Allen Wood notes that because, for Kant, the rational will is the source of all value and the sole thing possessing absolute value, "we have reason to regard as good the ends we ourselves set only to the extent that we (at least implicitly) respect and esteem our own rational nature as that which sets them" (Wood 1995, 310). It would follow that, if Tahitians are not setting their ends through the free exercise of reason, as Kant believes, their ends have no intrinsic worth. Wood wants to draw some positive conclusions that follow from Kant's principle that humanity is always an end in itself, claiming, for instance that since this formula "holds that all rational beings have absolute worth, it implies that they all have *equal* worth" (Wood 1995, 316). I acknowledged such positive implications in the first part of the present chapter, but also want to stress the moral failures to which this formula is prone.

[19] On the incoherence this ideal threatens to introduce into Kant's moral philosophy, see Langton 1992, 494–98.

While *Being and Time* sees Dasein as oriented toward the achievement of its ends, it also grants no independent worth to happiness. In fact, there is only one point at which it attributes value to any happy disposition, and that point refers to the "joy" (*Freude*) of seizing upon genuinely self-chosen possibilities, resolutely and courageously (BT 358). This joy is the satisfaction accompanying freedom and self-command, not the pleasure of fulfilling desires. Given that the anthropology of both Kant and the earlier Heidegger describes human life as a restless striving always driven by the anxious need to accomplish more, this life is not even compatible with happiness as a settled state of peace within the individual (cf. Shell 2003).

The anthropology of the later Heidegger, on the other hand, after the turn in his thought during the 1930s, would appear to be quite different. It abandons the stress on anxiety and worry characterizing the portrait in *Being and Time* of Dasein, who was described as accomplishing possibilities of being in an existence never free from care. Instead, the later works propose a more serene ideal, with authenticity being replaced by the calm composure of *Gelassenheit*, where a person is established outside the realm of "care" interpreted as the anxious attempt to secure one's own existence. The conceptual difference between these ideals may not be as radical as it first appears, since both the earlier and the later ideals involve a letting go of preoccupation with the immediate needs and wants proper to self-concern. But the mood is decidedly different, and represents a significant shift in Heidegger's understanding of the best way of being in the world at the present time.

In large measure, the shift responds to a sense that the present age, with all of its supposed advances, carries within itself a danger that the technological manner of approaching things, finally including even human beings, will shut out every other stance toward the world. Concomitantly, it may shut out every possibility of seeing things within the world as anything other than disposable resources. Adapting Husserl's idea that the constitution of objects varies according to the form of intentionality through which they are apprehended, Heidegger suggests that the modern Western subject primarily positions itself as standing over against the objects it sets out to master. These objects, correspondingly, are increasingly conceived exclusively as potential goods to be managed, put in the service of calculated ends with maximum efficiency. The alternative pointed to by Heidegger requires letting go of this exclusively assertive and exploitative relation to things, in favor of a more humble and respectful one, where human beings regard themselves not as masters of a reality wholly delivered over to them but as part of an unfolding process to which they belong, along with the things they encounter. Such a de-centering of the human subject is meant to restore worth to things in themselves, although the disclosure of that worth still depends upon the existence of human beings.

The problem, however, is that this critique of modern Dasein seems to suggest, as do elements within Kant's philosophy of history, that human beings are not ends in themselves after all, but exist for the sake of something else. That "man is the shepherd of being," as Heidegger puts it in the "Letter on Humanism" (BW 234/GA 9, 331), implies that human existence has some purpose other than that of tending to itself. Furthermore, the sense that human beings are "for" something begins to emerge in Heidegger's works of the early 1930s, leading up to his commitment to Nazism, and in these works the trope of humanity in the service of being does not have the same tone as in Heidegger's postwar writings. Rather, the language often suggests violence rather than gentleness and humility, as in these sentences from the *Introduction to Metaphysics*:

Man is forced into such a Da-sein, hurled into the need of such being, because the overpowering as such, in order to appear in its power, *requires* a place, a scene of disclosure. The essence of being-human opens up to us only when understood through this need compelled by being itself. The Da-sein of historical man means: to be posited as the breach into which the preponderant power of being bursts in its appearing, in order that this breach itself should shatter against being. (IM 162–63/GA 40, 171–72)]

Heidegger is offering in these lines an interpretation of the Greek conception of being as *physis*, a term usually translated as "nature." Within this interpretation, being is not another existent apart from humanity, and so not a "foreign" power that "makes" human beings to serve itself. Nonetheless, the rhetoric of the passage does suggest that being, as the overpowering, requires and uses humanity in order to appear, and that the essence of humanity – its destiny, so to speak – consists in being the space that enables this appearing. *Physis* is described as violently originating and ruling over the essence and destiny of humanity, and humanity as being for the sake of it, a means existing so that being qua *physis* may have a site of disclosure within human dwelling. Although being is never, for Heidegger, some other thing besides entities, there is an ontological difference between being and entities, and the resonances of the language Heidegger uses to describe this difference, as well as the relation between the two terms, are not irrelevant. The images are not meant to be taken literally, as indicating a relation between two entities where one is a means to the other's ends, but they do tell us something about Heidegger's sensibilities.

While the 1947 "Letter on Humanism" expresses the relation between humanity and being in gentler terms, it reiterates this sense that the former is needed for the sake of the latter. Man as subject seeks to be the tyrant of being, but in so doing, Heidegger suggests, he mistakes his true essence and destiny. Man is not the master of being; "man is rather 'thrown' from being itself into the truth of being, so that (*daß*), ek-sisting in this way, he might safeguard the truth of being, in order that (*damit*) beings might appear in the light of being as the beings that they are" (BW 234/GA 9, 330). Lines like these highlight the role of humanity as a vehicle for the truth of being, meaning the coming to light of the being of beings – the varying and multifaceted nature of things, constantly in the process of being discovered – through the medium of human thought and activity. Heidegger insists that this understanding of the unique destiny of humanity in relation to being actually elevates rather than demotes its status, a point to which I will return; but at times, his preoccupation with what he sees as the distinguishing excellence of human existence minimizes the everyday realities of individual human suffering and injustice.

To be sure, in his later works Heidegger is very much concerned with the plight of "mortals" in face of "the triumph of the manipulable arrangement of a scientific-technological world and of the social order proper to this world."[20] Only, this very concern often leads him to make remarks revealing an insensitivity to material needs and physical violence continuous with the lack of attention to these phenomena in *Being and Time*. In "Building Dwelling Thinking," reflecting on the problem of homelessness in the post-war period, Heidegger says that "the *real plight of dwelling* does not lie merely in a lack of houses," but is "older than the world wars with their destruction, older also than the increase of the earth's population and the condition of the industrial workers" (PLT 161/GA 7, 163). In "The Thing," the explosion of the atom bomb is said to be "only the grossest of all gross confirmations of the long-since-accomplished annihilation of the thing" (PLT 170/GA 7, 172).

The most disturbing instance of this genre of comment is Heidegger's notorious statement that "agriculture is now a motorized food industry – in essence the same as the manufacturing of corpses in gas chambers and the extermination camps, the same as the blockading and starving of nations, the same as the manufacture of atom bombs" (Heidegger 1983a, 25). In Heidegger's defense, it can be pointed out that his later writings use the term "essence" (*Wesen*) as a verb indicating the "coming to presence" of being. "Essence" names the correlative revelation of modes of human existence and aspects of the world reflected in the metaphysics of different ages. The "essence" to which Heidegger is alluding in this case is *Gestell*, "enframing," the dominant view of humanity and being in the present age. He is then referring to the total efficient ordering that gives the procedures and events he mentions their uniquely modern character of a cold-blooded, technologically ordered disposal of entities on an immense scale. The "essence" common to the mechanized agricultural industry and the production of corpses in gas chamber consists in

20 "The End of Philosophy and the Task of Thinking," BW 435/GA 14, 73.

this ordering disposal with the goal of maximum efficiency, the essence of *die Technik*, technicity.

I would take issue, however, with the following gloss on this remark by Albert Borgman:

Technology in Heidegger's sense was surely an ingredient of the Holocaust. Its bureaucratic and mechanized features have been widely noted. But to mention Nazism and the holocaust only in connection with technology is to suggest, wrongly, that technology was the nearly sufficient condition of those disasters or to let, reprehensibly, an incidental feature overshadow the moral substance at issue. (Borgmann 2007, 423)

The agriculture remark is morally insensitive, but it does not warrant the conclusion that Heidegger thinks technology is a "nearly sufficient condition" of the holocaust. He does not see technology as "an incidental feature," but neither does Zygmunt Bauman, when he suggests that "it was the spirit of instrumental rationality, and its modern, bureaucratic form of institutionalization, which had made the Holocaust-style solutions not only possible, but eminently 'reasonable' – and increased the probability of their choice" (Bauman 1989, 18). If Bauman's analysis does not seem morally objectionable in the way Heidegger's does, it is because he pays greater attention to the deployment of instrumental rationality, in its modern form, within the arenas of political management and social engineering. The same is true of Jaspers, Adorno, and Horkheimer, who all draw connections between modern rationality and the Holocaust, along with other totalitarian forms of social management. There is nothing either far-fetched or intrinsically immoral in the claim that technology, more precisely "technicity" as a way of relating even to human reality, was a necessary condition for the Holocaust and essential to the peculiarly modern character of this atrocity. Man's inhumanity to man is in itself nothing new, and history is littered with examples of grotesque political brutality. Heidegger's analysis is oriented toward what is historically specific about this modern form of inhumanity, and that point can be granted without denying his moral failings.

Yet this interpretation – which does, I believe, capture the intended meaning of Heidegger's statement – may still leave one with the legitimate sense that the statement is "scandalously inadequate," in Lacoue-Labarthe's words (Lacoue-Labarthe 1990, 34). Arnold Davidson comments:

For Lacoue-Labarthe, as for Blanchot and Levinas, Heidegger's silence concerning the Final Solution, his failure to pronounce the name of the Jews, is what remains beyond pardon. And I think that behind this silence, when one encounters Heidegger's 1949 pronouncement, one cannot but be staggered by his inability – call it metaphysical inability – to acknowledge the everyday fate of bodies and souls, as if the bureaucratized burning of selected human beings were not all that different from the threat to humanity posed in the organization of the food industry by the forces of technology. (Davidson 1989, 424)[21]

These events are "not all that different" only in the sense I explained above; but, the agriculture remark does reveal that the dominant point, in Heidegger's mind, about "the manufacture of corpses in gas chambers and extermination camps," or at least the point worthy of philosophical reflection, is the destiny of being that becomes visible in the coming to pass of this historical event.

There is then some justice in Levinas' claim that Heidegger "subordinates the relationship with the Other to the relation with Being in general," but it is not because he subordinates "ethics to understanding" (TI 46).[22] It is because his ethical position involves the claim that humanity's special place within the totality of beings is due to its possession, granted by a power not its own, of a distinctive capacity it is called upon to realize. The gift of this capacity bestows the "essence" of human existence, consisting in its being a "clearing" within which possible ways of understanding and shaping what-is are opened up over time. Whereas *Being and Time* analyzes Dasein as projecting and realizing possibilities of its own being, the later Heidegger thinks of human existence as a site where possibilities of being itself come to fruition through the medium of human worlds (though these possibilities are our "own" too, in that they are given to us in the place and time where we stand). This shift does not mark a radical departure from *Being and Time* but, as Löwith notes, "a subtle displacement of emphasis in the relationship between Being and Dasein" (Löwith 1995, 65).

Although in many respects there is a great distance between Kant's thought and that of the later Heidegger, they do still share this sense that the worth of human existence rests in the possession and realization of a particular capacity. For both, this capacity reveals itself in the fact that human beings are able to draw back from their immediate impressions and inclinations, so as to give themselves, and the world, a different form. There is some truth, then, in the charge that Heidegger's later writings promote an anti-humanism that fails to respect the priority of human ends because it positions humanity as a means. Notice, however, that this is also a danger for Kant, as revealed in his philosophy of history. It might seem odd to say of Kant's moral philosophy that what he cares about is human freedom rather than human beings themselves, as if the two could be separated. Surely, what he cares about is the freedom *of* human beings? But what one sees from Kant's philosophy of history, as well as his attitudes

[21] For some further discussions of the agriculture remark, see *Martin Heidegger and the Holocaust* (Milchman and Rosenberg 1996), particularly the essays by R. J. S. Manning ("The Cries of Others and Heidegger's Ear: Remarks on the Agriculture Remark," 19–38); George Leaman ("Strategies of Deception: The Composition of Heidegger's Silence," 57–69); and Elisabeth de Fontenay ("In Its Essence the Same Thing," 236–45).

[22] I deal at length with the relation between Heidegger and Levinas in Sikka 1998. For an overview of Levinas' critique of Heidegger, see Manning 1993.

toward non-Western peoples and races, is that the well-being of humanity is of moral concern only on the condition of being linked to the achievement of the freedom that defines this species in its difference from others – from happy pigs and sheep, for instance (Sikka 2011, 45–49). Granted, the freedom allowing human beings to be moral agents and to develop their gifts constitutes, for Kant, their very nature. The achievement of its true end, therefore, consisting not in happiness *per se* but in the worthiness to be happy, is a fulfillment of that nature. That is, however, exactly the sort of claim Heidegger makes in the "Letter on Humanism," with respect to the status of man as the "shepherd of being."

One might consider as well, in this context, that Kant manages to propose a theory of race according to which some human groups are incapable of fulfilling human destiny and are therefore doomed to extinction,[23] without worrying that this poses a problem for justified belief in a moral author of the universe. At the same time, he connects Jews with an attachment to worldly goods that runs counter to morality. Michael Mack points out, in relation to philosophies of progress such as those of Kant and Hegel,

> Worldly redemption does not necessarily imply an improvement of worldly life. Kant's and Hegel's philosophies did not accord priority to the melioration of material destitution. Kant downplayed the significance of worldly goods, with which he associated the Jews. (Mack 2003, 5).

It is reasonable to claim that human nature is defined by one or more ability whose exercise is required for properly human forms of flourishing, so that the institution and improvement of conditions enabling this exercise constitutes historical progress. It may also be reasonable to think that the human fulfillment thereby enabled is not best described as "happiness," even if it may belong within a wider conception of living and faring well, of *eudaimonia* in the Aristotelian sense. Perhaps it is better described as contentment with oneself (Kant uses the term *Selbstzufriedenheit* [CPrR 98]), or as a form of serenity, and it is worth differentiating such states from "happy" ones, where happiness is conceived as a matter of satisfying inclinations or self-centered desires (Guyer 2000, 11, 18). But a separate move, with a particular set of moral priorities, is involved in the contention that what matters most in history is the realization of this capacity and what it may bring to light or produce, rather than the well-being of individuals.

Heidegger does not hold a progressivist philosophy of history, and his understanding of what constitutes human flourishing, especially in his later works, is in significant respects opposed to that of Kant, as I will discuss in a moment. There is, however, a commonality between the two authors that leads both

[23] Larrimore 1999; see also Bernasconi 2011; Lagier 2004, especially pp. 123–30, "L'incursion de dispositions morales dans la raciologie."

of them to downplay at times the importance of individual well-being. The judgments leading to this outcome may have their ethical merits, but they also result in, perhaps because they arise from, some doubtful priorities and blind spots, as the shortcomings common to Heidegger's and Kant's conceptions of the good reveal.

Nihilism and the Need for Meaning

An adequate assessment of the decentering of the subject in Heidegger's later thought, however, must also consider his anti-humanism as a response to what he sees as the basis of modern nihilism. It is because tending to oneself alone results in nihilism that Heidegger insists the understanding of humanity he gives in the "Letter on Humanism," of man as the "shepherd of being," elevates rather than deprecates humanity's proper dignity. I have been underlining the fact that Heidegger sometimes emphasizes what "mortals" are *needed for* – the revelation of being through thinking, making, and doing – to such an extent that the ordinary afflictions of vulnerable bodies are rendered incidental. But the idea of humanity as for the sake of being is also a counterpoint to a subjectivism that robs life of meaning, precisely through a particular interpretation of humanity as an end in itself: a self-enclosed subject seeking to secure its being through a mastery of objects.

In later works, Heidegger analyzes the subjectivization of the human, and the correlative objectification of the world. He sees the development of this picture as grounding the imagination of ourselves as "representing" the world around us, while conceiving our primary relation to that world in terms of a comprehension led by the goal of redesigning it to fit our own ends. On Heidegger's reading of the history of the present age, this conception is radicalized by Nietzsche, singled out as a key figure in the formation of a modern Western (but increasingly global) understanding of self and world. What comes to expression in Nietzsche's thought is nihilism as a loss of meaning. In "The Word of Nietzsche: 'God is Dead'," Heidegger claims that this nihilism is "the fundamental movement of the history of the West," which has become "the world-historical movement of the peoples of the earth who have been drawn into the power realm of the modern age" (QCT 62/GA 5, 218).

While Nietzsche sees himself as struggling to overcome nihilism, on Heidegger's reading he is actually its highest pinnacle. Heidegger argues that the essence of nihilism does not rest, as Nietzsche thinks, in the loss of values resulting from increasing disbelief in a Christian God, so that it could be overcome by a new set of values, posited by a stronger and differently directed will to power. Rather, the very conception of human beings, and of life generally in terms of will to power, a desire for increase and domination, and the very notion of "values," which we design and posit, are for Heidegger extreme symptoms of nihilism. They exclude the possibility of understanding ourselves as anything other than self-assertive subjects, and of understanding nature as anything other than the field for the realization of our designs. They also exclude the possibility of finding significance within the world, and are profoundly opposed to Heidegger's understanding of humanity as a space within which possibilities of being are disclosed instead of being projected by subjects who see themselves as separated from being. "The value-thinking of the metaphysics of the will to power," therefore, "is murderous in a most extreme sense because it absolutely does not let being itself take its rise, i.e., come into the vitality of its essence" ("The Word of Nietzsche," QCT 108/GA 5, 263). Metaphysics is the history of the forgetting of being (QCT 109/GA 5, 263), and reaches its conclusion and fulfillment in the metaphysics of the will to power.

To understand these claims, we need rehearse the movement of thought that leads Heidegger from phenomenology to this critique of the subject-centeredness of all value thinking. On Heidegger's version of it, phenomenology is the study of the structure of the world and ourselves as given to us. It is thus the study of "appearances," but without the presupposition (an artificial philosophical construction, Heidegger thinks) that these are *only* appearances and thus not really real. "Being" includes, for Heidegger, appearing; it includes the process whereby something comes to light, thereby becoming a "phenomenon" for us. In *Being and Time*, Heidegger had sought to make explicit the kinds of being that we encounter, distinguishing between existence (our own kind of being), the being of tools, and the being of objects. He had examined how tools and objects come to appear for us through our organizing activities and our way of being toward the real. Via this analysis, Heidegger wanted to show that the subject-object distinction is based on an orientation toward only one kind of being, the kind presented to us by what we call "objects," things we apprehend as lying presently before us. Even the term "reality," Heidegger points out, comes from the Latin *res*, meaning "thing," and points to an interpretation where the being of objects has been taken for being itself, and so for the way of being of every kind of entity that presents itself to us (BT 96). Thus, one aspect of Heidegger's critique of the modern concept of nature involves, as Foltz puts it, "the critique of *Vorhandenheit*, or presence-at-hand, as a secondary, derivative mode of being that is originally apprehended in natural things, subsequently seized upon as the primary mode of being of nature itself, and finally identified with being as such" (Foltz 1995, 123).

The "subject" also gets taken as a thing in this sense, a substance, of a different sort than "material" or "extended" substance, as within Descartes' ontology, but a substance nonetheless. Forgotten here is the manifold presentation of being in its various modalities. Being is not *allowed* to reveal itself to us in its many forms, but is constantly forced to conform to the metaphysics of substance, in which all coming-to-appearance, all be-ing, understood as a verb and thus dynamically, is taken to be thing-like and concomitantly capable of being brought to a stand before us, represented as an object that could be investigated by the methods of science. Heidegger's later works add the idea, perhaps implicit in *Being and Time*, that we are not the ultimate source of this process of coming to light. We are included in it; being projects itself through us, and we can never get this process into our grasp, nor could we ever "master" being so as to know what "it" is in all of its possible modalities. We reveal and make what is given to us; *therefore* we are not the masters of entities but the shepherds of being. The statement in the "Letter on Humanism" means to describe a truth about the human condition, not just to propose a self-conception that would make our lives more agreeable.

The problem with Western metaphysics, then, is that it reduces all being to substance and seeks to bring all reality to a stand before itself, to know it, think it, and produce a single true description of it. In so doing, it supposes a particular view of ourselves as "subjects," somehow independent of the reality we seek to know and control, which we seem to, but actually do not, present to ourselves. This rather bizarre view of ourselves then takes the form – in, for instance, Nietzsche's thought – of seeing ourselves as value-positing agents imposing our designs on the world. Where these so-called "values" are supposed to come from, God only knows, and what would give them any binding power is unclear. This is the most extreme nihilism, where we find ourselves standing against a world bereft of all meaning, with nothing to guide us but the designs of our will – though again, where those designs come from, and how we are supposed to decide between them, is not known. Such a vision is guided, Heidegger suggests, by a conception of ourselves as isolated subjects separated by a gulf from what is not ourselves; the corresponding constitution of what stands before us as resource; and the underlying quest for certainty that consumes us in the modern age, a quest to secure knowledge and to secure at the same time the conditions of our own existence (QCT 82–84, 88–91, 107/GA 5, 238–40, 244–46, 262).

Nietzsche's interpretation of humanity and the whole of being in terms of will to power, where "values are the conditions of itself posited by the will to power" (QCT 75/GA 5, 231), is the most extreme expression of this quest. But Kant's understanding of humanity as the sole end in itself on earth, possessing the right to rank and order the rest of what-is by reference to its own aims, is a step on the way toward precisely this conception. Thus, while Heidegger's analysis in *Being and Time* adopts Kant's view of persons as ends in themselves, with its implications for our appropriate relations to one another and to the world, in his later works Heidegger reconsiders the understanding of autonomy on which this view had been based, judging it to be part of the "erring" of Western thought that has led to disaster on a planetary scale. The reconsideration is occasioned by what has happened in the meanwhile and what Heidegger thinks is happening now. It thereby illustrates the limited and fallible character of *every* purportedly universal view of ourselves and being, but without drawing the consequence that everything we say about how things are is "just" relative, and we should give up the quest for truth. Heidegger had struggled to articulate the truth about the meaning of freedom in *Being and Time*, and continues to do so, but response to what has come to light in the historical moment requires, he thinks, a turning.

That turning, needed to heal the unwellness of humanity in its present condition, involves a letting go of the insistence that the human subject, conceived as a special kind of animal equipped with reason, be at the center of being. After the turning, freedom no longer means the capacity to choose possibilities on the basis of nothing, as an "existential" interpretation of *Being and Time* might suppose. It means instead a mode of care that allows possibilities to come to light in the "clearing" of a self that no longer positions itself as the lord of all creation, having recognized that this is not the truth. Because Heidegger sees the true "end" of humanity as being this self, who is no longer the end of all things, he claims that "the highest determinations of the essence of man in humanism still do not realize the proper dignity (*Würde*) of man" (BW 233/GA 9, 330).

It emerges here that the sharpest contrast between Kant's moral philosophy and Heidegger's later thinking about what we are and how we should be rests on Heidegger's sense that the being well of entities like ourselves requires a proper relation to what is as a whole, including "nature," where that relation does not consist in mastery. And yet, Heidegger continues to agree with Kant's affirmation of a profound difference in kind, and not just degree, between humanity and every other being. I now turn to examine the status and nature of entities other than Dasein in light of these points, laying out Heidegger's understanding of the right relation between human beings and the rest of the world.

3 Animals and Other Beings

A major problem with positions linking morality to a capacity such as reason is that they exclude nonhuman sentient beings altogether from the realm of moral concern. For Kant, we have direct moral obligations only to "rational natures," meaning beings who are free and self-legislating, and therefore worthy of respect. While there can be an indirect reason not to behave cruelly toward animals, such as the effect such behavior could have upon our own moral characters (MM 6, 443), there is nothing about animals themselves that could impose upon us an obligation to be concerned about their welfare.

The point would seem to apply equally to Heidegger's analysis in *Being and Time*, which, as Simon Glendinning notes, "continues to think the essence of man through its absolute distinction from merely animal life" (Glendinning 1996, 75). Heidegger reasserts a radical difference between humanity and animality in other works, and gives an extended analysis of this difference in *The Fundamental Concepts of Metaphysics*, a lecture course he delivered in 1929–30. *Being and Time* only thematizes three kinds of being: "existence," the being of Dasein; "readiness-to-hand," the being of tools; and "presence-at-hand," the being of objects seen independently of practical concern. There is here no space for a proper consideration of sentient beings whose character does not conform to the structure of Dasein, or for discovering nature in any way other than either as raw material for use or as a field for scientific investigation. And yet, Heidegger's later thought has been appropriated by environmentalists and "green" thinkers due to its critique of the exclusively utilitarian and calculating relation to nature that he sees as a hallmark of the present age. In later writings, Heidegger does seem to propose a way of being toward the nonhuman world that is the opposite of this dominating one, inviting human beings to occupy the position of humble guardians, rather than masters.

I examine in this chapter Heidegger's views about the nature of animals and how we come to know it, asking what follows about how this category of nonhuman entities should be treated. I also explore the status of entities that are neither human nor animal, given Heidegger's reflections on nature and made things. Philosophers defending animal rights usually do so on the basis of sentience as a general property that gives rise to morally significant capacities and experiences, such as suffering, pleasure, and desire. Where do Heidegger's analyses of animality, nature, and human building stand in relation to these kinds of arguments? Does he assign the same moral status to both sentient and non-sentient beings when he calls upon humanity to be "the shepherd of being"? For that matter, why are we obligated to care about non-sentient beings at all, on Heidegger's account? Is it only to ensure the wellness of our own dwelling on the earth? I seek to answer these questions not only by presenting the relevant elements of Heidegger's analysis but also by drawing out implications that Heidegger may not have recognized.

Should We Care for Animals?

In defining the being of Dasein as care in *Being and Time*, Heidegger wants to emphasize that this is an entity for which its own being is an issue. That does not simply mean that we matter to ourselves. So do iguanas and beagles, whereas "care" is supposed to have a structure peculiar to Dasein. Animals can also be said to exhibit a concerned engagement with the world (Cave 1982, 253), but that is not what Heidegger has in mind when he describes Dasein as care. The term is meant to name the structure of an entity capable of standing back from itself, and relating to itself explicitly, so as to imagine being one way or another. Because of this capacity, Dasein can project possibilities for itself, through which it organizes and understands what it encounters. The "worldhood of the world" rests, on Heidegger's account, upon these projected possibilities. In other words, the complex of Dasein's projected ends forms the horizon against which things within the world are encountered. Dasein's capacity for projection then makes possible the appearance of the complex of definite meaningful things that constitutes the "world" in which we live.

As described in *Being and Time*, this capacity for "sketching out in advance" (the term *Entwurf*, "projection," also means "sketch" or "design") is fundamentally teleological and primarily practical. What we generally project in advance of our encounter with things are not categories through which we grasp substances, a form of projection proper only to highly specialized kinds of activity, but goals pertaining to the advancement of our own being. In *all* forms of activity, though, whether scientific or practical, having prior designs is a necessary condition for apprehending anything coherent. Because Heidegger connects the capacity for conceiving such designs, and organizing the world accordingly, with the ability to stand away from oneself, he often associates the understanding of entities *as such* with freedom, an odd move at first glance but one that makes sense within his overall epistemology. Animals, Heidegger claims, do not have this relation to things within the world. In fact, because they cannot stand away from themselves so as to project possibilities, they do not have a "world" at all, or not much of one.

In "Heidegger and the Question of Animality," Glendinning takes Heidegger to task for his descriptions of animals as either "worldless" (*weltlos*) or "poor in world" (*weltarm*) (Glendinning 1996, 75–79). Drawing on Derrida's critique of Heidegger's conception of animality in its alleged distinction from humanity, Glendinning complains that, by positing such a sharp break between human beings and the rest of nature, Heidegger remains trapped in the humanism he had claimed to overcome. Needed, instead, is a recognition that "human life is itself a manifestation of nature – relatively distinctive no doubt, but not absolutely so," a conception that "does not ignore the differences between human beings and other animals," but is "smoothly naturalistic" (Glendinning 1996, 83). On my reading, Heidegger's critique of humanism does not defend any contemporary form of "naturalism," which would presuppose a conception of "nature" that he historicizes and questions. Nonetheless, the difficulties highlighted by Glendinning, among others,[1] some of which are elaborations of points raised by Derrida, are apposite to the account Heidegger gives of the animal in both *Being and Time* and *The Fundamental Concepts of Metaphysics*.

A central problem, Derrida writes, is that "like most of those who, as philosophers or persons of good sense, speak of animality, Heidegger takes no account of a certain 'zoological knowledge' that accumulates, is differentiated, and becomes more refined concerning what is brought together under this so general and confused word animality" (Derrida 1987a, 173). For example, in *The Fundamental Concepts of Metaphysics*, Heidegger sets out to discover "what constitutes the *essence of the animality* of the animal and the *essence of the humanity* of man" (FCM 179/GA 29/30, 265). His formulation of this question supposes that "animality as such" can be defined, and Heidegger is explicit that his thesis about the "world-poverty" of animals "does not tell us something merely about insects or merely about mammals, since it also includes, for example, non-articulated creatures, unicellular animals like amoebae, infusoria, sea urchins and the like – *all* animals, *every* animal" (FCM 186/GA 29/30, 274–75).

Heidegger anticipates the possible objection that a proposition about animals ought to be based on zoological evidence, but counters:

> precisely because zoology deals with animals this proposition cannot be a result of zoological investigation; rather, it must be its *presupposition*. For this presupposition ultimately involves an *antecedent determination* of what belongs in general to the *essence of the animal*, that is, a delimitation of the field within which any positive investigation of animals must move. (FCM 186/GA 29/30, 275)

"The proposition does not derive from zoology," he adds, "but it cannot be elucidated independently of zoology either," and "thus it is that we find ourselves

[1] For another version of this critique, see Calarco 2008.

moving in a *circle*" (FCM 187/GA 29/30, 276). He is making the methodological point that, insofar as a discipline like "zoology" has a definite subject of study, it must already have some conception of the nature of that subject. Zoology does not study plants or human beings, and it must presuppose some understanding of animality that defines this category of entities, while distinguishing it from neighboring ones with which it may be classed under some more general category, such as "living beings."

The "circle" to which Heidegger alludes is the hermeneutic circle outlined in *Being and Time*, a necessary feature of all inquiry. Every investigation of entities must already have some preconception of what is being looked at and looked for, but will also be informed and corrected by what it finds through its examinations, as long as it is genuinely committed to discovering the truth. In the case of zoology, then, Heidegger is observing that this field of study must be mapped out beforehand in its fundamental concepts, the most fundamental of these being the concept of the animal. However much variety there may turn out to be among animals, they could not constitute a distinct field of study for the discipline of zoology, with its methodology, unless there were some perceived commonality among the entities falling within its field. That perceived commonality is the *a priori* of zoology, whose projection in advance secures the region of being that this discipline studies, and determines its character as a positive science.

Heidegger's descriptions of the essence of "animality" may accurately describe the *a priori* of zoology as it stood at the time, but this is a historical and culturally relative *a priori*, reflecting questionable views about the nature of animals, and the special status of humanity. The analysis Heidegger goes on to give reinforces those views, and its lack of adequate attention to the full range of beings comprising the category of the "animal" is a methodological flaw. The hermeneutic circle is unavoidable. However, Heidegger writes in *Being and Time* that "what is decisive is not to get out of the circle but to come into it in the right way" (BT 153). That must include allowing the things being investigated to speak back, as it were, challenging the preconceptions the investigator has brought to bear on them. Heidegger's uncritical reiteration of traditional Western tropes about animality, in combination with his strikingly narrow range of examples, then seems a very poor model for coming into the hermeneutic circle in the right way.

One flaw is that the majority of Heidegger's examples of animal life, and all of those for which he provides extended analysis, lie on the side of the "animal" spectrum that is furthest away from human beings. To support his claim that the essence of animality involves a kind of capability connected with drive, for instance, Heidegger speaks at some length about unicellular animals with no permanent organs. His point is that the capacities of these animals are prior to their organs, the latter forming themselves only temporarily in order to serve the former (FCM 224/GA 29/30, 326–27). To support his claim that the driven behavior of animals involves a "captivation," making them incapable of relating to the world in the way human beings do, he presents as evidence an experiment with bees (FCM 242/GA 29/30, 352). He refers elsewhere in his lectures to glow worms (FCM 230/ GA 29/30, 336), female insects (FCM 250/GA 29/30, 363–64), the embryos of sea urchins (FCM 261/GA 29/30, 380), and moles (FCM 237/GA 29/30, 345). On a couple of occasions, he does mention dogs, but simply assumes that they relate, or more precisely fail to relate, to things within the world, just as bees do (FCM 210, 269/GA 29/30, 308, 390). There is no serious attempt to observe dogs or any other animal that seems to be more like ourselves than are bees and amoebae, asking whether they truly fit the presumptions of the idea of animality Heidegger has inherited.

Heidegger's choice to focus on animals least like human beings is, moreover, deliberate. When seeking to illustrate the difference between animal behavior and human comportment, he states:

> In order now to bring the peculiar character of behaviour into view, we must take our methodological point of departure from a consideration of those forms of behaviour which are more remote, with respect to their consistent and intrinsic character, than those forms of comportment displayed by the higher animals that seem to correspond so closely to our own comportment. (FCM 240–41/GA 29/30, 350)

This would be a reasonable procedure, if Heidegger's task were only to analyze the concept of "animality" operative within the scientific discipline of zoology as it stood at the time, or within the wider discourses from which it had borrowed the concept – a worthwhile undertaking that could even lay a basis for critical questioning. But Heidegger engages in no such questioning. He assumes that all nonhuman animal species do in fact conform to the idea of the animal he is seeking to analyze, most clearly exemplified by such animals as amoebae and bees.

That idea is consonant with traditional iterations of the difference between humans and animals that have predominated in Western philosophical, scientific, and religious discourses. Central properties marking the difference, which human beings are said to possess while animals do not, include language, reason, tool use, free will, and culture. Instead of citing this standard list of properties, Heidegger attempts to pinpoint the distinctive feature of humanity that makes them possible. In *The Fundamental Concepts of Metaphysics*, that feature is described as the capacity to grasp something *as* something, to relate to entities *as such*, with an apprehension of their being. Explicating the difference between ourselves and lizards, he writes:

> The lizard basks in the sun. At least this is how we describe what it is doing, although it is doubtful whether it really comports itself in the same way as we do when we lie out

in the sun, i.e., whether the sun is accessible to it *as* sun, whether the lizard is capable of experiencing the rock *as* rock. (FCM 197/GA 29/30, 291)

Heidegger adds that "the lizard has its *own relation* to the rock, to the sun, and to a host of other things" and that "whatever the lizard is lying on is certainly given *in some way* for the lizard." The rock, however, "is not known to the lizard *as* a rock"; "it is not accessible to it *as a being*" (FCM 198/GA 29/30, 291).

This grasp of things *as* being is grounded in something yet more basic, being a function of the distance from things established by freedom. On Heidegger's analysis, the capacity for discovering truth requires precisely this distance, a standing away from things so as to inquire about their existence and nature, while binding oneself to respect for the results of such inquiry. That involves at the same time a certain distance from oneself, or rather, from the throng of immediate concerns that push a person this way and that, where being driven about by such concerns is not genuinely being one's self for a human being. In *Being and Time*, absorption in what is proximally ready to hand for accomplishing predetermined goals constitutes inauthentic being in the world, and I noted the continuity between Heidegger's interpretation of this way of existing and Kant's understanding of the phenomenal self that is continuous with "nature" insofar as it is propelled entirely by "inclinations."

Thus, there is a similarity between Heidegger's description of inauthentic Dasein in *Being and Time* and his description of animality in *Fundamental Concepts*. Indeed, in his analysis of boredom in the latter work, Heidegger remarks that we sometimes seek to eliminate the emptiness before which this mood brings us by occupying ourselves with things, where:

Being occupied gives our dealings with things a certain manifoldness, direction, fullness. But not only that: we are also *taken* [hingenommen] by things, if not altogether *lost* in them, and often even *captivated* [benommen] by them. Our activities and exploits *become immersed* [aufgehen] *in something*. (FCM 101/GA 29/30, 153)

Here, too, Heidegger's description links this way of being with animality, of which an essential moment, he says, is "captivation" (*Benommenheit*) (FCM 239/GA 29/30, 347). The animal is captivated, in that its manner of being is purely "an instinctual drivenness," and therefore not a "comporting oneself toward" but "behaviour." The term "comportment" (*Verhaltung*) suggests self-restraint, and Heidegger reserves it for the "doing and acting" of human beings in contrast with the "driven performing" of animals (FCM 237/GA 29/30, 345–46).[2]

[2] Cf. Kuperus 2007, 7–15, on "human poverty." In fact, though, human beings are never, for Heidegger "poor in world" as animals are, since their absorption in the world is always an evasion of their proper being.

The distinction again has methodological consequences for zoology, as well as for the humanities. The appropriate way to study animal life, it implies, is to observe behavior, searching for explanations in terms of instincts and drives oriented toward meeting the needs of an organism. This distinguishes the appropriate method and basic concepts of zoology from those of, say, physics, "for a drive is never present at hand ... as something which drives, it is essentially on the way to ... always driving on toward" (FCM 230/GA 29/30, 335). In that case, zoology cannot dispense with teleological explanations of animal behavior. It must also recognize sentience, for if the animal is not a human being, neither is it a stone. The lizard may not "touch" the rock it lies on in the same way that we touch something or someone, but nor can its relationship to the rock be described only in terms of one object exerting pressure on another, like a stone lying in the road (FCM 196/GA 29/30, 290). This difference makes the lizard, as an animal, "poor in world," while the stone is "worldless."

Given this poverty, zoology should not attribute to animals the same kind of acting and doing that is the subject of the humanities. And it follows from Heidegger's account that the reverse is equally true: human beings should not be treated – analyzed or handled – as if they were animals. Liberating solicitude is the appropriate way of being with those others who share a world with us, because they relate to themselves and things in the same way we do. They are never merely ready-to-hand, or present-at-hand, to use the terminology of *Being and Time*. Adding now the analysis in *Fundamental Concepts*, entities having the character of Dasein are also never captivated by their needs and therefore sunk into their environment, as Heidegger supposes animals to be. Heidegger's descriptions in *Being and Time* and *Fundamental Concepts* of a mode of occupation with the world in which human beings do seek a kind of absorption and captivation is presented as a fleeing, not a "natural" condition. In *Being and Time*, it is a fleeing from the anxiety that registers awareness of freedom and mortality; in *Fundamental Concepts*, it is a fleeing from the emptiness of boredom. The influence of Pascal's assessment of the human condition is palpable, summed up in the judgment: "Man's condition: inconstancy, boredom anxiety."[3]

In relation to animality, the point emerging from this part of Heidegger's analysis is that the comportment of human beings is never and cannot ever be like that of animals, who have no sleeping dread to be awakened or from which to flee, and no sense of emptiness they might seek to fill with distractions that are empty in another sense. Animals are also incapable of self-restraint, Heidegger thinks, and because there is no doubleness in their being, no relation to a self they could order to be this way or that, they have no conscience either

[3] See van Buren 1994, 174.

to follow or to evade. When human beings act as if they were like this, they are sometimes accused of behaving like animals, perhaps by their own conscience, but the fact that this is an accusation reveals that such conduct in human beings is fundamentally different from the behavior of animals. Heidegger therefore claims, in his lectures on Nietzsche, that "the human being can never be an animal, i.e. can never be nature, but is always either above the animal, or, precisely as human, below it, which is when we say they have been an 'animal'" (GA 34, 236). On account of freedom, humanity only has "the dubious advantage … of sinking beneath the animal," whereas the animal, for its part, is incapable of evil (ST 144/GA 42, 249).

In *Fundamental Concepts*, Heidegger likewise affirms that "no animal can become depraved in the same way as man" (FCM 194/GA 29/30, 286), and yet, at the same time, he questions distinctions between higher and lower in this area:

Every animal and every species of animal as such is just as perfect and complete as any other. Thus it should be clear from everything we have said that from the outset this talk of poverty in world and world-formation must not be taken as a hierarchical evaluation. (FCM 194/GA 29/30, 286)

Before considering this rejection of hierarchical judgments more closely, it is worth spelling out how characteristics traditionally thought to distinguish humanity from animality are grounded, within Heidegger's account, on the basic freedom he sees as the essence of humanity. That freedom involves a capacity for distance, from oneself and from things within the world, so as to have a relation to the being of these entities. This makes possible the apprehension of entities "as such," seeing a tree *as* a tree, so as to be able to name it and form sentences stating what it is by placing it within categories, describing its properties, and noting where it stands in relation to other things. Given this way of understanding the concept, freedom is the basis of human language, through which culture is formed and handed down across generations. It is also what enables human beings to project possibilities of being into the future, to imagine things being otherwise than they are. In practical reasoning, what we project into the future are pragmatic ends, and we imagine how we might redesign the material around us to serve those ends. Freedom is thus the basis for encountering things as possible equipment, necessary for the invention of tools.

Imagining being into the future brings with it the additional possibility of anticipating the final end of our lives, and so, freedom is also the basis for knowledge of our own mortality. Because the distance provided by freedom enables an individual's relation to his or her very own being, moreover, it is the basis of conscience, of myself calling upon myself to be otherwise and better. Freedom is simultaneously what makes it possible for a person to bind herself to that call. Last, but far from least, freedom makes it possible to see the other *as* other, another being whose projected ends are visible in the world I share with him, so that I may understand why liberating solicitude is the proper comportment toward this kind of being. It is fundamentally because I understand the other *as* other in this way that there is, for Heidegger, something uniquely human about "*that* touch which we experience when we rest our hand upon the head of another human being" (FCM 196). For the animal, by contrast, the other is never given as another, Heidegger claims, but is encountered only through captivation to needs. Consequently, animal behavior "is always intrinsically a form of elimination [*Beseitigen*]," Heidegger argues, as one can see from the example of some female insects, who eat the male after copulation. Here, the one animal is for the other first a sexual partner, then prey; it is never there for the other as simply a living creature (FCM 250/GA 29/30, 363–64).

At points such as this, the narrowness of Heidegger's examples is truly startling, given the broad conclusions he draws from them. Surely, before arriving at such conclusions about how others are given to animals, he might have considered more than insects. Careful observation of the social life of many other animal species, examining the multiple ways individuals within a group relate to one another and care for their young, would seem to reveal a different picture, as would observation of the relation between human beings and companion animals, such as dogs. Similar points can be made of all the properties that Heidegger's analysis endorses, in line with traditional views about what is supposed to separate human beings from animals. There are other animal species that use, and even design, rudimentary tools (Shumaker, Walker and Beck, 2011). Many animals communicate complex messages to one another, even if there is ongoing debate about whether any animal species is capable of what *we* define as language (Pinker 1994; Savage-Rumbaugh, Shanker and Taylor 2001; Hauser, Chomsky and Fitch 2002). Groups within certain animal species engage in transgenerational practices that are learned and local, generating a related debate about whether animals have culture (Laland and Galaf 2009). Dolphins, orca, and a number of primates appear to recognize themselves in a mirror, one test (though not the only possible one) for ascertaining self-awareness.[4] Elephants seem to exhibit an awareness of dying and death (Douglas-Hamilton, Bhalla, Wittemeyer and Vollrath, 2006). And some primates demonstrate a sense of fairness, even to the point of refusing a benefit for themselves under conditions of inequity (Brosnan 2013).

Such examples are often cited these days in criticism of the sharp divide Western moral discourses have, until recently, typically drawn between humans and animals. They would appear to be apposite objections to Heidegger's

[4] The Wikipedia entry for "Mirror Test" provides a good survey of the literature on this issue.

analysis, for as Glendinning notes, "Heidegger treats his distinction between Dasein and (any) entities whose character of Being is not that of Dasein as marking a distinction of absolute rigour and purity" (Glendinning 1996, 79). Given that Heidegger also makes no distinction among different species of animal in comparing them with human beings, Glendinning complains that "Heidegger's analysis passes over the possibility that different animals can be, in different respects, 'another like myself'" (78). On Heidegger's analysis, even our having sensory organs and bodily needs like other sentient living beings does not make us like animals in at least these respects, for freedom changes everything. The specifically human relation to being, grounded in the distance from entities that first makes it possible to grasp them as entities, means that animals cannot even be said to perceive and feel in the same way we do. Because beings as such are not manifest to them, so that animals can never apprehend something as something, Heidegger claims that "in a fundamental sense the animal does not have perception (*Wahrnehmung*)" (FCM 259/GA 29/30, 376). As a result, while human beings and animals both possess eyes with a similar anatomical structure, human seeing and animal seeing are not the same (FCM 219/GA 29/30, 320). Nor is the meeting of bodily needs the same in both cases; the dog "feeds with us – and yet, we do not really 'feed'... It eats with us – and yet, it does not really 'eat'" (FCM 210/GA 29/30, 308). We can feed *like* animals, but then we are precisely aware of doing so and of abandoning our humanity. That awareness is human. Pigs cannot reprimand themselves for behaving like pigs, nor is it appropriate to despise them for their piggish ways. Human beings who eat like pigs, on the other hand, can be considered contemptible precisely because, having the capacity for restraint, they are *not* like pigs. Because of this lack in animals, the dog is "with" us in a way, and yet not (FCM 210/GA 29/30, 308).

In relation to perception and activities responding to bodily needs, then, the difference between human beings and animals is rooted in the same fundamental feature: the capacity for restraint, allowing entities to be manifest as such, and thereby enabling comportment, as opposed to behavior. This is also the feature in virtue of which human beings are persons: "all comportment is only possible in a certain restraint [*Verhaltenheit*] and comporting [*Verhaltung*], and a stance [*Haltung*] is only given where a being has the character of a self or, as we also say, of a person" (FCM 274/GA 29/30, 397–98). According to Heidegger, "nothing of this kind is to be found in animality or in life in general" (FCM 274/GA 29/30, 398), and so "the animal is separated from man by an abyss" (FCM 264/GA 29/30, 384). We see here the contradiction between Heidegger's account and any naturalism analyzing human existence as an extension of animal life, different from it in degree but not in kind. For Heidegger, the capacity for distance that at the same time brings us before beings in a reflective manner involves not continuity but a disjuncture in being.

In light of this disjuncture, if being as a whole were still to be interpreted as "nature," the idea of nature would have to be comprehensive enough to accommodate such a break between animal life and humanity.

It is fair to object that Heidegger misrepresents a substantial spectrum of animal life, due to his highly problematic, and at times absurd, tendency to think in terms of "animals in general and insects in particular" (FCM 250/GA 29/30, 364). However, we need to see, first, that Heidegger sets the bar high for genuinely being Dasein. While Levinas writes that "to enjoy without utility, in pure loss, gratuitously, without referring to anything else, in pure expenditure – this is the human" (TI 133), for Heidegger's Dasein there is no "primal positivity of enjoyment," and "the gap between the animal and the human" does not lie in the fact that disquietude *can* trouble the human (TI 145) but that it does so from the beginning, and always. Release from grounds or causes, from the captivation by drives and their environmental objects to which animals are subject, enables human beings to project possibilities of being into the future, which in turn gives rise to the complex of references and assignments that constitute the being of "equipment." But when authentic, Dasein is *not* absorbed in manipulating equipment to accomplish a task. Rather, it draws back from immersion in the world and its fallen going along with conventions to feel itself suspended before the world. This enables it to make a resolution about its manner of being, a condition revealing at the same time the freedom that fundamentally makes it possible for Dasein to have that world within which it can make and use tools – and be absorbed in them – in the first place. The point of Heidegger's analysis of worldhood in *Being and Time* is to reveal this freedom, not merely to highlight the human capacity for using tools. "It never occurred to me," he remarks in *Fundamental Concepts*, "to try to claim or prove with this interpretation that the essence of man consists in the fact that he knows how to handle knives and forks or use the tram" (FCM 177/GA 29/30, 263)

Being an entity with the character of Dasein, therefore, means having the capacity to draw back from absorbed preoccupation so as to be placed before beings as a whole (FCM 283/GA 29/30, 410). Heidegger is interested in "attunements" like anxiety in *Being and Time*, or wonder in "What is Metaphysics?", or boredom in *The Fundamental Concepts of Metaphysics*, because "that attunement precisely makes *beings as a whole* manifest and makes us manifest to ourselves as disposed in the midst of these beings" (FCM 283/GA 29/30, 410). "The utter abyss of Dasein in the midst of Dasein discloses itself in this attunement," Heidegger says of boredom (FCM 283/GA 29/30, 411), as it does in the anticipation of death, to which the *Angst* described in *Being and Time* is especially attuned. This abyss makes Dasein the strange kind of being that it is, one for whom the "world" may slip away to reveal being in the world as such. The emptiness at the heart of Dasein is perhaps what Pascal interpreted theologically as "the infinite abyss," which can be filled only by God (*Pensées*,

VII/425; Pascal 1958, 113). Heidegger, in accord with phenomenological method, leaves it empty of God or any other explanatory posit.

Similarly, human language is not essentially a tool of communication to meet the shared needs of the "rational animal." It brings to language "the unspoken word of being," as Heidegger puts it in the "Letter on Humanism" (P 274/ GA 9, 361), giving expression to what is striking, wondrous, or uncanny. For Heidegger, the essence of human language is revealed in poetry, not in sentences like "pass me the hammer." The creative making that constitutes *poiesis*, moreover, also describes the "origin" or essence of art, which, when successful, sets into work the "truth" of what touches us in our being in the world. In line with this analysis, what we call "culture" is the product of Dasein's being in the world as a creature of distance, whose genuine inheritance of tradition consists in its finding in the collective past handed down to it possibilities for its own existence, which it can appropriate and transform, in light of what it is called upon to do by the needs of the situation in which it finds itself (BT 383). Accordingly, studying the past as history means understanding the existence of the Dasein that was once there, and that requires interpreting the remains of its world as the products of the imaginative, self-reflexive potentiality for being that Dasein fundamentally is.

Finally, the account Heidegger gives in *Being and Time* of conscience involves a readiness to hear its appeal and bind oneself to its call (BT 288, 294–97). This is holding oneself to the truth of being, as discovered by authentic being in the world. It includes authentic being-with, the comportment of liberating solicitude that genuinely recognizes the being of Dasein. It is essential to genuine science, which requires the investigator to respect what the investigation reveals. In later works, holding to the truth of being comes to mean the capacity to understand what is meet and fitting, given the character of what-is in each case, and to act accordingly – to act, that is, in a way that properly corresponds to the nature of things. This is what Heidegger understands as justice (cf. Dallmayr 1994).

The point I am leading up to is that Heidegger's interpretation of Dasein takes as essential to it features that nonhuman animal species do not seem to possess, as far as we know to date, however great a range there may otherwise be among them. The interpretation seeks to lay out what it genuinely means to be human, where "humanity" is not a biological category but an ontological one. In principle, there could be biologically human beings that do not have the basic structure of Dasein, and there could be entities having this structure that are not biologically human. While we know no cases of the latter so far, we do know cases of the former, and so the issue of "liminal" human beings must be confronted here, as it must in the context of any theoretical position wanting to confine the sphere of moral obligation to humanity in its difference from animality. What are the implications of Heidegger's analysis for the status of human beings with cognitive deficiencies and disabilities severe enough that they do not conform to the structure of Dasein? These would be living beings that are members of the biological species *homo sapiens* but do not exhibit the capacities Heidegger sees as defining *der Mensch*, humanity. Are such beings not properly human, on Heidegger's analysis, and if so, what are the moral consequences of such a judgment?

Heidegger does not pose this question but an answer can, I think, be reconstructed from his account. A hint is provided by the assertion in *Fundamental Concepts* that hierarchical *judgments* of "higher" and "lower" are questionable when we are comparing animals with ourselves, or animal species with one another, as "every animal and every species of animal as such is just as perfect and complete as any other" (FCM 194). There is an Aristotelian note here, connected to a conceptual point about evaluative judgments regarding different animal species. Heidegger is agreeing with Aristotle that every animal species has its own potential perfection, its own *telos*, in relation to which its possible defects are to be measured. In an important sense, appropriate estimations of the relative goodness of animal lives need to use the standard of what counts as proper functioning for a given species. A pig that eats in an unrestrained manner is a perfectly good pig; one that is unable to feed when presented with food fitting for pigs has something wrong with it. It would be inappropriate to blame a pig for the former behavior; indeed, if this living being is, like other animals, "captivated" by its drives, it is inappropriate to blame it for anything at all. But one can certainly make judgments about there being something "wrong" with a pig in a nonmoral sense, based on one's understanding of what a healthy pig is like. The Aristotelian insight is that negative judgments of this sort, involving the language of disease and deprivation, are parasitic on a positive idea of proper pig-being.

Given that Heidegger's interpretation of the essence of humanity also involves a positive conception of this entity's proper being, which requires the exercise of specific capacities, how would disabled human beings be analyzed in relation to the concept of Dasein? Physical disabilities, no matter how severe, are not relevant to this question, since there is nothing in Heidegger's interpretation of Dasein or humanity that requires any particular physical abilities. Though he speaks of handiness and hands,[5] what enables Dasein to encounter the readiness-to-hand of equipment is not any element of bodily structure, but the capacity to see the thing *as* for something, and to design and use it accordingly. Hands themselves could be designed and used as pieces

[5] In "What is Called Thinking?" Heidegger says that "apes, for example, have organs that grasp, but they have no hand," for "only a being that can speak, that is think, can have the hand and be handy in achieving works of handicraft" (WCT 16/GA 8, 18).

of equipment, and it is the capacity explicitly to order ends and means in this manner that distinguishes Dasein from animals.[6]

But severe cognitive disabilities that would make it impossible for a human being to make choices about his or her life, or to anticipate death, or to respond to conscience, or to learn a language, are another matter. Employing the framework of Heidegger's analysis, though, which I am suggesting is indebted to Aristotle, the language of disability and impairment is revealing, as it is in the case of any species. We recognize "disability" as privation of an "ability," and that still applies to the most severe forms of human disability, ones that deprive a biologically human being of all specifically human abilities. For Heidegger, potentiality is a true modality of being, fundamental to our understanding of what is. A human being lacking human capacities is then no kind of animal. She is, rather, a *disabled human being*, recognized as such in relation to the potentiality that defines being human, of which this living being has unfortunately been deprived. She can be nothing else; there is no proper good that could define this living being as an instance of some other species, and accordingly no form of animal flourishing she could attain if left alone by human beings. Being left alone could therefore not be what "letting-be" means in this case, as that is not a fitting response to the being of this being. So what *is* the fitting response to a being of this sort? Clearly, "liberating solicitude" would not be appropriate, as this is not Dasein, whether authentic or inauthentic, given that neither way of being would be possible for a biologically human being that is so profoundly disabled. Heidegger also does not tell us what he thinks is the right response to human beings that cannot arrive at Dasein through no fault of their own. His account entails, however, that these must be recognized as disabled human beings and nothing else, and there is every reason to suppose that some modality of love and care would be the appropriate response to such vulnerable members of our own species.

This reflection on liminal cases is also helpful for analyzing Heidegger's account of animals, and drawing out its moral implications. Heidegger describes the being of animals in terms of privation, and is conscious of doing so. The animal is "poor" in world, "deprived" of world, and yet Heidegger insists we should not be too quick to judge that the animal is therefore lesser:

[6] Cf. Kevin Aho: The animal can certainly take hold of and manipulate things, but it does not use "handy" (*zuhanden*) equipment because it does not encounter things in terms of a whole referential context or "totality of equipment" (*Zeugganze*)" (Aho 2007, 11). However, I disagree with Aho's claim in *Heidegger's Neglect of the Body* that Dasein is not "*a* being" but "a historical space or clearing of meaning on the basis of which things emerge-into-presence as the kinds of things they are" (Aho 2009, 18–19). It can be both, and it is hard to make sense of a good deal of Heidegger's description of authentic being in the world without conceiving of Dasein as *a* being, the being that each of us is, as he puts it himself (BT 7).

However ready we are to rank man as a higher being with respect to the animal, such an assessment is deeply questionable, especially when we consider that man can sink lower than any animal. No animal can become depraved in the same way as man. Of course in the last analysis this consideration itself reveals the necessity of speaking of a 'higher' in some sense. But we can already see from all this that the criterion according to which we talk of height and depth in this connection is obscure. May we talk of a 'higher' and a 'lower' at all in the realm of what is essential? Is the essence of man higher than the essence of the animal? All this is questionable even as a question. (FCM 194/GA 29/30, 286–87)

Heidegger does rank the capacity for freedom, which allows human beings to sink "lower" than any animal, as "higher" in a certain sense, one that will allow him to speak of animals as "deprived" of this capacity. At the same time, there is another sense in which one cannot speak of higher and lower as applying to an order of rank *between* beings, for judgments about a given species as lacking something can only be made in relation to the peculiar *telos* of that species. It is in light of such a *telos*, defining the essence of being human, that a profoundly disabled human being would be recognized as such.

What follows, then, about how animals should be treated, from the very different kind of lack by which they are characterized on Heidegger's account? In this case, the language of privation is not being used to describe a falling short of essence; the essence of animality itself is conceived in terms of a lack. We might ask why Heidegger speaks of privation and poverty at all this context, when he has said explicitly that talk of higher and lower is questionable "in the realm of the essential." Such a move would seem to rest on "a certain anthropocentric or even humanist teleology" (Derrida 1987b, 57), as Derrida objects, contradicting Heidegger's express reservations about humanism.

As with the concept of disability, though, at issue here is a point about the nature of our understanding of animality and animals. In *Being and Time*, Heidegger had written that "life, in its own right, is a kind of being; but essentially it is accessible only in Dasein," adding that "the ontology of life is accomplished by way of a privative interpretation" (BT 50). Phenomenologically, that is, we understand "life" through ourselves as living beings, subtracting elements of our existence to arrive at the idea of "mere aliveness" (BT 50). Heidegger's analysis of animality makes a similar point. Phenomenologically, we understand animals and animality in general through ourselves, subtracting from the existence of Dasein to arrive at the idea of a life that is in some respects like ours but lacking something essential to the definition of ourselves as human beings rather than animals: freedom, or rationality, or conceptual understanding. We have no immediate access to the sentient life of animals, after all, no experience of what it is like to be a lizard lying on a stone, or a dog bounding up the stairs. Yet we can see that these living beings are not like stones or stairs, and we imagine that they encounter what is around them in *some* way, which inanimate things do not. Heidegger's analysis suggests that we do actually see nonhuman sentient beings as like ourselves, in the sense that they are not things, or tools. At the same time, our interpretation of their fundamental being in terms of "captivated" life proceeds by projecting a version of our own being with some property negated. This is a form of life that sees but does not see *as* (FCM 219/GA 29/30, 219), that behaves but does not comport itself (FCM 247, 274/GA 29/30, 359, 397), that presses forward as drive and instinct but not through a self-reflexive projection of possibility (FCM 226–29, 362/GA 29/30, 331–35, 526–7). That is how we make sense of the nature of these strange intermediate beings, which are neither quite like stones nor quite like ourselves.

It remains true that Heidegger's own characterizations of animality are based on too narrow a spectrum of animal life and that he takes over uncritically a traditionally dominant conception of animals within Western thought, without adequate zoological investigation. A presupposed concept of animality may characterize zoology as an established discipline, but that does not rule out the possibility that the findings of zoological research may lead to a shift in the basic concepts and methodology of this science. That has happened through the work of revolutionary zoologists such as Jane Goodall, who saw the primates she observed as beings somewhat like herself, a perspective that was likely both a response to their behavior and a projected frame, including a mode of interaction, whose adoption made the behavior more comprehensible.[7] This is precisely how the hermeneutic circle ought to work in science, and Heidegger has been rightly criticized for imposing on animals a degree of homogeneity the category does not possess, thereby positing too sharp a difference between at least some animals, and human beings.

Granting the validity of these criticisms, however, we should not move too hastily to conclusions about the moral consequences of Heidegger's claims about the radical difference between humanity and animality. Many of his critics on this subject have done so, supposing that to posit such a sharp gap between human beings and animals entails our having no moral obligations toward the latter. But much depends on the nature of the difference being posited. Heidegger does set the bar high for counting as Dasein, and the comportment of "liberating solicitude," defined as authentic being

[7] Commenting on the resistance to her method and findings among her scientific contemporaries, Goodall states in an interview: "These people were trying to make ethology a hard science … So they objected – quite unpleasantly – to me naming my subjects and for suggesting that they had personalities, minds and feelings." She adds a point about intellectual honesty: "You cannot share your life with a dog, as I had done in Bournemouth, or a cat, and not know perfectly well that animals have personalities and minds and feelings … You know it and I think every single one of those scientists knew it too but because they couldn't prove it, they wouldn't talk about it" (McKie 2010).

with others, is appropriate only to the being of Dasein. That is because liberating solicitude amounts to respect for the freedom that defines the genuine being of the others who are there with us in a shared world. Supposing animals do not have such freedom, and liberating solicitude is therefore not a form of comportment that accords with their manner of being, it does not follow that they may be treated like stones or hammers, simply because, according to Heidegger's analysis of the being of animals, these entities are *not* objects or tools.

They are, Heidegger says, "poor" in world, held captive to their drives and unable to apprehend the being of entities, including themselves. As a result, they cannot truly speak. They cannot do science or metaphysics, or create poetry or art. They cannot feel anxiety, or boredom, or wonder in *such* a way that being as a whole becomes a question for them. They cannot encounter ready-to-hand things against the horizon of a meaningful world. And so? They do touch, and see, and press forward in their own ways, and we – who *do* have the capacity to apprehend and question the being of entities – understand this. We understand that they can suffer, for instance, as Bentham said, and we are capable feeling compassion for them. Derrida writes:

> Bentham said something like this: the question is not to know whether the animal can think, reason or speak, etc., something we still pretend to be asking ourselves (from Aristotle to Descartes, from Descartes, especially, to Heidegger, Levinas, and Lacan, and this question determines so many others concerning *power* or *capability* [pouvoirs] and *attributes* [avoirs]: being able, having the power or capability to give, to bury one's dead, to dress, to work, to invent a technique, etc., a power that consists in having such and such a faculty, thus such and such a capability, as an essential attribute). Thus the question will not be to know whether animals are of the type *zoon logon echon*, whether they *can* speak or reason thanks to that *capacity* or that *attribute* of the *logos* ... The *first* and *decisive* question would rather be to know whether animals *can suffer*. (Derrida 2008, 27)

What the "decisive question" is, though, depends on what we are trying to determine. If we are asking whether or not an entity belongs at all within the sphere of moral concern, then it is hard to see how the distinction Heidegger wants to draw between relating to things *as such*, and relating to them in *some* way, which sentient beings do and inanimate ones do not, should be decisive. It is one thing to say that certain human qualities – our capacity and need for self-determination, our ability to anticipate and remember events, our relation to death, the character of our bonds with others – entail *special* forms of moral obligation (although empirical investigation of various animal species will still be required to determine whether, or to what extent, they may share these qualities). It is quite another thing to claim that *all* moral concern is limited to these qualities, and therefore to entities that can say "I," or project possibilities and make choices.

Heidegger does not actually claim this, we should notice, nor is it anywhere entailed by his analysis. The implication of his analysis is only that *liberating solicitude* is not the appropriate mode of comportment toward animals on our part, given that they lack freedom. Admittedly, Heidegger also provides no account of what mode of care *would* be appropriate to beings that have drives, sensations, and feelings, but no capacity for distance from these, as is arguably true of many, if perhaps not all, nonhuman animal species. Add to this the fact that *Being and Time* only refers to animals in the context of an analysis of equipment (BT 70), while later writings continue to emphasize that the essence of humanity is separated from that of "living creatures" – plants and animals – "by an abyss" (BW 230), and it does seem that Heidegger is continuing rather than challenging a tradition that has differentiated human beings and animals, to conclude that animals indeed do not deserve moral concern and may be treated as tools.

I am arguing, however, that this does not follow from the analysis Heidegger gives of animality, even if he supposes otherwise. For Heidegger, the special dignity of humanity consists precisely in our ability to draw back from proximate drives, and correspondingly from immersion in things, so as to see precisely those things, and ourselves, as what they are in truth. That is what it means for Dasein to be a "clearing." It does not mean that Dasein is justified in subordinating all other beings to itself as the cleverest and most powerful of all animals – which would make it, in fact, still "only" an animal – but that it has the ability to comprehend the being of entities, and to let them be what they are.

In that case, what is special about humanity, establishing the radical break between the nature of this being and that of any other living creature, is that it can discern and respect the being of beings: its own being and that of other entities that are Dasein, but also the being of entities not like itself. Only human beings, for instance, can see and say that every animal species is complete and perfect in itself, measuring the wellness of particular animals in light of the *telos* proper to the kind of animal that they are. Only we can see and say that here are beings who are like us in this respect but not in that, who are not like stones or hammers, to which no world is given at all, but who do apprehend themselves and what is around them in some way. Consequently, we are not only able to feel compassion for them, but also to comprehend in what consists their proper flourishing.

I emphasized in the previous chapter that Heidegger, like Kant, does not focus on the bodily wants and afflictions of individual human beings. And Kant's moral philosophy emphatically does exclude in principle the claim that we have direct moral obligations to nonhuman animals because of shared capacities for feeling and suffering, since it is not these capacities, on their own, that warrant respect for persons. It can legitimately be objected that conceptions so sharply distinguishing human beings from the rest of the natural world draw rigid boundaries where there are in truth fuzzier ones, not only between kinds of living beings but also between the various dimensions of our own being, and that ethical systems based on such ontologies cannot help but reflect this flaw.[8] But similarity to ourselves is also not a prerequisite for respecting the being of other living beings. Foltz asks whether there is truly a "clear and direct relationship, as it is often assumed, between how we treat animals and whether – or the extent to which – we see ourselves as animals," and rightly answers that there is not (Foltz 1993, 89). Heidegger's phenomenological account positions animals as "essentially" not like us, practically by definition, since we distinguish ourselves from them and must have some criteria for doing so. It may be methodologically and empirically flawed in places (I believe it is), but even were it not, it would not follow that we are justified in treating animals in the same way we treat a "worldless" entity, such as a stone, to which nothing is given in any way. Nor would it be appropriate to treat them only as having a place within the network of our concerns, as if their being were constituted by those concerns, as is the being of a tool. To do so would be to behave in the way Heidegger describes animals as behaving, seeing these entities only as either useful or in the way, depending on the need that subjects them to itself. Thus, even were it true that all animals only ever behave in this way (which is highly doubtful), the moral consequence would only be that their being does not warrant a certain form of respect, insofar as we respect the capacity for respect itself – that is, the capacity to recognize the being of the other as independent of our needs and oriented toward its own ends. We can nonetheless recognize that an animal does have this orientation, and also that it has a place within a network of other living beings that have their own ends. Given this capacity on our part, we can also ask what justice requires of us in accord with these truths.

A full consideration of Heidegger's understanding of justice is reserved for the next chapter, but it is worth situating his position on animals here – or, more precisely, my reconstruction of the implications of his analysis of animals – in relation to current debates about animal rights, resting on conceptions of justice. For Heidegger, an understanding of the potentiality of a given kind of living being is essential to determining the truth about what it is. He also posits a radical difference between human beings and every other kind of sentient living being. Consequently, "rights" founded on the essence of humanity, supposing that there are such rights, could not be accorded to animals, and Heidegger's answer to the question of "liminal" cases of human beings would be that, although their actual abilities do not meet the criteria for human

[8] I argued precisely this myself in an earlier version of an essay comparing Heidegger and Kant; see Sikka 2006.

personhood, they are not reduced to the status of animals, since the truth about them can only be that they are disabled human beings.

This kind of position is usually associated with defenses of the special moral status of human beings. Some version of it is often adopted against proponents of animal rights, who argue that the confinement of rights to human beings through appeal to especially worthy properties exclusive to them will have to exclude severely disabled human individuals as well. The analysis I have given of Heidegger's position reveals, on the other hand, that the link of entailment between the view that only human beings have certain capacities and the view that only they deserve moral consideration is weak. Whatever Heidegger himself assumed about what we owe to animals, it emerges from his phenomenological findings that we are special precisely in our ability to recognize the manner of being of other living beings, which intrinsically involves a recognition of what is good for them. Heidegger's account does not answer the question of what precisely this means for how we should treat different animal species, but it does rule out treating animals as if they were something other than they are, inanimate things that do not feel, or tools with no ends of their own. To treat animals in this manner would be, quite simply, *wrong* – wrong about the character of the entity to which we are comporting ourselves, making the comportment itself a wronging of that entity.

We are here at the heart of what I have been describing as Heidegger's moral realism, which is not grounded in any affirmation of the "objectivity" of "values," whatever that means (and I will explore what it might mean in the next chapter). Rather, in relation to living beings at least, this realism involves a rejection of the distinction between fact and value. Understanding the "facts" about living beings means understanding their *telos*, and assessing how individuals are doing in relation to that *telos*. For animals, unlike plants (as far as we can tell), that includes understanding their being driven toward what is good for them in such a way that they will feel the privations they encounter. In spite of the "abyss" that Heidegger says separates animality and humanity, in certain respects his position can consistently be used to support animal "rights." Consider, for instance, the argument in favor of animal rights presented by Donaldson and Kymlicka in *Zoopolis*, when they state: "Our fundamental position, then, is that animals have inviolable rights in virtue of their sentience or selfhood, the fact that they have a subjective experience of the world," and "what matters to sentient beings matters because it matters *to them*" (Donaldson and Kymlicka 2011, 31, 33).

Heidegger does not use the language of rights or subjectivity, and he reserves the term "selfhood" for human beings, as he does the idea of "world." But he uses the latter terms in very specific senses, and acknowledges that things are given to animals in *some* fashion, that they sense and feel, and that they have their own ends as well as their own manner of *having* ends. If in all of these respects there remains an "abyss" between such properties and the way they are modified in an entity that relates to being as Dasein does, we may infer from this only what is in line with the character of that difference. We should not expect any animal, whether "higher" or "lower," to write poetry, or have an existential crisis, or recognize *our* rights, and it would be inappropriate for us to treat them as if they were able to do any of these things. We are, however, called upon to include them in our considerations of what is due to each being in light of what it is and within the design of what is as a whole, because we can grasp that the essence of animality is not constituted by being present-at-hand or ready-to-hand, and because we can understand that the places in which we dwell neighbor upon the spaces of these animal others or are coinhabited by them.

Nature, Things, and Artifacts

There are further questions to be raised about the status of these places and spaces themselves, and of the things within them that are "worldless," like stones and rivers, or ready to hand, like hammers and windmills. Is anything "due" to these entities, or to the environmental contexts in which they occur? According to Donaldson and Kymlicka, no, for "justice is owed to subjects who experience the world, not to things." Although "non-sentient entities can rightfully be the objects of respect, awe, love and care," they argue, and "there are many good reasons to respect and protect nature, including instrumental and non-instrumental ones," "only a being with subjective experience can have interests, or be owed the direct duties of justice that protect those interests" (Donaldson and Kymlicka 2011, 36). The reading of Heidegger I have been presenting could support the view that only sentient beings have "interests," but his later thought does seem to extend a duty of care to a wider range of entities.

Foltz goes so far as to claim that, for Heidegger, the Kantian injunction "that we should treat always at the same time as an end and never merely as a means … would not be limited to persons – indeed, it would not even be limited to sentient beings – but would extend to entities as a whole" (Foltz 1993, 86). He draws this conclusion from an interpretation of Heidegger's notion of *Gelassenheit* as "letting be," in conjunction with the relation to nature that emerges as an ideal from his later writings, and especially his critique of *die Technik*. I would challenge Foltz's claim that this ideal involves an extension of Kant's categorical imperative to all entities, but in his later writings, Heidegger does criticize the view of nature purely as a resource to be put into the service of calculated human ends. He even laments a change in the character of the things we make and use that goes beyond a consideration of their functionality. These critical observations are connected with concerns about the way human beings *are* within the modern worldview. They highlight the ills of our failure to dwell appropriately on the earth under the sway of technicity, this peculiarly modern way of being and seeing that turns us into dominating subjects, for whom every entity, and every region of being, is given as an object to be mastered and rearranged to suit our interests. We do not fare well ourselves under this paradigm, on Heidegger's analysis; but, the tone and content of his articulation of the problem, as well as of the hoped-for solution, resist an interpretation that would cast the matter purely in terms of human interests. It therefore seems as if not only sentient beings, but also "things," and certainly the things that belong to the self-producing activity of nature, demand from us some kind of "letting be."

This is a significant development over *Being and Time*, where nature is said to be discovered first as raw material, out of which ready-to-hand things are made, which can then be stripped of significations constituted by involvement in human projects to become, second, a field of present-at-hand objects of the sort investigated by science. *Being and* Time identifies no way we can be toward nature except using or knowing and, correlatively, no way nature can appear to us except as potential tool or object. And yet, Hubert Dreyfus is right to suggest that there are "at least three ways of encountering nature" in *Being and Time*, citing as evidence the following passage:

> As the "environment" is discovered, the "Nature" thus discovered is encountered too. If its kind of Being as ready-to-hand is disregarded, this "Nature" itself can be discovered and defined simply in its pure presence-at-hand. But when this happens, the Nature which 'stirs and strives', which assails us and enthrals us as landscape, remains hidden. (Dreyfus 1992, 179; BT 70)

The trouble is that Heidegger does not realize he is presenting more than *two* ways of encountering nature here. The passage is confused, as the next sentence illustrates: "The botanist's plants are not the flowers of the hedgerow; the 'source' which the geographer establishes for a river is not the 'springhead in the dale'" (BT 70). The contrast Heidegger is trying to draw is exclusively between nature as ready-to-hand (encountered through concerned activity), and nature as present-at-hand (encountered through scientific investigation). The theoretical content of the text does not provide space for a nature that fits neither of these varieties of being, nor for a mode of reshaping nature to which scientific representation and calculation are not essential.

The third mode of being of nature to which Dreyfus refers actually breaks through and disrupts the categories being presented in the text. Heidegger does not see at this juncture that "the Nature which 'stirs and strives', which assails us and enthralls us as landscape," or greets us in our everyday world in the form of "the flowers of the hedgerow," or "the springhead in the dale," is not encountered as ready-to-hand, any more than as present-at-hand. Some modes of being, linked to ways of discovering and making, that will become central to Heidegger's later thought are not thematized in *Being and Time*: art, as a special kind of work related to the apprehension of beauty, for instance, and the experience of the holy. Missing also, as Dreyfus notes, is the dimension of what Heidegger will later call "earth" (Dreyfus 1992, 177), the aspect of nature on which the world of human production and concern depends, but which at the same time resists it. "Earth" is also encountered via concern, and it both offers itself to, and resists, transformation into the artifacts of the humanly constructed world.

Precisely the dimensions of nature that had eluded Heidegger's categories in *Being and Time* become key preoccupations in his later reflections. Nature is now seen as self-standing, entering the human world as its basis but incapable of being mastered. It is associated with experiences of the beautiful and the sacred, and calls for a response that respects the diverse natures of "things," both produced and self-producing. These things include animals ("heron and roe, deer, horse and bull"); non-sentient elements of nature ("tree and pond . . . brook and hill"); and works of human craft ("the jug and the bench, the footbridge and the plow"; "mirror and clasp, book and picture, crown and cross") ("The Thing," PLT 182/GA 7, 183–84). While the latter are not "natural" things in the usual sense, they do depend upon nature, as do we. What differentiates the made things that Heidegger appreciates and contrasts with the products of technology is that the material and manner of their construction remain within, and reflect, the bounds of this relationship.

Heidegger describes technicity as an overstepping of proper boundaries, effecting an assault upon nature that turns it into stock or standing-reserve (*Bestand*). Many commentators have construed this as a critique of an approach to nature that views it only in relation to human needs, as opposed to respecting what it is in itself. Ladelle McWhorter, interpreting how things are under the reign of technicity, writes:

> All is here simply for human use. No plant, no animal, no ecosystem has a life of its own, has any significance, apart from human desire and need. Nothing, we say, other than human beings has any intrinsic value. All things are instruments for the human will. (McWhorter and Stenstad 2009, 12)

Letting things be does not, however, mean removing them from all relation to ourselves. It is true that, while there is a phenomenological version of Kantian ethics in *Being and Time*, Heidegger's later writings emphatically reject the view that the worth of all nonhuman entities is dependent upon the ordering activity of the human will; but, technicity is not contrasted with leaving nature alone. Rather, appropriate human dwelling on the earth is supposed to reveal and respect the place of every thing within a network of relations to which humanity belongs, but of which it is not the foundation. Human beings are still regarded as special, but in virtue of their capacity for understanding the what and how of entities within what Kenneth Maly describes as the "living connectedness" of the earth, which they are called upon to reenact in their own way of dwelling (McWhorter and Stenstad 2009, 52). That requires us to recognize our proper place in relation to nature, and to refrain from transgressing its limits in a way that we alone can.

That proper place is still an exceptional one, as Thiele points out, but in the sense that "for Heidegger, it is precisely our capacity for ontological shepherding that distinguishes human beings from other life forms" (Thiele 1995b, 185). "Ontological shepherding," moreover, requires determining the proper order of things in relation to one another and within the design of what is as a whole. Thiele rightly observes that Heidegger's position does not constitute a biocentric egalitarianism or deep ecology (Thiele 1994, 286), and that "Heidegger is unwilling to equate humans, ontologically or ethically, with all other organisms" (Thiele 1995b, 182). Heidegger offers, rather, a model of benign stewardship (Thiele 1995b, 183), where "if ... we understand our freedom and dignity to rest with our capacity to let beings be" rather than master them, "our relation to nature may bear the fruits of a symbiotic integration" (Thiele 1995, 184).

Much has already been written about Heidegger's philosophy of nature and the environmental ethics entailed by it. My question here is limited to whether, in light of his understanding of nature and the place of humanity within it, Heidegger thinks we have a duty of care toward non-sentient beings. The short answer is yes, for reasons that cannot be described either as instrumental or non-instrumental, because Heidegger's understanding of the relation between humanity and nature disturbs that binary. For Heidegger, we have seen, the essence of humanity, the achievement of which constitutes its *telos* and special dignity, consists in being a shepherd of being. In that case, the being well of human beings cannot be separated from their taking care of the earth and all that is on it, including non-sentient beings in a way that preserves the proper relations between entities. It might seem odd to speak of "achieving" an essence, but within Heidegger's account, the essence of living beings is defined by a *telos*, and humanity is the one entity on earth that can turn toward or away from its essence. We therefore also have the possibility of being in a way that is out of joint with ourselves and with other beings. We "are" not just rational animals, distinguished from other animals only through the possession of a faculty that gives us vastly greater power than any other predator. But we can "be" that, nothing greater than the most fearsome of beasts, seeking to secure our own being through total domination of nature with the ultimate (and in fact unachievable) aim of acquiring control over the very basis of our existence. This project is doomed to failure, and will lead to being unwell, for us and the other entities to which we relate in this heedless manner. Thus, it can be said that such a relation pushes us out of our essence. The point is not that we should care about other beings rather than only about ourselves. It is that our being well requires a right relation to the being of what is around us.

Instead of being rational animals, we can understand the power of disclosure given to us as a kind of gracious enabling, and move, in Gail Stenstad's words, from "disconnection toward connection … from our panic-stricken obsession with control (and the violence which all to often accompanies it) toward the strength and wisdom to care for things in accord with how they show themselves to us" (McWhorter and Stenstad 2009, 68). Things show themselves to us in light of their own ends and their relatedness to one another. Right understanding then means recognizing how entities are in view of their good *and* how they best fit together, where that is, for Heidegger, the essence of justice. On this interpretation, there can be obligations of justice toward non-sentient beings not because they have their own interests, but because there is a way things best fit together to enable the well-being of all that lives on the earth, including ourselves as the ones called upon to heed our essence by taking care of things.

Justice, then, even includes made things, in a way, because how we relate to the earth and the world in our activities of crafting and building can be fitting or not. Heidegger sees *die Technik*, technicity, as a particularly unfitting manner of relating to ourselves and nature, not in accord with the truth of the way things are. He sometimes finds in ancient Greek thought possible alternatives to this modern conception of ourselves and the world, and of what we call "nature," but interpret in a specifically modern fashion. To be sure, Greek philosophers are very much complicit in Heidegger's narration of the history of Western metaphysics, ending in nihilism. That history begins with them, and Heidegger tells a number of stories about how it does so, and how the seeds for the modern conception of being and humanity were contained within the writings of, for instance, Plato and Aristotle. As Zimmerman says:

> The technological understanding of being, the view that all things are nothing but raw material for the ceaseless process of production and consumption, is merely the final stage in the history of productionist metaphysics. Heidegger read Plato as the initiator of this metaphysics. Fascinated like other Greeks by human making and producing, Plato conceived of the being of entities in terms drawn from human manufacturing. (Zimmerman 1990, xv)

But Heidegger also sometimes finds at the origins of Western philosophy possibilities for thinking otherwise, paths that might have been followed, and could provide for the present not models for simple imitation but sources of inspiration, material for imagining a different way of being in the future.

In "The Question Concerning Technology," for example, Heidegger retrieves from Aristotle a different conception of production than the one that guides modern technology, involving an alternative understanding of nature, and of human making in relation to nature. For the Greeks, he proposes, making is not an imposing of self-created human designs on a nature conceived as raw material. It is a form of *poiesis*, a bringing-forth, where *physis*, the Greek word for what we now call nature, is also a *poiesis*, "the arising of something from out of itself" (QCT 10/GA 7, 12). Human craft, therefore, whether the making of handy things and buildings, or the making of poetry and art in their narrower modern senses, is not a process standing against nature, finding its source purely within the so-called "subject." It belongs to the broader process of bringing-forth as *poiesis*. It is a bringing-forth through the medium of another, the craftsman or artist (QCT 11/GA 7, 13), rather than the bringing-forth of itself proper to *physis*.

When right to how things are, and right *about* how they are, the crafting of things by human beings not only respects but also reveals our proper relationship to nature and to one another in our common dwelling on the earth. This idea underlies the difference Heidegger sees between the products of modern technology and the constructions of earlier ages, as well as his understanding of art as a way truth is revealed. It also has implications for the significance of these made things and for why their being matters, even though it does not matter to the things themselves. In "Building Dwelling Thinking," Heidegger contrasts the old stone bridge that "gathers the earth as landscape around the stream," and thus "guides and attends the stream through the meadows" with "the highway bridge ... tied into the network of long-distance traffic, paced and calculated for maximum yield" (PLT 150/GA 7, 155). The old stone bridge relates earth and world to one another, reflecting the belonging together of the natural and the human. It also makes space into place, for it arises out of, and makes reference to, a kind of living or dwelling in common with a local history and geography. The highway bridge, on Heidegger's description, does neither.

Similar observations apply to the contrast Heidegger draws between an old windmill and a modern hydroelectric dam, in "The Question Concerning Technology" (QCT, 14–16/GA 7, 15–17). Here, too, the contrast has to do with an appropriate relation between nature and the human world, and with the significance of place. We might note as well that Heidegger's descriptions of appropriately made things evoke the sense that they, unlike the highway bridge and the hydroelectric dam, are beautiful. This is a genre of things whose beauty is intimately linked to being well in the world, a kind of flourishing that includes a recognition of our relatedness to nature, along with a sense of what it means to live together as a community. These things are to be respected and cared for in virtue of their enactment of appropriate human dwelling, which their being expresses and preserves.

They also matter because they occupy and disclose a place of significance within the human world. Works of art effect such a disclosure directly, whereas things of use do so indirectly, as illustrated by Heidegger's reading of van Gogh's painting of a pair of old shoes. He interprets them as the shoes of a peasant, disclosing the world of their wearer.[9] In themselves they are *Zeug*, ordinary things of use, whose significance is given by their location within the patterns of concern that make up human lives as led in a given place and time. *Being and Time* describes things of this sort as referring also to an environing nature out of which they are made, from which they provide protection, and to which they give access (BT 70–71). In other words, things that are made and used, like shoes, refer to both nature and culture, emerging at the intersection between these two dimensions. Accordingly, the shoes in van Gogh's painting evoke what Heidegger now terms earth and world: "This equipment belongs to the *earth* and it is protected in the *world* of the peasant woman" (PLT, 33–34/ GA 5, 19).

Another example Heidegger gives in "The Origin of the Work of Art" is that of an ancient Greek temple. This work, too, reveals the intersection of earth and world in the leading of human lives at a given time and place. It reveals "the world of this historical people," Heidegger writes, and at the same time the rocky ground on which the temple stands, the storm raging above it, "the light of the day, the breadth of the sky, the darkness of the night" (PLT 42/GA 5, 28). The work testifies to what touched the people who constructed and used it, and sets forth the materiality of nature in a special way. While materials disappear into inconspicuousness in well-functioning tools, in a work of art "the rock comes to bear and rest and so first becomes rock; metals come to glitter and shimmer, colors to glow, tones to sing, the word to speak" (PLT 45/GA 5, 32). Such works are then worth preserving for their disclosures of the human world, present and past, in its essential relation to nature.

If Dasein is here still the final "for the sake of which," an end in itself, that end consists in its caring for the being of all entities in a manner that preserves and safeguards their truth. In the case of animals, that would mean adopting a mode of care appropriate to beings that are fundamentally different from us but that also, we can see, have ends in relation to which their flourishing is determined. In the case of non-sentient natural beings, living and non-living, it means taking care of the relational expanse essential to dwelling on the earth. In the case, finally, of made things, it means preserving the right relation between humanity and nature, while respecting the significance of the human world that strives against the earth but still has to be established, always, upon its basis.

[9] Heidegger interprets these as peasant shoes, which they may not have been. For one analysis of the debate on this question, see Thomson 2011, 106–20.

4 Justice in Light of the Good

I have briefly discussed Heidegger's rejection of the fact/value distinction, and pointed to his conception of justice as achieving appropriate relations between entities. This conception is linked to the ethical prescription that every entity ought to be treated in a manner that recognizes and respects the truth about its character as the kind of entity that it is. I now want to focus more deeply on these themes, first examining in greater detail Heidegger's critique of "values," before going on to show how this critique, far from undermining the possibility of any "objective" conception of justice, actually lays the ground for his own realist position.

The Danger of Values

Although a popular misperception of Heidegger as a relativist or amoralist persists, I am not the first to claim that Heidegger is in truth a kind of moral realist, who rejects the modern distinction between fact and value. Julian Young, to whom I have referred before on this point, also argues that Heidegger's rejection of "values" in many of his works means to challenge rather than support subjectivistic relativism. Heidegger's worry, Young observes, is that "values are simply our own goals in disguise," making them dependent upon human willing and therefore optional, "things that can be affirmed (i.e. chosen) or not" (Young 1997, 207). Young underlines Heidegger's "insistence on the inseparability of *Sein* and *Sollen* ('Being' and the 'ought' or, in more familiar terminology, the 'is' and the 'ought') in the *Introduction to Metaphysics*" (207). He also notes Heidegger's indication of an alternative possibility in the "Letter on Humanism," where human beings would receive their binding directives from the "truth of Being," in which values are given along with facts (209). Young concludes that "Heidegger is no amoralist or value-nihilist, but rather, in terms of the (perhaps not very helpful) categories of analytic meta-ethics, an ethical 'realist' or 'cognitivist' " (209).

Similarly, Frank Schalow observes that, while "we speak of 'values' almost uncritically to designate either preferences that are culturally relative or norms that are grounded in the natural order of things" (Schalow 2001, 250), "from

Heidegger's perspective, we must consider first what seems almost alien to values, namely, Being itself insofar as our understanding of it arises prior to the schism between ought and is, value and fact" (255). Ingo Farin examines the development of this perspective through Heidegger's early engagement with the neo-Kantian value philosophy of Windelband and Rickert. The latter did not conceive of values either as objects or as dependent upon human faculties, Farin points out (Farin 1998, 259, 272), and in these respects there is some continuity between Heidegger's position and theirs. "Heidegger's crucial objection," though, Farin argues, "is that Windelband and Rickert work with the theoretically denatured concept of a 'given' or 'fixed' value – the theoretically declared values –, whereas the real phenomenon is to be found in the event of valuing" (274). That event, in which "historically embedded subjects are enveloped by the unfolding of value-soaked life worlds" (274), is not dependent upon the voluntary act of a subject. Thus, "by dissociating validity from subjective forms of approval, Heidegger interprets values, so it seems, as objective forces whose objective validity does not depend upon subjective recognition and appropriation" (275).

Although they may be used loosely to describe Heidegger's position, speaking more strictly, terms like "objective" and "realist" are inapt when applied to Heidegger's position, scholars recognize, because of his phenomenological questioning of how these terms picture being. The word "objective" refers literally to objects, and while we do not always mean to speak so literally of objects when we use it, Heidegger suspects that its usage presses us to imagine objectlikeness, as long as what *else* we might mean remains unclarified. We imagine that being is equivalent to constant presence, and that what truly is must be a substantial entity lying about somewhere or other. In philosophy, this unanalyzed idea of true being as *realitas*, or "thinglikeness," generates pseudoproblems, and this is true of debates about the metaphysical status of value. If we think that "values" are "real," or "objective," we cannot help but imagine that they are objects – "ideal" objects, but objects nonetheless – or properties or relations pertaining to objects, that "are" present somewhere, and to which our thinking about values, when true, accurately corresponds. Such a confused picture of the possibility of truth in relation to judgments about what is good and right gives rise to the scenario in which a philosopher such as John Mackie may argue that there cannot be "objective values," because if there were, "they would be entities or qualities or relations of a very strange sort, utterly different from anything else in the universe" (Mackie, 1977, 38).

From Heidegger's perspective, Mackie's objection is muddled as a refutation of the possibility of true ethical judgments, not because there *are* in fact "objective values" but because picturing ethical judgments in terms of correspondence to things existing in the universe, as planets and protons do, is already muddled. Heidegger is not a naturalist, if that requires accepting a picture where only entities of that sort, existing in that manner, can be said truly to "be." But he is also not an anti-naturalist, if that means someone who posits additional "real" entities. On Heidegger's analysis, it does not make any sense to say, as Ronald Dworkin does, that "values are real and fundamental, not just manifestations of something else; they are as real as trees or pain" (Dworkin 2013, 13). Values *are* not in the same as trees or pain – Mackie is right at least about this – and they are consequently not "real," if being real means being present in such a manner.

Neo-Kantians such as Windelband and Rickert also did not take values to be existing objects; but, Heidegger's complaint is that tacitly they still do, and in any case, they do not provide an adequate ontology of what else – or better *how* else – values might "be." Faris points out that "Rickert himself associates his value idealism with Plato's Idea of the Good, which is, like the values and the ought, beyond all Being" (Faris 1998, 272), and that Heidegger criticizes both this reification of values and the lack of clarity within neo-Kantian thought about the experience of the "ought" upon which the validity of values is supposed to rest (273). Eventually, Heidegger will reject the neo-Kantian scheme altogether, arguing that "values" can be nothing but subjective, because the concept of value is intrinsically linked to human positing. In a section of the *Introduction to Metaphysics* called "Being and the Ought" (*Sein und Sollen*), Heidegger traces the history and prehistory of the concept of value, from its inception in Plato's idea of the good, to the contemporary understanding of values in terms of validity. This is a history in which "being" is interpreted as presence and actuality, and thereby necessarily distinguished from potentiality and the "ought." In the form of the good, the "ought" is first placed *epekeina tes ousias*, beyond being, and interpreted as "idea" (IM 197/GA 40, 206). In the modern era, Kant, who understands what is as a whole through a specific idea of "nature," opposes to this nature the "ought" of the categorical imperative, determined by reason (IM 198/GA 40, 206). But now, the status of the "ought" is in danger, especially given the predominance and prestige of the empirical sciences, which study "facts" about this or that region of reality. There is then an attempt to ground the force of the "ought" in "values," asserted to be the foundation of morality. Finally, these values are said to possess "validity":

> The values have validity. But validity is still too suggestive of what is valid for a subject. Exalted as value, the ought was again in need of bolstering up. To this end a being was attributed to the values themselves. *At bottom* this being meant neither more nor less than the presence of something already-there, though not in so vulgar and handy a sense as chairs and tables. With the being of values a maximum of confusion and uprootedness was achieved. (IM 198/GA 40, 207)

The "confusion and uprootedness" are a result of no longer knowing what we are talking about. We take it as obvious that what *is*, is a fact, and that what *ought* to be, is not yet and therefore cannot be included in being. If we are bound to realize this "ought," we have come to think, it must be because of something that in fact is, and imposes an obligation upon us. There must be, in other words, "objective values," although we fall into nonsense when we try to describe the being of such queer things.

The only alternative left to us, within this view of being with its radical separation between fact and value, is to conclude that there are *no* objective values and that all values are therefore merely "subjective," a product of our own all-too-human preferences and perspectives. That is what Nietzsche concludes about "values" when he interprets them as a function of will to power, but this interpretation also clearly reveals the essence of the concept. Nietzsche understands value as a "point-of-view … posited at any given time by a seeing and for a seeing" ("Nietzsche's word: 'God is Dead'," QCT 71/GA 5, 228). This positing is in turn a function of the will to power that Nietzsche takes to be the essence of all life (QCT 74/GA 5, 230), and even "the innermost essence of being" (QCT 79/GA 5, 236). "Value" is taken back into being, but being is interpreted as "nature," and nature as "will to power." Values are then "real," insofar as they are in fact posited by the needs and drives of living beings seeking to preserve and enhance their being.

On this view of being and value, "justice" can only be a function of will to power, and that is exactly what Nietzsche proposes. "The justice thought by Nietzsche is the truth of what is – which now *is* in the mode of the will to power" (QCT 92/GA 5, 247), and modern humanity now "completes its last step … it wills itself as the executor of the unconditional will to power" (QCT 95/GA 5, 251), "set before the task of taking over dominion of the earth" (QCT 96/GA 5, 252). Nietzsche sees the self-conscious setting and taking charge of this task as an overcoming of nihilism, but to Heidegger, it reveals the essence of nihilism, because it is the culmination of a historical process through which being is degraded to a value, and we are left, in the end, with no goal other than that of securing our existence, and no measure to guide us except what we posit ourselves in order to further this goal. Heidegger thinks the emptiness of this condition, reflected in a loss of meaning and sense of having become unmoored, cannot be reversed by deciding on a different set of values. As long as "values" are "decided" by us – and the very nature of the concept makes it hard to see how else they could arise – and as long as we take ourselves to be the measure of all things, giving value to an otherwise valueless world, we will persist in our current state. The solution is not the adoption of different values, but a giving up of "values" in favor of an experience of the "truth of being" that is more original than the distinction between fact and value. This thought lies behind the claim in the "Letter on Humanism" that "only so far as man, ek-sisting into the truth of being, belongs to being can there come from being itself the assignment of those directives that must become law and rule for man" (BW 262/GA 9, 360–61).

What does it mean, though, to take our "directives" from "being"? Heidegger's "being" is not something like a god who issues moral commandments. We might identify it with "nature," instead, but then we will have to ask, what is this "nature" such that we could take from it those directives that become law and rule for us? The answer is not obvious, given that nature, as we have come to understand it, hardly presents a model of justice. Nietzsche also proposes conformity to "nature" as an ideal, but the nature he describes is a struggling mass of antagonistic relations, a vision that does reflect an observed aspect of nature. Where we are supposed to stand in relation to "nature" is likewise an open question, whose meaning depends on the definition of the term. It is interesting that both Young and Schalow discuss Heidegger's critique of values, but Young suggests that Heidegger's alternative is founded on the insight that "*humanity is part of nature too*" (Young 1997, 211), whereas Schalow claims that, for Heidegger, "Dasein is not just a natural being, an entity embedded within nature" (Schalow 2001, 253). These claims are not necessarily incompatible. Humanity is "part of nature," if "nature" is the overpowering power that rules in *all* that is, including the process of disclosure that happens with us, through our knowing, acting, and making. But "Dasein is not just a natural being," if "natural" means being immersed in things so as to exclude the self-reflexive distance that makes possible specifically human forms of understanding and doing.

Furthermore, while Heidegger seems at times to be proposing something like a theory of natural justice, he cannot mean that "values" are embedded in "nature" like the perceptible properties of some thing, given that he has criticized precisely this phenomenologically inappropriate way of imagining the objectivity of values. Nor can he mean that we can "read off" how things ought to be by examining the facts about how they are. Meaning does require projection, and in spite of his critique of Plato's idea of the good as having set Western philosophy on the long path that ends in subjectivistic nihilism, the "truth of being" is, for Heidegger too, discerned in terms of a "for-the-sake-of." In *The Metaphysical Foundations of Logic*, after providing an ontology of Dasein essentially consonant with the analysis in *Being and Time*, where the "world" is dependent upon Dasein's projection of a "for-the-sake-of," Heidegger ends by saying that he has only led us back to where Plato stood, when he wrote:

"And so you must say that knowing is not only present for and with known beings, present namely on the basis of the good (the good establishes for beings not only knownness and thereby world-entry) but also being and being-a-what is assigned to beings from that (namely the good). The for-the-sake-of (*Umwillen*), however, (transcendence) is not being itself, but surpasses being, and does so inasmuch as it outstrips beings in dignity and power." (MFL 219/GA 26, 284)

The truth of being – the character of entities in their proper natures and relations to one another – is disclosed in light of a "for-the-sake-of," and this "for-the-sake-of" does not lie "in" things as they are actually configured. It lies "beyond" them, as the good for which they strive. True knowledge requires a transcendence toward this good, a surpassing of actuality toward the potentiality of a given entity and of what-is as a whole. Because Heidegger will question the distinction between *Sein* and *Sollen* that reduces being to actuality, he also comes to conceive of potentiality as itself an aspect of being, intrinsic to revelation of the truth about things. But potentiality requires projection. In order to estimate the relative fitness of an entity, that is, or the fitting relations between different entities, there must be a standard – a good – according to which the estimation is made. Who projects that good according to which we measure things, if not the human subject? If we are supposed to project it, but in accordance with being, and yet being is neither nature nor God (or such terms are so obscure that they are of no help), then where do we find the measure to which we should cleave?

Justice as Correspondence with Being

I have already presented part of the answer to this question. In relation to human and animal others, their own being, whose truth we are capable of apprehending, provides the measure for appropriate comportment toward them. "Projection" is how the being of these entities is grasped in advance of one's comportment toward them. Right projection involves, simply, an understanding of their being that genuinely corresponds to how it is. But knowing how it is with human beings and animals requires a reference to the good *for them*, since in different ways, both of these ranges of entities strive forward toward a form of ideal being, in relation to which the constitution of their actual being is measured. The case of human beings is special, because, according to the analysis of *Being and Time*, there is no single form of the good that defines their flourishing. Rather, what has to be referred to in understanding persons appropriately is their self-reflexive capacity to set ends for themselves and decide upon them, a capacity which defines their being, and which Heidegger seeks to lay bare in the analytic of Dasein he undertakes in *Being and Time*.

This means that there is an ethical component to phenomenology itself, since it is charged with the task of fundamental ontology. For Heidegger, phenomenology is not confined to describing appearances as opposed to things in themselves, a distinction he rejects. An adequate phenomenology struggles to make manifest the phenomena as they show themselves in themselves (BT ¶7). All human understanding proceeds through interpretive forestructures involving advance projection (BT ¶32), but coming into the hermeneutic circle in the right way means "working out these fore-structures in terms of the things themselves (*aus den Sachen selbst*)" (BT 153) – in terms, that is, of the phenomena as they present themselves to us. That requires close attention to "the things themselves," and withholding the tendency to *impose* preconceptions. Consider these lines from *Being and Time*, where Heidegger criticizes Descartes' interpretation of the being of things within the world:

> The kind of being which belongs to entities within-the-world is something which they themselves might have been *permitted* to present; but Descartes does not *let* them do so. Instead he *prescribes* for the world its 'real' being, as it were, on the basis of an idea of being whose source has not been unveiled and which has not been demonstrated in its own right – an idea in which being is equated with constant presence-at-hand. (BT 97; my italics)

Heidegger is accusing Descartes of having superimposed the being of objects, understood as substances with properties, upon the being of ready-to-hand things, whose structure points back to the existence of Dasein. This is a cognitive error, but the language Heidegger uses also strongly suggests that there is a kind of violence in this gesture, an insistence that things conform to the pattern the observer has prescribed for them and expects to find in them. This is a failure to be "true" to how things are, because such insistence involves a measure of decision. Appropriate understanding, which is "just" to the phenomena, will hold back from precisely this kind of insistence, allowing what-is to speak for itself. That still involves projection, for understanding is not a mere mirroring of things. It requires interpretation, and "an interpretation is never a presuppositionless apprehending of something presented to us" (BT 150). However, the projection that constitutes the fore-structure of understanding will, when appropriate, be worked out with due diligence through close assessment of the self-presentation of things. This is being in the truth, for a phenomenologist.

Ethical comportment, which Heidegger understands as a fitting response to being, does not require doing phenomenology, but it does require, in relation to the being of others, a self-restrained openness where a person holds himself to the truth of the other, being willing to recognize (in the multiple senses of that term) the true nature of that other. As Heidegger understands the matter, we do not first know the "facts" about what a person is in order to subsequently, or independently, add judgments of value about these facts. Revealing the truth of the being of Dasein means recognizing the freedom essential to that being, and holding myself to this truth means comporting myself in accordance with it. That is what "correspondence" means, in relation to morality; it does not mean comprehending ideal objects called "values."

This form of correspondence does not exhaust the idea of justice, however, which also requires judgments about the right order of being as a whole. The question of justice, that is, pertains not only to my personal conduct toward particular others, but has to do with judgments about how things generally ought to be in relation to one another. Heidegger's answer to this question is also a realist one, particularly in his late works, where he suggests we can find guidelines for an appropriate order of things within the order of being itself. This suggestion is advanced partly through a hermeneutic retrieval of ancient ideas about natural justice. An important example is Heidegger's interpretation of a pre-Socratic fragment attributed to Anaximander, which, he states, "is considered the oldest fragment of Western thinking" (EGT 13/GA 5, 321). Heidegger begins his own analysis of the fragment by citing a translation given by the young Nietzsche. It runs: "whence things have their origin, there they must also pass away according to necessity; for they must pay penalty and be judged for their injustice, according to the ordinance of time" (EGT 13/GA 5, 321). This rendering agrees with other modern translations in supposing that Anaximander's saying reflects a primitive natural science, in which moral and juridical notions are mixed up with the view of nature (EGT 20/GA 5, 330).

Heidegger is acutely aware that we are currently inclined to dismiss all such ancient ideas as anthropomorphic, supposing that they belong to naive and long-since superseded views of nature, which project onto it features of human subjectivity and society. As I have argued, though, he repeatedly challenges this modern supposition by exposing what he sees as the questionable, but largely unquestioned, metaphysical picture upon which it rests. According to this picture, human beings are subjects standing over against objects, and the latter define what is really real. In my discussion in Chapter 1 of Heidegger's lectures on Schelling, I emphasized Heidegger's claim that we do not have good grounds to assume this is our relation to being "in itself," as if we arose independently from what is real rather than belonging ourselves within the process of its unfolding. This is the point Young articulates, saying that, for Heidegger, "humanity is part of nature too," but humanity is special because we are able to relate ourselves explicitly to the being of beings, reflecting on the way things are and the way they go. We are a "part" of nature in the sense that we also come to be within, not outside, that way.

Heidegger's reading of what the Anaximander fragment says about "justice" in relation to being needs to be interpreted in this light. On Heidegger's analysis, we are actually too quick to translate the words *dike* and *adikia* in the fragment as "justice" and "injustice," for we thereby assimilate them to modern understandings of ethics and jurisprudence. These words are saying something about the being of things, and the way they speak of being precedes the modern boundaries between regions of reality that generate the distinct disciplines such as physics, ethics, philosophy of law, biology, and psychology

(EGT 21/GA 5, 331). Heidegger proposes a different translation, whose oddness is a function of his attempt to communicate, in the terms of a modern language that resists such communication, what he sees as an original experience of being that happened before its historical splitting into "is" and "ought," and long before the emergence of the modern form of the subject-object distinction.

In attempting to understand and describe this original experience of being, Heidegger is still engaging in a species of phenomenology, though one that bears a rather distant relation to its Husserlian ancestor. He has by now fully absorbed the insight, formulated in *Being and Time* but not always consistently observed in its methodology, that going back to "the things themselves," as phenomenology seeks to do, cannot be accomplished merely through a decision on the part of the investigator to set aside or bracket his presuppositions. The language we inherit, housing how we think about being, necessarily imposes upon phenomena the history of the way they have been interpreted. Consequently, getting back to the things themselves requires examining the roots of our concepts, tracing their history to understand how things have been represented by them. Heidegger's creative interpretations of texts lying at the origins of Western metaphysics, like the Anaximander fragment, seek to uncover what he sees as the earliest and freshest engagements with being in this tradition of thought, and at the same time to discover possibilities for thinking otherwise of being than we currently do – otherwise, for instance, of "justice."

With this adapted phenomenological goal in mind, and having rejected the opening and closing pieces of the Anaximander fragment as not certainly authentic, Heidegger's own final rendering runs: "... along the lines of usage; for they let order and thereby also reck belong to one another (in the surmounting of disorder)" (EGT 57/GA 5, 372). Let us examine the key stages in the development of this weird translation. Anaximander's saying brings to language the being of beings – the way things are – and as the earliest fragment of Western thought, it therefore belongs at the beginning of the history of being that Heidegger identifies with the history of (Western) metaphysics. The latter is, Heidegger claims, the history of an error – *Irre* – not in the sense that it results from an avoidable human mistake, but in the sense that a species of erring lies at the basis of its unfolding. This erring, Heidegger claims, is established by being itself, through a self-withdrawing revealing that he names the *epoche* of being (EGT 26–27/GA 5, 37). "Being withdraws itself as it reveals itself in beings," so that "the unconcealment of beings, the brightness granted to them, obscures the light of being" (EGT 26/GA 5, 337). Heidegger also calls this self-withdrawing revelation the "destiny" of being and says that, each time it occurs, "world suddenly and unexpectedly comes to pass" (*sich ereignet*) (EGT 27/GA 5, 338). Dasein is appropriated for this event of disclosure, establishing the character of various historical epochs, in each of which entities are revealed in a different manner, while being itself withdraws from view.

The language of looking and light – "glance of being" (*Blick des Seins*), "glance of light" (*Lichtblick*) (EGT 26/GA 5, 338–39) – recalls Heidegger's commentaries on Schelling. In *The Ages of the World* (begun 1811), moreover, Schelling describes the decision at the root of "the history of the realization, or of the real revelations of God," in terms strikingly similar to the ones Heidegger employs in the Anaximander essay to characterize the moment of appropriation in which the essence of humanity is established, and disclosure occurs.[1] As in the lecture courses on Schelling, Heidegger uses a cluster of German words containing the root *Fug*, whose meanings connote joining, structure, order, dispensation, and justice. In addressing itself to the being of beings, he writes, Anaximander's saying is concerned with the presencing of what is present (*das Anwesende*). It says that what is present is in *adikia*, translated by Heidegger not as "injustice" but as "disorder," *Unfug*. What is present is then said to be *aus der Fuge*, out of order, or out of joint (EGT 41/GA 5, 355), meaning that presencing happens in such a way that what is present is allowed to be out of joint. Bringing into presence means: allotting to a being the specific "while" of its stay between arrival and departure. Through this allotment, the present being is delivered into its "place," so that its being is determined by the relations in which it stands as the being that is precisely there and then. What is present is then the one that lingers awhile in this place, *das Je-Weilige*, the specific being.

But the saying says, according to Heidegger, that the presenting of this being, which is the "ordering" of being itself that delivers a being into its place, actually delivers it over to dis-order. That is because what lingers awhile tends to persist in its presence, and may do so willfully in a manner where it no longer concerns itself with what else is present. It stiffens, and insists on continuing as it is, as if this were the proper way to while (which it is not) (EGT 42/GA 5, 355). The saying does not say, however, that the presence of what is present consists in disorder. It consists, rather, in the surmounting of disorder. Heidegger adds that the experience of being that comes to language here is neither optimistic nor pessimistic, but remains tragic (EGT 44/GA 5, 357).

Schelling speaks of the sadness that clings to all finite being, which can be overcome only by love, the joy of harmony, the consideration of the whole of being as a gathering together in which difference is preserved. Heidegger's corresponding term in his translation of Anaximander's statement about how things may be in relation to one another is *Ruch*, "reck," the opposite of being without "reck" or reckless. Heidegger comes to this term by reflecting on the word *Rücksicht*, "consideration," as a possible rendering, but one that "means for us too directly that human trait" and lacks not only the necessary breadth,

[1] See SW 1:8, 223–25, 245, 302f.

but above all the gravity to speak as the translating word for *tisin* in the fragment, and as the word corresponding to *dike*, or order (EGT 46/GA,5, 359). In proposing *ruch* instead, he traces this word back to the Middle High German word, *ruoche*, meaning "solicitude or care" (*Sorgfalt, Sorge*) (EGT 46/GA 5, 359–60), where "care tends to something so that it may remain in its essence," and is associated with esteeming something so as to let or allow it to be itself (EGT 46/GA 5, 360).

As a dispensation extending to the whole of being, *ruch*, "reck," does not name "care" as a specifically human way to be. Instead, it names the way entities surmount the disorder to which they are prone. They do so by lingering in such a way that consideration pervades their relationship with one another, as opposed to insisting on their own being and seeking to expel others from presence (EGT 47/GA 5, 360). Paul Tillich writes, in commenting theologically on Schelling, that "sin is the attempt of the individual to resist the recurring process of the annulment of all individuals in the unity of the absolute synthesis," and it is overcome through the love that corresponds to this synthesis (Tillich 1974, 104). In his 1936 lecture course on Schelling, Heidegger explicitly connects Schelling's interpretation of being as structure and ordering (*Gefüge, Fügung*) with Anaximander's understanding of *dike* and *adikia*, adding, though, that "here we must keep at a distance all moral and legal and even Christian ideas about justice and injustice" (STF 50/GA 42, 86). These are claims about the nature of being, and therefore not "moral" or "legal" claims as we usually understand these terms. But Heidegger's reading also suggests that they point to possible ways of taking our directives about morality and justice from the nature of being, from the way things "are" in their coming to be and passing away.

The Anaximander fragment says further that order occurs *kata to chreon*, translated by Heidegger as "along the lines of usage," *der Brauch*. The German term *Brauch* usually means "custom" or "tradition," but Heidegger uses it to designate the way being itself presences: "As the dispensing of portions of the jointure (*Fuge*), usage is the fateful joining (*das zuschickende Fügen*): the enjoining of order (*die Verfügung des Fugs*) and thereby of reck" (EGT 54/GA 5, 368). Since, in enjoining this order, usage de-limits (*be-endet*) the being of what is present, it hands out boundaries. But as the dispenser of boundaries, it is itself without boundary, *to apeiron*, "the unlimited" (EGT 54/GA 5, 368). In *Basic Concepts*, another, slightly earlier, work where Heidegger comments on Anaximander, he translates *to apeiron* as "the refusal of 'boundary'" (*die Verwehrung der 'Grenze'*), as the closing off of presencing in some final and conclusive presence, or in the subsistence of a mere presence (GA 51, 114). This ordering of presencing, as what sends to beings the presence of their while, is at the same time a preserving and protecting (*Wehrung*) of boundaries. The ordering of the un-limited, then, both sends and refuses limits. It is an un-limited limiting that sets beings free into their while, but in so doing also releases them into the danger of insistence, and therefore disorder. Thus, in a sense it can be said that usage itself decrees (*fügt*) the dis- of disorder (EGT 54/GA 5, 368).

The peculiarities of Heidegger's interpretation arise from his attempt to avoid a kind of reading that would, in light of modern assumptions, incline his audience to judge from the start that the ideas he is presenting involve an anthropomorphization of nature. Nietzsche's translation, with its talk of "penalty," and "injustice," does precisely that, setting the modern reader up to conclude that one is dealing here with an ancient text in which, typically of archaic modes of thought, moral and juridical ideas are projected onto a nature that is in itself free of them. This judgment presupposes the modern Western worldview Heidegger seeks to question, according to which "nature" is delimited in contradistinction to "spirit" or intelligence, *Geist*, the "subject" to which the character of the objective world that constitutes this "nature" is radically alien.

Whether or not the details of Heidegger's translation are accurate, a question I leave aside, the broader hermeneutic assumption behind his interpretation is that early Greek thinkers did not see the matter in this way. They reflected on the character of be-ing, presencing, the process that gives rise to and governs all that is, including ourselves, and struggled to articulate their observations about the character of this process. But there is a moral implication to the account, for we, the ones who understand being, are in virtue of that capacity able to come into accord with our understanding of it, or not. We can, in other words, respect the nature and boundaries of what-is within the dispensation of being, or we can refuse to do so, in various ways. We can insist, willfully and egoistically, that a specific entity be more than the boundaries defining its nature permit, and more than its place within a harmonious order of being could allow. The understanding of being, which arises as a moment within being itself, makes such overstepping and disorder possible, since it releases us from the necessity by which other entities are mastered.

These ideas are incorporated into Heidegger's own view of the (Western) history of being as "error," which involves a form of injustice that culminates, Heidegger's story implies, in a refusal to occupy our appropriate place in relation to being. All finite revealing of beings involves a simultaneous concealing of alternative possibilities, as well as of the ultimate source of the process of revealing. Error therefore belongs to truth, which Heidegger understands as disclosure. The realm of error is opened up by the event in which we are set free to reveal what-is through the understanding of being that constitutes our essence as human beings. This event, however, is the source of possible disorder as well, since it permits a finite being to overlook the unlimited that is the source of the limited and constantly holds the possibility of the new. The history of metaphysics is an example of such erring, because each of its epochs involves the assertion of a limited understanding of being as absolute, as "truth" of a sort that no individual, and no age, could ever possess. In so doing, it fails to do justice to the unbounded character of being as a continual presencing, which will always exceed the limited character of our being in time. The assertions of metaphysics are not therefore "wrong" in a simple sense, and overcoming metaphysics may not require rejecting all philosophy and philosophizing. But it will require understanding past metaphysical systems differently than they have understood themselves. And giving up the attempt to master being in thought – a renunciation that constitutes a clear-sighted way of holding ourselves to the truth of being – will constitute a change in the essence of philosophy qua metaphysics.

The needed change is the subject of Heidegger's essay, "The Turning," providing the answer to "The Question Concerning Technology." The modern way of being and seeing that the *Contributions to Philosophy* calls "machination" becomes, in "The Question Concerning Technology," the comportment of "enframing." Enframing, Heidegger claims, is beset by an ambiguity pointing to the mystery of all revealing or truth because, on the one hand, enframing is the "constellation" of truth that threatens all revealing with the possibility that it will be taken exclusively as positing and ordering, while what is revealed is taken correspondingly as what is ordered, the "standing reserve" of what can be employed and manipulated. The danger is that this mode of revealing will be seen as the only possible one, with humanity being viewed exclusively as the rational animal possessing the capacity for calculation, and that what-is will be taken as the nature posited in such calculation. On the other hand, though, enframing, as a historical "destiny" of being, also holds within it the "saving power" because, through thoughtful reflection upon it, humanity may come to see it as a mode of revelation, and to see itself as the one through whom the revelation occurs (QCT 32–34/GA 7, 33–34). When this is seen, the unlimited self-assertion of man as the calculating animal, and the endangerment of the essence of being in its degeneration to standing reserve, may be surmounted, along with the desolation of the earth delivered over to this conception of humanity and being.

It is important not to forget that the technological assertion of humanity is still a revelation of being. What is "wrong" is only that it is not comprehended as such. The error consists in a refusal of finitude that distorts the relation between humanity and being, a possibility granted by being itself when it breaks into understanding through human existence. Only in this breakthrough is the being of beings revealed, but being itself, at the same time, withdraws from view as the source of unlimited-limiting revealing. That makes it possible for humanity to assert what it discloses at a given time as fixed and final, perfect in its comprehension of the whole, and in this sense unlimited, and to assert *itself* as unlimited. For Heidegger, this is the perverse relationship that constitutes the greatest danger of the modern age.

In "The Turning," Heideger says that being dis-places (*ent-setzt*) its truth into forgetting, as it reveals itself in the epoch of enframing (QCT 43/TK 42). This is the danger, but once it is seen as such, the possibility of reversal is already there. It comes about through "insight into that which is" (*Einblick in das was ist*), where what genuinely "is" is being, and insight is not the discriminating examination of a human subject but the "glance" or "look" of being itself. In the "view" of being and humanity that comes to presence in technology, that is, being catches sight of a possibility of itself. The understanding of this view *as* a view is a flash (*Blitz*), in which the true nature of humanity and being as correspondents in the revealing process is revealed, and the danger of technology thereby surmounted. This flash comes to pass in and through – indeed, *as* – the being of humanity. Thus: "Human beings are the ones caught sight of in the insight" (*Die Menschen sind die im Einblick Erblickten*) (TK 45; cf. GA 42, 219, 235–36, and GA 49, 126).

The relation between the vision of humanity and the vision of being, then, involves a certain "identity" or belonging together. Within Schelling's ontotheological idealism, this identity was conceived as a pantheism, with humanity as the relatively independent reflection of being qua God, the site where being's creative "imagination" of itself comes to pass. A human perspective is therefore nothing "merely" human, because humanity arises within being, is "built into" being in such a way that its understanding corresponds to being. Correspondence requires difference, the positing of humanity as a free center, and this, for Schelling, in a position Heidegger adapts in a non-ontotheological fashion, is the source of the possibility of perversion, where an individual refuses to accept limitation and seeks to be the ground of all that is. Heidegger contends that this possibility is, in the end, the stumbling block for Schelling's thought, as it means there is something in being that cannot be incorporated within a system.[2] Heidegger does not attempt any such incorporation himself, and that is why the turns in the history of being are, on his account, sudden and inscrutable. They cannot be foreseen, so the shift that could heal the distress of this age is not inevitable, but only possible, "necessary" only in the sense of being called for. One cannot count on historical shifts, as this is precisely the element in being that cannot be calculated, given the truth of human freedom.

If the truth of freedom is taken seriously, that is, if we hold that freedom is not reducible to causal necessity, then history cannot be seen, or foreseen, as following any kind of logic, for its turnings are dependent on decision.[3] At the

[2] That Schelling does not see this, and does not give up the attempt to produce an absolute system is also a central point made by Karl Jaspers in his criticism of Schelling (Jaspers 1955, 217).

[3] This forms a central difference between Heidegger's philosophy of history and Hegel's, as Bernasconi points out (Bernasconi 1985a, 7).

same time, since we *are* historical beings, fundamental changes in how we think and act come about through our struggling to respond to the needs of our time, given the intellectual resources handed down by tradition. There simply is no other way of imagining new possibilities of being; to think that there could or should be is to misunderstand the fundamental character of human thought. Finally, the essence of human freedom is such that there is never any guarantee of a just conclusion. If the character of decision is always free, and the basic decision is between accepting a limited place in the order of things or refusing to do so, no historically constituted progress of human understanding can ever eliminate the possibility of perversion, of what Schelling understood as "evil." We may hope, but cannot be certain, and Heidegger does not share Hegel's optimism about history, with its belief in inevitable moral and political progress.

Yet he holds out the possibility of "corresponding" to the dispensation of being by following an order discernable in the way things are. This is a kind of "natural" order, interpreting "nature" as the overpowering power that reigns in all things, giving rise to harmony by imposing limits on the disharmony to which entities are prone in virtue of their tendency to insist on themselves and push out other beings. While this limitation happens of necessity among all other beings, humanity is privileged in having been released from necessity, but also thereby made responsible for observing limits it alone has the ability to overstep. This is a very general conception of justice, and we do not find in Heidegger's thought any detailed prescriptions for how things should be ordered precisely in relation to one another, so as to accord with the way of being. Nor should we expect to; Heidegger is not that kind of "practical" philosopher. He does, however, stake out a position in relation to the metaphysics of justice, with practical implications for determining the appropriate conduct of humanity and its rightful place in nature.

This position undergoes some evolution. In *Being and Time*, Dasein is described as "the sole authentic for-the-sake-of," who encounters "nature" largely as raw material for its tools, whereas in later works, humanity is the site for the disclosure of beings, whose dignity consists in tending to what is as a whole. Accordingly, corresponding to the truth of the essence of humanity – what Heidegger comes to describe as "letting be" – would seem to mean something different in the two cases. And it does, although there is a measure of continuity as well. *Being and Time* posits "liberating solicitude" as the authentic mode of comportment toward Dasein, which is "in the truth," insofar as it recognizes the truth of this entity who "is" as a future-oriented potentiality for being. I argued in Chapter 2 that Heidegger's analysis of this point is indebted to Kant, and that liberating solicitude is similar to Kant's imperative of respecting persons as ends in themselves. However, although this does involve a certain respect for "choice," Heidegger's account of the highly situated character of being-in-the-world, where the call of conscience directs a person to a particular task, suggests that the range of choices for a person is in fact limited. The respect in question, moreover, is not fundamentally for the capacity to choose between a number of options for action – there may even only be a single "destined" course – but for the ability to decide between the either/or of responsibility and irresolute falling. What liberating solicitude respects and seeks to advance in the other is his or her own "fate"; that is, a person's efforts to follow conscience in finding her appropriate place in the world. Read retrospectively from the perspective of Heidegger's later thought, "letting be," as applied to Dasein in *Being and Time*, would mean helping the other to find this place, rather than respect for "free will."

"Justice" for persons, on this model, does not quite conform to liberal principles based on respect for individual choice, but nor does it agree with frameworks assigning persons a place in virtue of their birth. It involves, rather, the idea that persons do have "places" where they fit, assigned to them not by a god but by the dispensation of being in time – the potentiality given to them as the persons they concretely are – but that there is also a possibility of things being "out of joint" in such a way that the fit is not achieved. Justice as letting be would then mean allowing the fit to occur, limiting the tendency on the part of this or that being to overstep its allotted space or obstruct the path of others. The ideal of justice here is of achieving the right order of things, and in this sense, Heidegger is profoundly conservative; but, the "order" is supposed to respect the character of every entity in its potentiality. Concretely, a politics furthering justice would seek to establish the conditions for such respect. It could concur with a liberal politics in wanting to allow persons to find their own way, but its underpinnings would be significantly different, since the ideal guiding this conception of justice is that of achieving a harmonious accord, not of respecting "freedom" understood as the exercise of free will. At the same time, respect for "freedom" in another sense, where it means the freedom to realize a situated potentiality, is central to Heidegger's idea of justice. Implemented as a politics, this idea would promote a "freeing" where every being is given the best possibility of achieving its "essence," of occupying the place to which it is best suited, while being respectfully considerate of the rightful place of all others.

This is an intrinsically relational model of justice. While *Being and Time* focuses on entities having the character of Dasein, giving short shrift to other beings except in terms of their involvement in Dasein's projects, the later works emphasize the need to establish harmonious relations between all manner of beings. Steven Davis writes that *dike*, or justice, is understood here as "a relating or order wherein the overpowering as dike reigns and disposes in such a way as to compel adaptation and compliance to one another to the articulated whole or ensemble" (Davis 1992, 45). Only, in the case of humanity alone, *dike* does not quite "compel," or at least not in the same sense as it does with respect to other beings. It issues a form of imperative whose authority human beings may respect or not, although failure to do so bears a penalty. The penalty is not imposed by a supernatural being who acts as a divine judge, but is a consequence of the natural order of things. Human beings may upset this order by overstepping their bounds, as they do when they set themselves up as lords of the earth. But in the end, they cannot succeed in this venture, as it would require getting into their grasp the very power that allows *them* to be, while mastering the whole of reality, as if they were themselves its overpowering power and the origin of its possibility, which is impossible.

The attempt to accomplish the impossible is, however, possible for a free being, although it can only result in devastation:

> The unnoticeable law of the earth preserves earth in the sufficiency of the emerging and perishing of all things in the allotted sphere of the possible which everything follows, and yet nothing knows. The birch tree never oversteps its possibility. The colony of bees dwells in its possibility. It is first the will which arranges itself everywhere in technology that devours the earth in the exhaustion and consumption and change of what is artificial. Technology drives the earth beyond the developed sphere of its possibility into such things which are no longer a possibility and are thus the impossible. The fact that technological plans and measures succeed a great deal in inventions and novelties, piling upon each other, by no means yields the proof that the conquests of technology even make the impossible possible. ("Overcoming Metaphysics," EP 109/GA 7, 96)

Human beings are released from "the law of the earth," in the sense that they *may* correspond to this law or not, but not in the sense that they *can* actually alter it. The resolute readiness to follow conscience described in *Being and Time* has by now become willingness to follow the commanding guidance of nature by observing the boundaries it prescribes to all beings in bestowing upon them the possibility defining their specific being here for a while. This is a command that only human beings have the ability to respect freely, or refuse at their own peril.

I would argue that Heidegger also connects the harmonious order to which nature directs us with beauty, even though he disconnects art from beauty by analyzing it as a mode of disclosure rather than in terms of pleasing forms. While this analysis of art rightly makes space for works that are not beautiful in a conventional sense, as many great works of art are not, Heidegger describes beauty as "one way in which truth occurs as unconcealedness" (PLT 56/GA 5, 43). And his descriptions of the things he holds up as examples in positive contexts often evoke a beauty connected with harmonious order, a point to which I alluded in Chapter 3.

An example is Heidegger's account of "things" in "The Origin of the Work of Art." On the wider meaning of the term, he observes, a thing is anything whatever: "the stone in the road," "the clod in the field," "a jug," "the water in the well." "These too are things," Heidegger writes, "if the cloud in the sky and the thistle in the field, the leaf in the autumn breeze and the hawk over the wood, are rightly called by the name of thing" (PLT 20/GA 5, 5). Notice, first, that with the exception of the jug, each thing mentioned here is placed somewhere (and in truth jugs are always placed somewhere as well, in a context of use). The stone is *in the road*, the hawk is *over the wood.* Second, the examples, as Heidegger lists them, increasingly lean toward the beautiful. The leaf in the autumn breeze and the hawk over the wood are simple, beautiful things. The same tendency is illustrated when Heidegger delineates the narrower meaning of the term "thing," where it means *mere* thing. We do hesitate, he notes, to call God, or persons, "things," and even "the deer in the forest clearing, the beetle in the grass, the blade of grass" (Heidegger 1971, 21). The examples are again drawn from a familiar local landscape, one we know Heidegger held dear and found to be beautiful.

That same local landscape is also frequently evoked when Heidegger talks in other works about built things, as in his remarks on bridges in "Building Dwelling Thinking," discussed earlier. He does give examples of different kinds of bridges, including the city bridge and the highway bridge, but there is clearly, in the tone of his comments, a partiality for the bridge that "gathers the earth as landscape around the stream," and thus "guides and attends the stream through the meadows." This would be "the old stone bridge," not "the highway bridge … tied into the network of long-distance traffic, paced and calculated for maximum yield" (PLT 152/GA 7, 154–55). Once again, beauty is not mentioned, but is evoked in the descriptions Heidegger gives of bridges that: a) relate earth and world to one another, expressing the belonging together of the natural and the human; and b) that make spaces into places, being the product of and expressing a living, or dwelling in common, that happens *here*, and has a specific history as well as geography. The highway bridge does not fit this description.

Similar points can be made about the contrast Heidegger draws between the old windmill and the modern hydroelectric dam, in "The Question Concerning Technology" (QCT 14–16/GA 7, 15–17). Here, too, the contrast has to do with a particular relation to nature, and with the significance of place. And here, too, beauty and its absence are at play. The old stone bridge and the windmill are beautiful. The highway bridge and hydroelectric dam are not. Why? Heidegger does not say directly, and in fact does not mention beauty in these contexts at all. But it would seem that the beauty of the built things he describes rests in their expressing a harmonious and salutary relation to nature, on the one hand, and on the other in their evocation of human significance, the patterns of concern belonging to lives led in a given place. Making room for ourselves in a given place, in a way that saves the earth, is precisely what Heidegger describes as appropriate living or dwelling (*Wohnen*).[4] It is implicit in Heidegger's account, I believe, that things establishing, promoting, and expressing such dwelling are beautiful. There is then a sense in which truth, goodness, and beauty are intertwined in Heidegger's thought, for the "truth" of things is revealed through reference (not always conceptual) to the good, and beauty shines through those harmonious relations that best reflect that good, whether in art or in nature.

From Plato to Hitler (in Heidegger's Mind)

I have painted a rather sunny picture of Heidegger's conception of justice so far in this chapter, but we know that his own path took an exceedingly dark turn in the 1930s. The political regime he supported was the very antithesis of justice in the senses I have been outlining, neither respecting human beings as ends in themselves, nor fostering harmonious relations between beings in general. It was violent and dictatorial, murderous toward persons and hardly a model of the good shepherd of being that Heidegger holds up as an ideal in later works. Granted, the latter ideal evolved as a reaction to Nazism and the planetary horrors of World War II. Given that I have been arguing for a measure of continuity between Heidegger's earlier and later works, however, and given also that the idea of justice I have seen as implicit in *Being and Time* seems equally remote from Nazi ideology, it has to be asked what Heidegger was thinking when he lent his enthusiastic support to National Socialism in its early years.

The answer still lies, unfortunately, in Heidegger's way of associating the truth of being, including its right order, with insight into the good, during one phase of his career. It is a phase in which he was much taken with Nietzsche. In the early 1930s, and up to the time of Heidegger's resignation as Rector from the University of Freiburg in 1934, Nietzsche's positive influence on him increases, and so does his agreement with the current ideas that would lead him to support National Socialism, and take up the Rectorate in 1933. This is not to say that the Nazi appropriation of Nietzsche was accurate, or that Heidegger ever judged it to be so; but, the fact is that the period of Heidegger's strongest agreement with Nietzsche is also the period of his unequivocal commitment to Nazism.

At the height of this period, immediately preceding and during his tenure as Rector, Heidegger adopts the language of will, hardness, greatness, and self-assertion – his Rectoral Address is titled "The Self-Assertion of the German University" – combining it with nationalist themes. A notebook entry from

[4] *Wohnen* is an ordinary verb in German, used, for instance, to ask someone where he lives. The noun *Wohnung* just means "apartment" or "home," and one way to understand Heidegger's reflections on the word is to see them as exploring what it truly means to be at home somewhere.

1932 reads, "A glorious awakening national (*volklicher*) will thrusts into a great world darkness" (GA 94, 109), and entries from the year of the Rectorate are full of a similarly militant, heroic rhetoric: "relentless towards the hard goal" (GA 94, 111); "to be ready, with the great will to shatter against everyday tumult" (GA 94, 112); "only where [there is] a *stronger* will – a *law* and *resistance*" (GA 94, 119); "a long-striding spiritual-historical will to the future must waken" (GA 94, 121); "education – the rousing and binding imposition of state power as the will of a people to itself" (GA 94, 121); "the sealed will to form (*Gestaltwillen)* of the people" (GA 95, 135).

In imagining that his task was to "educate the leader" (Bambach 2003, 79 n. 13), Heidegger did at this time think of himself as one of an enlightened and enlightening few, often expressing contempt for the superficiality and averageness of the chattering many, in a way that echoes the distinction between authenticity and inauthenticity in *Being and Time*. In 1931, he asks himself in a notebook entry: "Can an individual still accomplish something essential? Is not the community of the few lacking, who would carry the burden?" (GA 94, 16). In 1933, it seems, he saw himself as one of those few who possessed the vision to shape "the masses" into a proper "community of people" (GA 94, 114), resisting mediocrity (GA 94, 128, 135) and the standards of the petty bourgeois (*Kleinburger, Biedermänner*) (GA 94, 120). At this juncture, the superficiality of small men who believe they know extends, Heidegger thinks, to prevailing interpretations of Nietzsche: "*Nietzsche*! He is raided arbitrarily and by chance – but no effort to bring his innermost will (*Wollen*) to ground, to put it into work and get it underway" (GA 94, 39).

By the time he resigns the Rectorate, Heidegger's relation to Nietzsche has already started to change. He continues to see him as widely misunderstood and misappropriated, but begins a period of critical confrontation that will lead to an interpretation of Nietzsche as the culmination of Western metaphysics, a thinker who brings to light in an especially clear way the (errant) understanding of humanity and being that holds sway in the modern age. The language of will, hardness, greatness, and so forth largely falls away and is criticized as part of the *Gerede*, the unthinking popular chatter, of the times. In his notebooks from late 1934 onwards, it is the ideology of Nazism, of the form that effectively took shape in Germany, that Heidegger increasingly treats with contempt, in language decidedly reminiscent of his descriptions of inauthentic discourse in *Being and Time*. Virtually every significant term in its lexicon is targeted as a perversion of truth in one manner or another: "nation" (*Volk*), "race" (*Rasse*), "community" and "national community" (*Gemeinschaft, Volksgeimenschaft*); "culture" (*Kultur*), "life," and "close to life," or "realistic" (*Leben, lebensnah*); "greatness" (*Größe*), "will" (*Wille*), "decision" (*Entscheidung*), "struggle" (*Kampf*), "hero" (*Hero, Held*), and "hardness" (*Härte*).

Heidegger had once heard in this language a new relation to being he wanted to support, but now decides that it was ambiguous, as idle talk tends to be, and meant something quite different than he had thought. For instance, he had been attracted to the Nationalist Socialist idea of community and emphasis on shared culture, but now says:

There must be those who believe that "national community" is equivalent to the prattling harmony of a foolish mediocrity, whose empty noise is then taken to be a following. (GA 94, 164)

The much invoked "community" does not yet guarantee "truth": "community" can also go astray and persist more greatly and stubbornly in error than the individual. (GA 94, 174)

"Culture politics" (*Kulturpolitik*) is the last disguise for barbarism. (GA 94, 319)

He had endorsed a return to concreteness over speculation disconnected from being in the world, but now:

Under "life" one understands the readily comprehensible bustle of immediate everyday life and its tangible utility and everyday needs. (GA 94, 222)

"Realistic philosophy" – that is like a bridge sunk in the river. (GA 95, 358)

… the uncritical adoption of the distinction between what is being and what is becoming (Parmenides – Heraclitus! flattened for textbooks) as the foundation for establishing "life" *("des" Lebens*) and for the interpretation of "life" itself. (GA 95, 218)

He had been stirred by the language of greatness, hardness, heroism, and struggle, but:

The current generation is and will not be hard, as one likes to profess, but only obtuse. (GA 95, 376)

To want to strive for "greatness" is a dwarfish beginning. (GA 95, 288)

An age in which the boxer counts as the great man and conventional honours are deemed worthy, where mere bodily manliness in its brutality counts as heroism – where the frenzy of the masses is taken for community and this is given as the ground for everything. (GA 94, 183; cf. IM 38/GA 40, 41)

In "heroic" ages that know nothing of their own origin, "peace" counts as weakness, because the heroism is mistaken about the essence of mastery and does not know that "peace," which is something other than the mere abandonment of war, needs for its establishment and preservation higher forces than the cleverness of powers breaking loose. (GA 96, 173)

He had spoken himself of the need for decision, a central theme in his own philosophy, but:

The "totality" of the superficial ("nation," "politics," "race") and the destruction of every making-space and indeed grounding of the possibility of a decision about the essence of truth and beyng. (GA 94, 461)

As long as we speak only of the "decisions" of human beings and of human beings who move within the received – and more and more gone astray into dis-essence – "essence" of being human (rational animal), the word "decision" is not a word but a way of speaking that only disguises that one wants to go *back* to what has already been decided and held for a long time as decided … (GA 95, 291)

In short: "political world-view, invented heathendom, helplessness, idolatry of technology, idolization of race etc. etc. … one *does not want* to be clear about oneself, and how much talk there is of 'will' " (GA 94, 261). This is the inauthentic language of the "they" in the age of "vulgar National Socialism." Apparent in the above quotations is the implication that there is some understanding of these words and the thoughts they harbor that Heidegger would himself endorse, and once did, but that within the public discourse of the day they are being employed in a conventional, thoughtless, and shallow manner. Occasionally, he makes direct reference to misunderstandings of his own work, as in the following assessment of the current understanding of heroism:

An exceptional or perhaps just eccentric endeavour is the preoccupation with the "metaphysical" grounding of "heroism"; presumably a quite unheroic expenditure of "time." One even acknowledges occasionally the treatise "Being and Time," that it began a grounding of heroism, but did so naturally only entirely from a distance and in a preliminary manner that is entirely insufficient measured against today's standards and advances; one points here to "resoluteness" (*Entschlossenheit*).

That such stupid intentions do not guide "Being and Time" can the thinker (but *who* is still able to *think*?) gather from the first sentences of this treatise. (GA 95, 424)

Yet, Heidegger himself held up dubious models of heroism only a short time earlier, in his lauding of characters like Leo Schlageter[5] and in his support for Hitler himself. These judgments point to serious flaws in Heidegger's intellectual and moral character, including a tendency to overlook the concrete realities of the current situation out of a sense of having some special vision, and inattention to the everyday realities (not the "essence" or ideal forms) of social and political power.[6]

[5] Leo Schlageter was executed in 1923 by French authorities for acts of sabotage against the occupying French forces in the Ruhr after World War I. He was turned into a hero by the Nazis. In 1933, Heidegger gave a memorial address celebrating him; the text is translated in *The Heidegger Controversy* (Wolin 1993, 40–42).

[6] In making this statement, I am aware that Heidegger does reflect on power in a certain fashion. His analysis of "machination," *Machenschaft*, in works like the *Contributions to Philosophy* is a critique of the dominant modality of power in the modern age, as Dallmayr notes (Dallmayr 2001). But it does not address the kinds of concerns about power that practical politics needs to

This was a sense of having a special vision for the good, revealing at the same time what needed to be done in response to the distress of the historical moment. Thus, the judgments Heidegger made do reflect an application of his conception of the relation between the good and the true at this point in time. As formulated in *Being and Time*, this conception involved the thesis that the meaningful givenness of entities, their showing up as being so and so, is dependent upon a prior projection of their being, linked to the envisioning of possibility that belongs to Dasein as care. The basic epistemological point is easiest to grasp in relation to Heidegger's account of the "world" of everyday concern. The structure of this world – the way things within it are ordered, their place within patterns of signification – is a function of the shared, interrelated goals Dasein projects in its historical being with others. These shared "ends" form the horizon against which things appear. They give form to things, and in this sense are the source of the "light" that makes things "visible," though the metaphor of seeing is too oriented toward theoretical knowledge to be quite apt for all forms of understanding. At a humble level, a hammer is grasped immediately as a hammer when we use it, but its presenting itself as a hammer is enabled by the projection of the goal of constructing something that will be good for something else. The final good, the end of all these ends, is Dasein itself, our own existence, imagined in one way or another.

At a less humble level, properly grasping the shape of the human world also requires an understanding of what that world is good *for*, and if it is a space for the realization of Dasein's possibilities of being, disclosing the world in its truth requires a grasp of what are taken to be the highest possibilities of human existence. When it is a matter of *shaping* something, then, be it a hammer or a social institution, one must understand (project rightly) the "for the sake of" in light of which the thing in question is to be constructed. Projected in this case is the end determining the proper form of something and enabling us to judge whether a given form is suitable or not. That is why Dasein's being transparent about its own being in authenticity is a precondition for revealing the "truth" of the world, for discriminating what is right and wrong about its present shape, and for projects of setting it in order. We can see, then, how Heidegger came to the conclusion that authenticity is required for politics, and that politics needs the guidance of those who are especially able to discern the form of the good.

Heidegger's engagement with Plato before and during his Rectorate is no coincidence, and his reading of Plato's allegory of the cave in relation to the concept of truth plays an important role in the formation of his ideas at this time. In *Being and Truth*, a set of lecture courses delivered in 1933–34, Heidegger connects being in the cave, watching the shadows of things while not knowing

take into account, such as the institutions, checks, and balances needed to limit governmental power to prevent domination and corruption.

they are shadows, with everydayness (BTr 105/GA 36/37, 133). Emergence from the cave, accordingly, requires an authentic will to know in which a person is not dazzled by what is directly before him. For Plato, the one capable of this is the philosopher (BTr 131/GA 36/37, 168). To exit the cave so as to see clearly and know the shadows for what they truly are means grasping the ideas, the highest idea being that of the good. Heidegger's phenomenological reading of this philosophical parable looks at it not as offering an explanation by way of metaphysical postulates, but as a descriptive interpretation of the nature and structure of right knowing, and of the making that follows it. Viewed through this lens, Plato's idea of the good is connected with the essence of art, whose purpose is not to give pleasure or enjoyment, but to "reveal the *possible*, that is, the free, creative projection of what is possible for the being of humanity" (BTr 127/GA 36/37, 164). The projection of the good that is possible is a necessary condition for understanding the character and order of what is, for estimating the actual and creatively envisioning the better. This is the "good beyond being," on Heidegger's intended dismantling and recovery of what Plato means in saying that the idea of the good is the source of the light by which we see the true forms of things, and the highest power that both gives and binds (BTr 153/GA 36/37, 200; cf. MFL 184–85/GA 26, 236–38).

The projection of the good, which is in turn dependent on the existence of Dasein, thus allows to beings "world-entry," as Heidegger puts it in *The Metaphysical Foundations of Logic* (MFL 194/GA 26, 251). Again, it is not a matter of adding value-properties to things that are given without them. Rather, the very *being* of things is disclosed in terms of possibilities – in terms, that is, of their ideal forms. I would therefore take issue with Laurence Paul Hemming's claim that "Heidegger is uninterested in the ideal form of anything, let alone existence or being" (Hemming 2016, 110). Certainly, Heidegger is focused on the "actual, factical, concrete forms of existence as we find ourselves already within them" (Hemming 2015, 110), but the truth of these very forms of existence is known through a projection of the good. That good cannot be for Heidegger an eternal metaphysical "first principle," to which we could have the same kind of access as we do to the principles of mathematics. Heidegger is, of course, not a Platonist in that sense, and denies the possibility of finding any such *arche*, given the finitude of our understanding and the need for constant revisioning in response to the times. Moreover, it is true, as Schalow writes, that in Heidegger's eventual critique of the concept of value, "we can see the extent to which Plato's idea of the Good, the exemplar of all exemplars, provides the first step in shifting thinking in the direction of values" (Schalow 2001, 256). But Heidegger also drew on Plato in his alternative way of thinking about the good, which plays a crucial role in the evolution of the blend of "spontaneity and receptivity" that characterizes his understanding of ethical and political action (Schalow 2002, 36). There is in this account a certain rejection of empiricism, maintaining that we do not come to know merely by abstracting from sense-data. The world is organized into meaningful wholes, and those wholes, along with the relations between them, are given order by projected ends or ideal possibilities. This enables unconcealment, without which "correctness" is impossible. Part of Heidegger's point is that mere facts unrelated to one another do not yet constitute meaning. In human affairs, the meaningful whole is the context of action, the "situation" described as the authentic present in *Being and Time*, requiring a projection that is, at the same time, response.

Heidegger's understanding of the right form of politics, which issued in his support for an autocratic leader who was supposed to be (but in fact was not at all) interested in being educated by a philosopher, is rooted in this revised Platonic understanding of knowledge, production, and action. In *Nature, History, State*, the transcript of another seminar Heidegger delivered in 1933–34, he says that "ruling involves power, which creates a rank order through the implementation of the ruler's will," but that "under this true rule, there are ruled people who are not oppressed" (NHS 61/NGS 86). There are some rather obvious practical questions about "true rule" that Heidegger does not seem to have considered. Perhaps a dictator who truly saw and willed the good under the tutelage of enlightened philosophers could indeed do a better job of shaping a society than a ragtag bunch of democrats, muddling through in response to what seems good to the many at a given time. But then so could a god; that is beside the point. One does not have to believe democracy always provides excellent or even good results to prefer it over a Platonic model of government by superior beings. The practical political question is how we are supposed to come by these superior beings, supposing they exist, and how we are to ensure they are what they seem to be, and not disguised and dissembling, to others as well as themselves. Most important, how do we replace them, if they turn out to be not far-sighted and benevolent but stupid, wicked, or corrupt? It is hard to understand how an intellectually gifted, twentieth-century philosopher could fail to pose such questions to himself when reflecting on politics. But Heidegger did just that, and while he changed his mind about the reality of Nazism, he does not seem to have changed his mind about democracy.[7] The

[7] I am alluding to the following statement in "Only a God Can Save Us":

> For me today it is a decisive question as to how any political system – and which one – can be adapted to an epoch of technicity. I know of no answer to this question. I am not convinced it is democracy. (Heidegger 1981a, 55)

To be fair, Heidegger does not himself propose an alternative political system here, and in light of current environmental concerns, a person might share his skepticism about the capacity of democracy to deal with the problem (even if she has no better idea). Cf. Thiele: "A successor to liberal ideology that remains equally effective at opposing fascism and other antidemocratic forms of rule has yet to gain a full voice. But I believe it has begun to show its colors, and they are mostly shades of green" (Thiele 1995a, 256).

fact is that the problem of power as it pertains to political authority and social relations is barely registered in Heidegger's thought, except to be lightly dismissed in favor of a naïve collectivist idyll.

That said, Heidegger's writings after his resignation from the Rectorate do drop the language of hardness, will, and resolve (in its ordinary sense), and subject to criticism the aggressive stance underlying such language. Increasingly, the ambiguity of concepts such as "projection," "care," and "resoluteness" in *Being and Time* is resolved in favor of a stance of composed receptivity that is meant to be the opposite of worried, egoistic assertion. This notebook entry on "care," written in the late 1930s, illustrates the shift nicely:

> "Care" – the awkward space for that in-standing of humanity in the there … almost the opposite then of what "one" knows as "cares" – hurrying and attachment in desire and acquisition. Care – but it means the gatheredness of human beings from the simplicity of that undriven (*begierdelos*) simple–creative relation to beyng – almost releasement (*Gelassenheit*)… (GA 94, 495)

Heidegger's attempts to recover a premodern idea of justice as not a "moral value" invented by human beings but written into the nature of things, emerging as an imperative for humanity, is also a reaction to what he sees as the subjectivism of Nazi ideology, reflected in a much more sophisticated way in the metaphysics of their favorite philosopher. Nietzsche's grounding of value in will to power is only the clearest expression of the danger of this concept, for "value is the objectification of needs as goals, wrought by a representing self-establishing within the world as a picture" (QCT 142/GA 5, 202–103). The concept of value, then, entails the view that *we* decide the truth about what ought to be, and may engage in a revaluation of values when it suits us.

The idea of natural justice Heidegger finds in the Anaximander fragment, where *dike* is a true saying of the being of beings, is offered as an alternative to this relativistic notion. Charles Bambach is right that what Heidegger found most problematic in contemporary interpretations of the Anaximander fragment (and of pre-Socratic writings generally) "was the tendency to read the fragment metaphorically as a projection of an anthropomorphic notion of justice onto the cosmos" (Bambach 2013, 133). But his motivation was not merely defensiveness about the justice of post-war Allied military rule over Germany (Bambach 2013, 98). That Heidegger did indeed worry about "victor's justice" can be seen from the following notebook entry:

> Victory over the enemy does not yet prove that the victory is in the right. But this "truth" no longer cuts any ice if "right" is interpreted as that which is not only confirmed and enforced through victory, but is in the first place established and produced by it: right is then the power of the victor, the power of the overpowering. (GA 96, 15)

These lines date from 1939, though, appearing in an entry where Heidegger reflects on what is truly needed for "overcoming the age of unconditional violence" (GA 96, 16). He concludes that the answer lies not in "moral indignation" (GA 96, 16) but in understanding that this age is rooted in a self-understanding and way of being that found the possibility of God-lessness (*Gott-losigkeit*) (GA 96, 17). The loss of "God" is here a measure for humanity's having lost its measure, its no longer being able even to ask: "Who is man? Only a value positing animal or the shell for a soul that floats off into eternity – or the singular place for the truth of being and the relation to beings?"(GA 94, 285). Heidegger claims the latter, and in that case, the measure of justice is not humanity but being, as the Anaximander fragment suggests, at least on Heidegger's interpretation.

This means that justice is not "up to us." As I have pointed out, the reason Heidegger does not affirm the "objectivity" of "values" is only that such talk is, on his analysis, uprooted nonsense, because the notion of "value" is dependent upon being posited by someone who values, and "objective" is a characterization of being drawn from the observation of entities present-at-hand. Given the birth certificates of these concepts, the idea of standards of valuation lying present somewhere is the product of a confused picture that we do well to dismantle, if we truly want to overcome subjectivism. As long as we continue to think of the good as some kind of present-at-hand object we apprehend, this overcoming will not happen. On the contrary, what has happened historically – and this is the "destiny" of the modern West – is an increasing recognition that there is no such object and never was, leading to the mistaken conclusion that values are "relative" to the needs and drives of the human subject. Heidegger tries to say, instead, that being disposes entities in a certain manner over time, a disposition we are capable of apprehending and following, and he suggests that this is something ancient thinkers tried to say, but that we find it hard to hear in the present age. Under the modern presuppositions about humanity and being that constitute subjectivism, we can only interpret what these ancients say as involving a primitive anthropomorphization of the world. But in the notebooks, as elsewhere, Heidegger asks, "What do we know of ourselves – who we are? *Who is man*?" (GA 94, 98 [1931]).

5 Cultures, Peoples, Nations

Heidegger's view of justice between different peoples and nations (the German word *Volk* can mean both) imagines the right relation between these collective entities as akin to the proper relation between persons in *Being and Time*. Considered on its own, this conception is common enough in modern German political philosophy. Kant writes in "Perpetual Peace" that "as nations (*Staaten*), peoples (*Völker*) can be regarded as single individuals who injure one another through their close proximity while living in the state of nature" (PP 115/AA 8, 354). In the fullness of time, he predicts, these individual nations will make the rational decision to give up their "savage (lawless) freedom, just as individuals do" (PP 117/AA 8, 357), by forming a federal association in which they agree to respect one anothers' freedom. Because such an association is supposed to guarantee the independence of each nation, Heidegger does not think he is breaching its principles when he claims, in one of his 1933 appeals supporting Hitler, that Germany's withdrawal from the League of Nations is not a turning away from the "community of nations" (*Völkergemeinschaft*), because such a community can be formed only through "the parallel observance by all peoples of [the] unconditional demand of self-responsibility."[1] The philosophical ideal embedded in this idea of a community of nations is thought to be, in Heidegger's words, "equally far removed both from an unrestrained, vague desire for world brotherhood and from blind tyranny" (Wolin 1993, 48). The model Heidegger advances here is consonant with his account of liberating solicitude in *Being and Time*, which implies that respect is owed to Dasein in virtue of the manner of its being, and that true respect consists in letting the other be what it genuinely is. Heidegger's interpretation of Anaximander presents another version of the same model of justice, reflecting a paradigm of identity and difference, where diverse entities are gathered into a harmonious whole while retaining and developing their unique characters.

However, the term "community of nations" is in this case an extension of the Nazi term "national community" (*Volksgemeinschaft*), which Heidegger

[1] November 10, 1933, published in the *Freiburger Studentenzeitung*, trans. William S. Lewis in *The Heidegger Controversy*, Wolin 1993, 48.

uses elsewhere,[2] and has highly unsavory connotations in this historical context. We know the outcome of Nazi views of the nation, and even once the gap between Heidegger's "Freiburg National Socialism" (Neske 1977, 245–46) and the historical reality of the Nazi regime is acknowledged, his enthusiasm for the National Socialist idea of the *Volk*, as he understood it, is alarming. Yet Richard Velkley is wrong to claim that Heidegger's version of a Kant-inspired notion of freedom "no longer supports Kant's Enlightenment-universalist idea of human dignity, but instead after 1932 ... undergirds a romantic exaltation of particular people or folk (the Greeks, the Germans) who have a universal mission of a philosophical nature" (Velkley 2011, 87). This claim, advanced in a chapter of Velkley's book on Heidegger and Strauss called "Freedom from the Good," is far too simplistic in its assessment of Heidegger's relation to the Kantian notion of human dignity, and to universalist ideas of justice generally, and in the either/or that it posits between universalism and cultural particularism. Heidegger was indeed influenced by "romantic" ideas of the *Volk*, articulated in a German tradition that centrally includes Herder and Fichte. However, not only is this a complex line of thought comprising a variety of conflicting positions, but its central philosophical proponents – precisely thinkers such as Herder and Fichte – inherit Kant's concern with a just formula for international relations. They do not simply abandon his cosmopolitanism, but adapt it in light of the normative implications they draw from an increasing recognition of the nature and significance of culture.

I argue in this chapter that Heidegger's thought in the 1930s and beyond is continuous with this tradition,[3] reflecting both its strengths and weaknesses, as well as Heidegger's own foibles and insights. Heidegger's conception of the constitution of cultures, peoples, and nations, as well of the relations between these groups, is flawed in important respects, and his specific judgments about nations and cultural groups reflect reprehensible personal prejudices. But his reflections on cultural identity also contain valuable insights, from which the implications he drew in supporting National Socialism do not necessarily follow. It is possible to reject ethnic or cultural nationalism, and certainly fascism, while recognizing that cultural identity is an essential component of selfhood in some of the ways Heidegger describes, and that *place* is relevant to this component.

[2] For instance, in the Rectoral Address; Wolin 1993, 35.

[3] Cf. Gadamer's accent on the importance of Fichte in understanding Heidegger's rectoral address, when agreeing with Derrida's claim that "there is a German tradition that is very old and deep, in which all the themes of the rectoral address were already hammered out since the beginning of the nineteenth century" (Calle-Gruber 2016, 72). Derrida is referring specifically to "the discourses in philosophy concerning the university," but his point applies equally well to discourses about nation and culture more generally.

In making my argument, I follow the opposite course to the previous chapter, first reconstructing the views about *Volk*[4] and state that underlie Heidegger's political speeches and writings during the 1930s, before moving to the analysis and assessment of this theme in his postwar philosophical works. Explicit references to *Volk* become quite infrequent in Heidegger's later writings, no doubt because of the overtones the term came to have through its contamination by Nazi usage and Heidegger's participation in that usage during the period of his political involvement. The issue, however, remains one of his abiding concerns.

Volk in the Rectoral Address and Other Political Works

In 1945, Hannah Arendt, commenting on Heidegger's political actions from 1933 onward, wrote:

> Heidegger is, in fact, the last (we hope) romantic – as it were, a tremendously gifted Friedrich Schlegel or Adam Mueller, whose complete irresponsibility was attributed partly to the delusion of genius, partly to desperation. (Arendt 1946, 46)

Arendt does not specify what she means by "romantic," but it is evident from the context that she has in mind the sort of unprincipled opportunism or "occasionalism" that Carl Schmitt, whose primary models were also Schlegel and Müller, criticized in *Politische Romantik* (1919). The accusations Schmitt leveled in this work against what he understood as "political Romanticism" have been directed by others at his own mature position, though, which is essentially anti-normative.[5] Karl Löwith, among others, sees a parallel between the "occasional decisionism" of these works and Heidegger's earlier thought, in *Being and Time* as well as the political writings and speeches of 1933–34 (Löwith 1984, 62f.).

For those familiar with Heidegger's writings over the course of his career, the label "Romantic" is likely to bring to mind a host of other implications and associations as well. In the minds of many people, German political Romanticism is a broader and less well-defined category that it was for Schmitt. It might be thought to include, at its incipience, Herder's reflections on the nature of culture and ethnic identity as embodied in language and literature. It certainly develops through the Romantic nationalism of Schleiermacher and the later Fichte, and takes a decidedly odious turn with Wagner. One also cannot think

[4] As the term has no precise English equivalent, I will mainly leave it untranslated in this chapter.

[5] Schmitt's position in *Political Romanticism* is still normative. He criticizes Romanticism for an "organic passivity" that cannot distinguish between right and wrong, and says that "in the Romantic, the 'organic' conception of the state rests on this inability to make a normative evaluation" (Schmitt 1986, 116–17). What I am referring to as his "mature position" (which, however, alters again in the mid-1930s) is expressed in *Political Theology* (1922) and *The Concept of the Political* (1927).

of Romanticism without opposing it to the rationalism of the Enlightenment. In the German tradition, this opposition includes the conflict between "culture" and "civilization," where the latter is rational and universalizing, the former particular, organic, often associated with sentiment and imagination, and with that medley of forces that Spengler, for one, names through the vague and ominous term "blood."

Heidegger's understanding of *Volk* belongs within the German Romantic tradition, and the brand of German nationalism that produced Nazism is also indebted to this tradition. Belief in the monoethnic state common to the strand of German political thought originating from Herder, and a lack, in some quarters, of the political realism that understands the necessity of checks and balances for any organization wielding power, played a role in creating the conditions that would allow an absolute and oppressive dictatorship to arise historically, while not necessarily legitimizing it philosophically. The idea of *Volk* is central to these various flaws in the political philosophy of many German Romantics, which Heidegger's thought shares to a considerable extent.

Heidegger's occasional political texts and lecture courses from 1933–34 clearly exhibit many of the fundamental themes and tenets of German Romantic nationalism, in its fascist incarnation. Above all, there is the emphasis on the deeply rooted unity of the *Volk*, so central to the Romantic tradition from Herder onwards (NH 202).[6] The concept of the *Volk* as bound together into an organized unit underlies the National Socialist idea, as Heidegger understands it at this time, of a *Volksgemeinschaft* ("national community") in which all members are *Volksgenossen* ("national comrades").[7] The creation of such a unified cultural and national community requires, in the words of the Rectoral Address, that each person share in "the effort, striving and ability of all the estates and members of the *Volk*" (SU 15). This is to be accomplished through "labor service" (*Arbeitsdienst*), and Heidegger repeatedly expresses support for the newly established "work camps." "Labor wins back for the people its rootedness" (NH 148); labor service provides the experience "of hardness, of closeness to the soil and to tools," and puts to the test "one's sense of social origin and of the responsibility that devolves upon the individual through the ethnocultural common bond (*volkhaften Zusammengehörigkeit*) of all" (NH 180).

Labor service is meant to unify the *Volk* into a single articulated entity, in which each individual and each profession have assigned places and functions. The unity of the people, therefore, is not just naturally occurring but

[6] I have also consulted, and in many cases reproduced, William S. Lewis' translations of selected texts from the volume edited by Schneeberger, *Nachlese zu Heidegger* (Heidegger 1962b). These are published as "Political Texts, 1933–34" in Wolin 1993, 40–60.

[7] Perhaps it is this sort of idea that leads Gadamer to say, "I would propose calling Heidegger, in truth, a National-Bolshevik," adding "that is not simply a joke" (Calle-Gruber 2016, 73).

also created. It is then akin to the unity of a work of art, as opposed either to a mechanical construction or a biological organism. The form of unity Heidegger envisages is similar to Nietzsche's idea of "culture" as "unity of artistic style in all the expression of the life of a people,"[8] as well as to the ideal advocated by Wagner in *The Artwork of the Future*.[9]

The *Volk*, moreover, is realized in the state, so that participation in the life of the *Volk* means participation in the state. The will of the *Volk* is embodied in the state, and insofar as the *Volk* is unified, that will is single and is in turn represented by "the towering will of our *Führer*" (NH 202). The relation between people, state, and leader is also a major theme in *Nature, History, State*. In these lectures, delivered during his tenure as Rector, Heidegger rejects the notion of "organism" as inappropriate to describing the proper form either of people or of state, since "we are asking about the essence of man, and not about the essence of an organism" (NHS 38/NGS 70). This rejection of biological concepts in descriptions of humanity is a recurring theme and becomes crucial to Heidegger's critique of race, as discussed in the next chapter. For Heidegger, neither people nor state are "natural" in the sense a biological organism is so. Rather, their shape and inner arrangement are a function of specifically human ways of being.

This means that their order does not just happen of itself but is a result of decision. "The being of the state is anchored in the political being of the human beings who, as a people support this state – who decide for it" (NHS 45/NGS 73). Heidegger rejects the idea that the decision founding a genuine state takes the form of a social contract, however, "based only on each individual's striving for his own welfare" (NHS 52/NGS 79). For Heidegger, this kind of contract actually abandons "political being," as the latter involves being in common, being a community, which is something more than a collection of self-interested individuals. A genuine state does not merely represent the inclinations of a mass of individuals, nor does such a mass constitute a true *Volk*. Rather, by *Volk* is meant: "the nation, and that means a kind of being that has grown under a common fate and taken distinctive shape within a *single* state" (NHS 43/NGS 73). The decision for the state on the part of a *Volk* involves commitment to a future sharing of a common fate. The constitution and law according with such a decision are "factical attestations of what we take to be our historical task as a people, the task that we are trying to live out" (NHS 48–49/NGS 76). Knowledge of and dedication to this task establishes the proper order of the world of a people, where "order is the human way of being and thereby also the way of being of the *Volk*" (*Ordnung ist die Seinsweise des Menschen und somit auch des Volkes*) (NHS 49/NGS 77):

[8] "On the Uses and Disadvantages of History for Life," Nietzsche 1983, 79.

[9] See "*Das Volk und die Kunst*" ("*Volk* and Art"), Wagner 1907, 46–50.

This order is not merely organic … but is something spiritual and human, which also means something voluntary. It is based on the relations of human beings in ruling and serving each other. Like the medieval order of life, the order of the state today is sustained by the free, pure will to following and leadership, that is, to struggle and loyalty. For if we ask, "What is rule? What is it based on?" then if we give a true and essential answer, we experience no power, enslavement, oppression or compulsion. Instead what we experience is that rule and authority together with service and subordination are grounded in a common task. Only where the leader and the led bind themselves together to *one* fate and fight to actualize *one* idea does true order arise. (NHS 49/NGS 77)

Thus, while "the will of the leader first transforms the others into a following, and from the following arises a community" (NHS 63/NGS 87), "the true implementation of the will is not based on coercion but on awakening the same will in another, that is, the same goal and engagement or accomplishment" (NHS 62/NGS 87).

These statements reflect an application of the ideal of authenticity developed in *Being and Time*. The state produced by a social contract could only represent the "inauthentic" being of a mass of people, because it would owe its existence and form to the narrow egoistic concerns of everyday being in the world. The genuine self of a people and its self-ordering in the form of the state, by contrast, are established by willingness to respond to a higher calling directing a people toward its historical mission, determined by what is required of it in view of its character and the needs of the present moment. There is an adaptation of the temporality of Dasein as well here, transposed to the level of community. A people realizes its true self in being attuned to the lack of its present being, and responding to that lack by envisioning a better future through a creative recalling of its past. Genuine being with one another is then neither jealous competition nor distracted chattering but the solicitous solidarity that comes from voluntary commitment to a common task. Added is the idea of a leader who will awaken the will of a people toward its common task, and therefore serve as its conscience, guided by the especially discerning vision of philosophical guardians. At the same time, Heidegger's idealistic conception of "the medieval order of life" illustrates all too well his incomprehension of the realities of power and subordination.

While Heidegger rejects the idea of the people or the state as literally like an organism, his conception of the *Volk* resembles Romantic conceptions that did employ this metaphor. Herder is a prime example, although he was deeply suspicious of state power, which he saw largely as a mechanical force in opposition to the "organic" unity of the *Volk*. For the later Fichte, and for Schleiermacher and Müller, on the other hand, the state is the natural form of the *Volk*. This is form understood not as separate from content and imposed onto it, but as the "shape necessitated by content," one might say, borrowing a phrase from Nietzsche.[10] What distinguishes this view from liberal conceptions of the state is most fundamentally the idea that the state is the embodiment of a cultural community, and not the result of a historical or ongoing contract between individuals. That Heidegger does support the monoethnic state, including the need for a revision of boundaries or resettlement of populations where necessary, is clear from his statement that it is necessary "to know what is entailed in the fact that 18 million Germans belong to the *Volk* but, because they live outside the border of the Reich, do not yet belong to the Reich" (NH 200). In the end, Herder, too, felt that the only kind of political organization which could safeguard the unique identity and way of life of a given people was a state governed by those people and corresponding to its cultural borders.

One very common complaint against conceptions of the *Volk* like that of Herder, whose ideas were appropriated by Nazi ideologues, is that they rely on an overly homogeneous and unified conception of the "people" who are supposed to form the basis for a state.[11] While Herder is not quite as essentialist about peoples or nations as is sometimes supposed, he does tend to imagine them as wholes possessing a certain character, expressed in the facets of a given culture and, especially, its language. Language is therefore the primary criterion for identifying and distinguishing different peoples, but Herder did not see it as a self-enclosed system of signs. Language is bound up with the *life* of a people, unfolding in a given place, with which the identity of a *Volk* is intimately connected. Herder did recognize that peoples, and so cultures, migrate and adapt, but he nonetheless saw geographical place – the natural environment from which people originally draw the material elements of their existence and within which they make a home for themselves – as integral to human culture (Sikka 2011, 160–91).

Heidegger's reflections on space in *Nature, History, State* advance a similar view of the relation between *Volk* and place. In this case, space does not mean "measurable, extended area" (NHS 53). It is not the geometrical space of the physicist, in which all points are alike, nor is it the natural environment to which specific plants and animals are adapted that is studied by the botanist and zoologist (NHS 54). It is, rather, "the space of the people rooted in the soil," the "fatherland" or "homeland" (*Heimat*) (NHS 55). The influence of Herderian ideas is evident in such statements as "every people has a space

[10] "Richard Wagner in Bayreuth," Nietzsche 1983, 216. See also "The Uses and Disadvantages of History for Life," Nietzsche 1983, 82.

[11] Peter Trawny claims this is an anachronistic criticism to make against Heidegger, as at the time, it was common to view peoples as singular wholes (Trawny 2014, 27). I am not so sure that alternatives to a strong notion of each people having a single, national character were unimaginable for Heidegger, or even, much earlier, for Herder. In any case, the purpose of criticism is not necessarily to assign individual blame. One may also simply be trying to discriminate between better and worse ideas.

that belongs to it," for "persons who live by the sea, in the mountains, and on the plains are different" (NHS 55). An informed listener might also hear in such statements an echo of the roles played by nature, tools, and production in *Being and Time*'s analysis of the constitution of the "world." Herder, moreover, affirmed the value both of cultural rootedness in a native place and of non-violent forms of interaction between peoples through study, travel, and trade. Likewise, Heidegger favors a relation to space that includes both "rootedness in the soil and interaction," for "it is no less necessary to rule over the soil and space, to work outwards into the wider expanse, to interact with the outside world" (NHS 55/NGS 81).

Heidegger's pejorative remarks on "nomads" follow from the importance he grants in these lectures to a people's establishing itself in a place. He makes two seemingly disparate comments on the subject. The first is that "history teaches us that nomads have not only been made nomadic by the desolation of wastelands and steppes, but they have also often left wastelands behind them where they found fruitful and cultivated land – and that human beings who are rooted in the soil have known how to make a home for themselves even in the wilderness" (NHS 55/NGS 81). The second is that "the nature of our German space" will perhaps never be revealed to "Semitic nomads" (NHS 56/NGS 82). Given the context, in which Jews were being considered and treated as not true members of the German *Volk*, these remarks are dreadful. In the editors' introduction to the English translation of *Nature, History, State*, Richard Polt and Gregory Fried note as obvious "the implied characterization of Jews as aliens," adding that "Heidegger does an injustice to nomads: nomadic people can be very much at home in the landscape through which they travel, and their practices may well be ecologically superior to those of settled agriculture" (NHS 9). Against this reading, Zaborowski argues that when Heidegger speaks of "semitic Nomads," it is not clear that he means to include twentieth-century Jews living in Europe, as he is referring specifically to those who have no fixed space (Zaborowski 2009, 255). But I think he does mean modern European Jews (although perhaps not only them), who are, in his mind, "nomads" in another sense: cultural nomads not truly at home anywhere in the world, who have a way of thinking that reflects their condition of uprooted wandering.

Outlandish as it may seem (and is), Heidegger connects this alleged way of thinking, stemming from a history of exile, with empty rationalism. A notebook entry from the late 1930s reads:

> The temporary increase in the power of Jewry (*Judentum*) has its source in the fact that the metaphysics of the occident, especially in its modern unfolding, offers the starting point for the spread of an otherwise empty rationality and capacity for calculation, which in this way finds lodging for itself in the "spirit," without ever being able to grasp the hidden regions of decision independently. The more original and initial the future

decisions and questions become, the more inaccessible do they remain to this "race" (GA 96, 46)

That is what one would expect, apparently, from a people with a history of living in exile and being nowhere at home: they will think abstractly about everything. It is then not surprising, Heidegger speculates, if they are inclined to think of space in a geometrical fashion, as everywhere alike, or to look for universal principles.

Heidegger wants to re-root thinking, a task he sees as an essential component in the destiny of the German people as "a nation of poets and thinkers" (GA 94, 501). The following ghastly passage, occurring in the version of "On the Essence of Truth" that Heidegger delivered as a lecture course in 1933–34, is consistent with this aim:

> An enemy is each and every person who poses an essential threat to the Dasein of the people and its individual members. The enemy does not have to be external, and the external enemy is not even always the more dangerous one …
>
> The enemy can have attached itself to the innermost roots of the Dasein of a people and can set itself against this people's own essence and act against it. The struggle is all the fiercer and harder and tougher, for the least of it consists in coming to blows with one another; it is often far more difficult and wearisome to catch sight of the enemy as such, to bring the enemy into the open, to harbor no illusions about the enemy, to keep oneself ready for attack, to cultivate and intensify a constant readiness and to prepare the attack looking far ahead with the goal of total annihilation. (BTr 73/GA 36/37, 91)

These remarks are made while interpreting Heraclitus' saying that struggle or war (*polemos*) is the father of all things. In light of Heidegger's criticisms of Nazi ideology for its violence, thoughtlessness, and reduction of the human to a predatory animal in the following years, it cannot be that he is literally endorsing the "total annihilation" of Jews as persons (supposing he is referring to Jews obliquely in this passage). We should notice, too, that in the passage cited above, connecting *Judentum* with empty rationality and calculation, Heidegger goes on to mention Husserl as an example of someone who took an important step in the right direction but did not quite reach the realm of essential decisions (GA 96, 46). Husserl is still an illustration of the Jewish mentality Heidegger is describing, but he mentions neo-Kantianism and Hegelianism as well, adding:

> My "attack" on Husserl is not directed against him alone and completely inessentially so – the attack is rather against the neglect of the question of being, i.e. against the essence of the metaphysician as such, upon whose basis the machination of entities is able to determine history (GA 96, 47)

This entry is made several years later than the statements about "the enemy" in *Nature, History, State*, and well after Heidegger's disillusionment with

Nazism. The two remarks are consistent, though, in that the earlier passage can be seen to fit with the goal of a *cultural* annihilation of enemies of the people: that is, with "cleansing" the German *Volk* by ridding it of alien rootless ways of thinking. If *Judentum* is one of these, as Heidegger implies, there is a resemblance here to Kant's proposal for "the euthanasia of Judaism" (Kant 1992, 95), an infamously unfortunate choice of words. Kant uses the term *Judentum* rather than *Juden*, as does Heidegger in the majority of his anti-Semitic remarks, for he does not mean the literal destruction of human beings but the extinction of a religion he views as based on law alone and devoid of ethics. Although their views of what is supposedly wrong with the Jews are different, Kant and Heidegger have in common the sense that *Judentum* does not quite fit the ideal future of Europe, and needs in one way or another to be made to disappear.

Heidegger's behavior toward actual Jews in the academic contexts where he primarily engaged with them is a matter of some dispute. In light of his views on the character of the Jewish manner of thinking, though, and the importance he attaches to the university as a site for the education of the German *Volk*, he might well have thought that decreasing the influence of Jews within German universities would be a good thing. After all, within the new order Heidegger envisages, the university is to be "the highest school of the German *Volk*," which "educates and disciplines the leaders and guardians of the destiny of the German *Volk*" (SU 9–10). It must therefore "be integrated again into the national community (*Volksgemeinschaft*) and be bound with the state" (NH 74). This requires that all faculties and disciplines participate in "the same ultimate necessities and afflictions of existence as a *Volk* and a state" (SU 17), a statement reminiscent of Wagner's notion that the *Volk* is the epitome of all who experience "a common distress" (*eine gemeinschaftliche Not*), which Wagner also associates with "need" and "necessity" (*Notwendigkeit*) (Wagner 1907, 48). The term *Not*, "distress" or "need," plays a significant role in Heidegger's political addresses, as it does in many of his philosophical works. The situation calls for "the experience of distress (*Not*)" (NH 75), and teachers and students are called upon to "stand firm in the face of German destiny in its extreme distress" (SU 10). The statements can be seen as typical of the crisis mentality of the times, and resemble Schmitt's description of decision in the face of a state of exceptional emergency (*Notfallzustand, Ausnahmezustand*).

For Heidegger, however, the experience of distress is not limited to states of emergency. It is what motivates historical change in general, being linked to the perception of "destiny," which requires understanding what is called for in response to the condition of distress. The historical readiness of a people to respond to this call, analogous to the readiness of an individual to hear the call of conscience in *Being and Time*, is described in the Rectoral Address as the "will to essence" (*Wille zum Wesen* – SU 10). Thus, fulfilling "the historical and spiritual task of the German *Volk* as a *Volk* which knows itself in its state" (SU 10) is tantamount to realizing the essence of that *Volk*, occurring insofar as the *Volk* wills that essence and thereby wants to be itself (SU 19). The essential mission of his *Volk*, Heidegger thinks at this time, is to answer the distress of "this decrepit sham-culture," that of contemporary Europe, so that whether this culture survives or falls apart "depends solely on whether we as a historical-spiritual *Volk* still and once again will ourselves" (SU 19). This idea is not new in the history of German nationalism. Fichte's *Addresses to the German Nation* (1808) also express the belief that the unity and self-sufficiency of the Germans are the best means for obtaining their salvation, and thereby the salvation of Europe (Fichte 1846, 467). The contexts of Heidegger's and Fichte's claims are different, though, and so, accordingly, is their understanding of the character of the German *Volk*'s mission.

For Heidegger in 1933, that mission consists in responding to the distress of the times, as expressed in Nietzsche's proclamation that "God is dead" (SU 13). In response to this situation, the mission of the German *Volk*, and therefore of German science (in the broad sense of *Wissenschaft*) as the guide for the spiritual destiny of this *Volk*, consists first of all in fashioning an *ethos*, in contrast to the Christian one and as a renewal of the Greek beginning, in which the *Volk* experiences "the hardness of its existence" (NH 64) through constant work and struggle (*Kampf*). Such hardness and struggle mean willingness to persevere in the face of what is. For Greek knowledge, this perseverance meant wonder and admiration; given the crisis of the age, the transformative repetition of this past in future German science will mean exposed and constant questioning in the face of uncertainty and danger (SU 13). In addition, science will be integrated into the common life of the *Volk*, since knowledge is not contemplation of an otherworldly realm but means "knowing one's way around the world in which we are placed, as a community and as individuals" (NH 201). Knowledge is thus a form of service, and genuine research, as opposed to the empty and idle pseudoknowledge commonly pursued at universities, is "linked with the whole through its rootedness in the *Volk* and its bond to the state" (NH 75). This is also a renewal of Greek science, which was "the innermost determining centre of the spiritual world of the *Volk*," not the "superstructure of a culture" but "the power that comes from the most profound preservation of the forces rooted in the soil and blood (*erd- und bluthaften Kräfte*) of a *Volk*" (SU 14).

Many of these notions are also prefigured in the nineteenth century. In *The Characteristics of the Present Age*, Fichte complains of the deterioration of intellectual life into "a camp of mere formal knowledge," a "republic of letters" in which "intellectual freedom" means nothing more than the license to indulge in unfounded and unsettled opinions (Fichte 1847, 81). However, while he asserts, like Heidegger in 1933, that each individual should devote himself to the state and be honored according to his performance of this service in the mode assigned to him (Fichte 1847, 239–40), he believes that the higher branches of culture cannot become purposes of the state, and that science is inevitably estranged from the state (Fichte 1847, 174). Müller, on the other hand, laments the false independence of the sciences from the state (which he simply identifies with civil life) among contemporary Germans, in contrast with the ancients (Müller 1922, I, 45–47). The opposition to a certain species of cosmopolitanism evident in Heidegger's appeal to "blood and soil," a familiar Nazi slogan, is also a commonplace among his *völkisch* predecessors. Herder evinced a marked enthusiasm for pastoral life, in contrast with the "pestilential atmosphere of the cities" (Herder 1989, 315), and Heidegger's support for an apparent policy of reversing urbanization through resettlement (NH 200) reflects a similar preference. However, one does not find in Herder's writings the mood that led Heidegger to advocate hardness and praise the virtues of a polemic, agonistic existence. These are Nietzsche-inspired responses to what Heidegger sees as the decline foreseen by Nietzsche and seen in the present by Spengler (although it is hard to imagine Nietzsche supporting anything so profoundly philistine as National Socialism, which Spengler was in fact unwilling to do).

Finally, it is important to underline the ideal of the relation between different peoples that emerges from Heidegger's political texts during the Rectorate. I deliberately wrote above that figures such as Herder oppose a *certain species* of cosmopolitanism, because there is also, among all the major figures I have mentioned, a form of cosmopolitanism accompanying their nationalist and *völkisch* sentiments. They are often drawn to the rural over the urban, but more fundamentally, they oppose historical developments or forms of thought that would level the differences between peoples into a blank identity, although they often underestimate, at the same time, the heterogeneity within what they characterize as single nations. The resulting ideal is not usually one of complete separation between peoples, but of a harmony that would preserve difference.

In Herder's thought, the preservation and cultivation of distinct national identities takes place within a universal ideal of furthering "humanity" (*Humanität*), although what this term means remains rather vague. For Schleiermacher, each *Volk* is a particular aspect of the divine image, with its own definite vocation (*Beruf*). Therefore, while each *Volk* should keep to its own without taking in foreign elements, every *Volk* should also be respected as having a place within the divine order.[12] Fichte, who also held a strong notion of the unique place and vocation (*Bestimmung*) of every individual being, including every *Volk*,

[12] See the pieces collected in the Nazi volume, *Patriotische Predigten*; Schleiermacher 1935, 22, 58, 69.

advocates a Christian republic of nations based on mutual recognition (Fichte 1847, 205). This internationalism complements rather than contradicts the nationalism of the *Addresses to the German Nation*. Following Kant's formula for perpetual peace, Fichte's model is that of a league of nations (*Völkerbund*) that preserves difference, not an international state (*Völkerstaat*) that would dissolve them (Fichte 1970, 160). The Germans, he feels, are particularly good at respecting the individuality of other peoples (*Addresses*, Fichte 1846, 471) and so, one assumes, especially well-suited to produce a formula for such a system, which would also be a formula for eternal peace (Fichte 1970, 162). This may seem an ironic judgment in view of later events, but it would not have seemed so to someone who saw the German character expressed by such thinkers as Kant and Herder. Müller's ideal for a league of nations is similar in its recommendation of a unity that preserves difference, except that, for him, the preservation of *Völker*, as opposed to a disintegration into *Masse*, requires not perpetual peace but a state of "living, i.e. militant (*kriegerisch*) equilibrium" (Müller 1922, II, 197).

Herder had explicitly conceived of each *Volk* as a kind of self-evolving monad with an assigned position within a global harmony, and this Leibnizian idea remains the basic model in all of the variants I have discussed. He did not see peoples as windowless, and he made significant room for the positive role of cross-cultural interaction, but others did not. Fichte's model of the "closed commercial state," in the text of the same title (1800), projects the nation as an almost absolute isolate, politically, economically, and culturally (Fichte 2012). This truly windowless monad, which claims to be an ideal of independent self-realization, might well seem instead a formula for stagnation.

Heidegger's views on the relation between nations fit squarely into this line of thinking, as is clear from the nature of his appeals for a "yes" vote in the plebiscite on Germany's withdrawal from the League of Nations. The decision to withdraw from an organization that he sees as stifling independence accords with "the primary demand of all existence, that it preserve and save its own essence." This legitimation of what Heidegger at this juncture sees as cultural self-defense does not, however, simply divide the world into "us" and "them," with no thought of justice. The will to self-responsibility requires "that each *Volk* find and preserve the greatness and truth of its vocation (*Bestimmung*)," so that every people has an assigned mission within the international community, just as every individual and estate does within the national community" (NH 145, 149). Heidegger's ideal during these years is a militant one, like Müller's, stressing the role of military service in maintaining "the honour and destiny of the nation in the midst of other *Völker*" (SU 15). But it does not propose a war of all against all, nor is it supposed to be isolationist. It is supposed to involve a form of interaction based on mutual recognition and respect: "if the will to self-responsibility becomes the law for the coexistence of *Völker*, then each *Volk* can and must be the master who instructs every other *Volk* in the richness and strength of all the great deeds and works of human being (*Sein*)" (NH 150). As I noted, this ideal clearly applies the model of liberating solicitude among individuals sketched in *Being and Time* to the level of appropriate relations between nations.

The ideas about the nature and role of *Volk* and *Völker* presented in Heidegger's political speeches are not particularly original or complex. Given the situation in which they were uttered, they are, of course, much worse than that. If I have stressed the philosophical background of these ideas rather than the actual political situation to which Heidegger made this profoundly unintelligent contribution, it is because I believe that, in spite of his call for closeness to the demands of concrete existence, Heidegger remained closer to an intellectual stratosphere that was removed from the real circumstances of the day.[13] In this respect, one cannot help but feel that if he had spent less time dwelling on the "essential" in the early 1930s, and more time paying heed to the everyday scribbling and talk he despised, he might have been better able to see what was truly coming to presence.

He did see it eventually, a little too late, and he was far too late in abandoning the absurd belief that Hitler was better than the officials surrounding him, or that the actual movement might still be brought into line with his own vision of what National Socialism ought to be.[14] As demonstrated in the last chapter, however, his notebooks after 1934 do repeatedly draw attention to the vast distance between "vulgar National Socialism" and the ideals he originally saw in the movement. He now complains about its reductive view of the role of universities, its egoistic making of the nation into an end in itself, its lack of questioning, and its destruction of village life. These events prove "that 'one' *no longer* wants to be the 'Volk' of poets and thinkers" (GA 94, 501). "One preaches 'blood' and 'soil' and yet executes an urbanization and destruction of village and square" on an unprecedented scale (GA 95, 361). Whatever Heidegger meant to promote, he does not see it in all this blather about *Volk*, and the fashion for Herder (GA 96, 41). Yet he never renounced the "National Socialism" he had imagined as agreeing with his own ideas about *Volk*. I now want to examine these ideas further on the basis of their articulation in Heidegger's philosophical works, beginning with the crucial topic of language.

[13] I discuss this point at further length in the final chapter of this book.

[14] See Karl Löwith's report of his final depressing meeting with Heidegger in Rome in 1936, during which Heidegger wore a swastika and continued to express support for Hitler, while describing the Nazi anti-Semitic tabloid, *Der Stürmer*, edited by Julius Streicher, as "nothing more than pornography" (Löwith 1988, 116).

Volk and Language

Charles Taylor argues that Heidegger stands within the tradition of the "constitutive-expressive" theory of language that has its original source in Herder (Taylor 1992), according to which language is not merely an instrument for communicating representations of an independent reality but in some sense constitutes that reality. Moreover, like Herder, Heidegger views language as essential to being human, although "while Herder … still speaks in terms of 'reflection' (*Besonnenheit*), which sounds like a form of consciousness, Heidegger clearly turns the issue around, and sees language as what opens access to meanings" (Taylor 1992, 256).

Taylor argues further that, for Heidegger, the constitution of reality effected by language is at the same time, in line with the constitutive-expressive tradition, a manifestation or expression of something beyond the self, so that Heidegger is actually "an uncompromising realist" (Taylor 1992, 263). Consequently, in lines such as, "strictly, it is language that speaks," Heidegger is not invoking "a super(non)agent," but articulating an antisubjectivist stance in which creative language establishes the space of disclosure while being "a response to a call," and thus bringing to light something outside of itself to which it is intrinsically related (Taylor 1992, 262–3). Not only does language open the "clearing" in which things are lit up, but the *telos* of the human essence, since it is defined in relation to language, consists in this power to reveal (Taylor 1992, 263).

I largely agree with this reading of Heidegger on language, which rightly situates Heidegger within the Herderian tradition to which Taylor's own philosophy of language is strongly indebted, with a few qualifications and extensions. First, Heidegger's critique of subjectivism and its culmination in the notion of "will" as the basis of reality – a notion informing the metaphysics of German Idealism, as well as that of Schopenhauer and Nietzsche – should not mislead us into overlooking the fact that things (in the broadest sense of anything that in any way *is*) reach the space of the clearing through *care*. What becomes manifest within the world of Dasein is presented through care, which in turn is made possible by primordial temporality, the basis of care as "ahead-of-itself-already-being-in (the world) as being with (entities encountered within-the-world)" (BT 327). As noted before, in *The Metaphysical Foundations of Logic*, Heidegger claims this temporal structure is a necessary condition for "world-entry," and so for anything to be manifest as a phenomenon (MFL 208–9/GA 26, 270–71).

In his later works, Heidegger's thought shifts away from the suggestion that the "being" of entities is constituted exclusively through their involvement in human projects, whether pragmatic or moral, but he never rejects the idea that things come to light through one mode or another of care. Language, as "the house of being," is the preserve of such care, and any particular language presents a world of care. It both establishes and reveals how the being of "what is" is disclosed through its coming close, its *mattering*, to the people whose world is articulated in that language.

Being and Time describes Dasein as the entity for which its own being is an issue (BT 12), and Dasein encounters its own being in the mode of a self-reflexive mattering to itself. This encounter is the basis of its having a world, in Heidegger's sense of the term, because Dasein's caring self-grasp founds its grasp of what it encounters within the world. In spite of Heidegger's rejection of any and all notions associated with "consciousness," this analysis is close to Herder's notion of "reflectivity." Human language, Heidegger writes in the "Postscript to 'What is Metaphysics?'," is a response to the soundless voice of being (P 237/GA 9, 106–107). Its origin rests in the capacity to "hear" the speaking of this voice, and so, in responding, to bring "soundless saying to the sound of language" (OWL 129/GA 12, 249). The word is indeed not a label for something already present, for it brings beings into the open in a creative fashion. But it is evoked by the "needfulness" of being, which seeks – through us and as us – to come to word and thereby into manifest presence. *Logos* (word, speech) as a human faculty is originally our need to respond truly to the *logos* of *physis*, the "nature" that comes to presence in all that is. The human utterance, then, is the corresponding response to what evokes the word and is then housed within that word.

Herder's notion of *Besonnenheit* or "reflectivity" also involves a capacity to hear and respond to being, rooted in the same relation to being expressed, in *Being and Time*, with the claim that Dasein is distinguished by the fact that its own being is an issue for it. This is a reflective relation, of the sort that Herder saw as enabled by the capacity to stand back from the press of immediate impressions and inclinations. The ordinary meaning of the German term *Besonnenheit* is "calm" or "prudence," and it is often used to translate the Greek term *sophrosyne*, meaning the wisdom connected with self-restraint. Herder saw the capacity to step back from the immediacy of being as foundational for the reflective relation to things that gives rise to language. Heidegger's analysis of the structure of Dasein in *Being and Time* is comparable, and the connection he later draws between freedom and truth develops the same point. The change in Heidegger's later works consists in the notion that Dasein's being is intimately related to and enabled by being itself, which comes "first," so that the struggle for creative expression is the struggle to let what is be, by building for it the appropriate words. This notion lies at the heart of the turning that Heidegger both experiences and calls for. Although he does speak later of the poet as established outside the precinct of care, and therefore as *sine cura*, or secure, this is freedom from care meant only in the sense of self-assertive desire. The poet is still "touched" by being, and his words are a response to that touch

(PLT 120, 125/GA 5, 299, 303). The realization that being comes first means that the concernful reflection of human beings is in a way the self-reflection of being, and this gives Heidegger's thought a strong affinity with the nineteenth-century metaphysical tradition Taylor invokes.

The above-outlined understanding of humanity, being, and language shapes Heidegger's conception of language in relation to *Volk*. Disclosed to humanity not primarily as an object of knowledge but as a matter of care is "our" being, and "our being is not that of an isolated subject, but ... historical being-with-one-another as being in a world" (H 174).) This is the presupposition for being able to understand one another, and it is original community (*Gemeinschaft*), as opposed to mere association (*Gesellschaft*) (H 72). Language builds and establishes the historical being of a community; it "opens" that being. And because language, as a form of bringing into the open or revealing (*Offenbarmachen*), is creative, it is originally poetizing (*Dichten*) (H 30). The poet is therefore the founder (*Begründer, Stifter*) of being, and since this is the being of a historical community, poetry (*Dichtung*) is "the primal language of a *Volk*" (H 64). In his writings after the war, Heidegger tends to drop the term *Volk* and sometimes speaks instead of "neighborhood." The latter is also constituted by a form of nearness arising from dwelling with common concerns, and articulated by the saying (*Sage*) rooted in these concerns (see OWL, 103, 120/GA 12, 198, 239). Both of these conceptions of community belong within the line of thought inaugurated by Herder, and both seek to explicate the phenomenon that has sometimes been described in terms of the metaphor of "organic unity," although Heidegger rejects the metaphor itself.

The life of a *Volk* is rooted in its *Heimat*, which is not a mere place of birth and familiar countryside, but "the power of the earth, on which man "dwells poetically" at any given time" (H 88). This "native earth" (*heimatliche Erde*) (H 195) is founded in poetry, broadly understood as the literature, both oral and written, of a people. On Heidegger's analysis, the appearance of the earth as presented in such poetry is not constructed through the use of physical features to represent something else. Rather, "this appearance is historical and it is history, discovered and grounded in poetry and myth and thus an essential area of our world" (IM 105/GA 40, 112; see also H 254). The poet speaks the truth of a *Volk*, for "earth becomes earth and landscape becomes landscape first in the poem" (H 226). This is the earth in which the life and traditions of a *Volk* are "rooted," and the "forces rooted in the blood and soil of a people" that Heidegger speaks of in the Rectoral Address, which he does not intend in any crudely biological sense, are the powers of this earth and its history. These are also the fundamental powers of poetry, the nature of which, by the time of the 1935/36 Hölderlin lectures, Heidegger feels is not comprehended by the prevailing talk of "folk and blood and soil" (*Volkstum und Blut und Boden*) (H 254).

Poetizing, moreover, founds the earth on which a *Volk* dwells by establishing the possibility of humanity's settling "between the earth and the gods," where this is what it means to be a *Volk* (H 216). The gods belong to the space of the holy, which Hölderlin, Heidegger notes, names *das Uneigennützige*, the "unselfish," meaning not the sacrifice of self-interest for the general interest, but that which does not stand in the region of what is useful in terms of such interest at all (H 84). The *Volk* is not properly a *Volk* without this dimension, so that the world of the *Volk* established and revealed in poetry is not equivalent to the sum of what is involved in people's "projects," whether individual or collective. The form of dwelling Heidegger speaks of here in terms of lightning and storm, the gods, the earth, and the *Volk*, he expresses later, again drawing on Hölderlin, in his notion of "the fourfold" of earth and sky, divinities and mortals.[15]

If "language is the primordial poetry in which a people speaks being" (IM 171–72/GA 40, 180), then the language, and that means the *world*, of a *Volk* belongs to the self-revealing of being, which Heidegger understands as the essence of truth. To it belongs not only poetry in the narrow sense, but all poetizing, all language in the broad sense of any disclosive articulation of being, and therefore all art (see PLT 57, 71–3/GA 5, 44, 59–61). To it belongs also "the act that founds a political state," "the nearness of that which is not simply a being, but the being that is most of all" (i.e. God), "the essential sacrifice," and "the thinker's questioning" (PLT 62/GA 5, 49–50). All of these events are the historical revelation of the life of a *Volk*, whose ultimate origin rests in the same nameless power that gives rise to and governs all that is.

In later essays, such as "Building, Dwelling, Thinking" and "The Thing," Heidegger no longer talks about the *Volk*, but his understanding of the relation between being and truth on the one hand, and the things and works of the world on the other, remains fundamentally unaltered. Insofar as the event (*Ereignis*) in which these things and works come into being is the event of the occurrence of truth, what is brought to light each time, in a unique and unrepeatable historical fashion, is a manifestation of something that is in itself not only human – and is certainly not the substance of the self-enclosed "subject," with its needs and ideas – but is disclosed through the dwelling of human beings. Given the nature of the fourfold, and the sorts of "things" of which Heidegger speaks – "the jug and the bench, the footbridge and the plow," tree and pond, brook and hill," "heron and roe, deer, horse and bull" (PLT 182/GA 7, 183–84) – the world and way of being he primarily associates with appropriate dwelling can still be described as *völkisch*, although Heidegger distances himself from what that term means within "vulgar National Socialism."

[15] See "Building Dwelling Thinking" and "The Thing," in *Poetry, Language, Thought*.

It is not, however, only the language of *Volk* that changes in Heidegger's writings after the war. In the *Introduction to Metaphysics*, the 1935 set of lectures that Habermas describes as "fascist right down to their stylistic details" (Wolin 1993, 200), the poet, who takes upon himself the "need" of *logos*, is called "the violent one" (*der Gewalt-tätige*) (IM 163/GA 40, 172). For the Greeks, Heidegger says in this work, *techne*, "the knowing embodiment of being," demands a decision for being that will persevere against the pressure of the everyday and commonplace, and this decision must use violence (IM 168/GA 40, 177). Moreover, the way *physis*, nature, posits the essence of Dasein and thereby posits the *techne*, making, that brings *physis* to stand in the work, is also described in violent terms (IM 162–63/GA 40, 171–72). The relation between man and being is therefore one of a kind of mutual violence. Later, as we have seen, violence gives way to *Gelassenheit*, an attentive paying heed that lets be. This is not indifference; in the mood of *Gelassenheit*, human beings still struggle to formulate being in word and work, but the struggle is now described as a composed gentleness that receives rather than as a battle of forces.

A final aspect of Heidegger's philosophy of language highly relevant to his understanding of *Volk* is its tendency to "fall" over time, a process *Being and Time* terms *Entwurzelung*, uprooting or deracination, and describes as a feature of inauthentic or unowned existence. Uprooted language is empty talk because, in the way it is spoken and heard, the truth it originally contained is no longer appropriated. With explicit reference to the section on truth in *Being and Time*, Heidegger remarks in the *Introduction to Metaphysics* that "in the transmission [of language] the truth detaches itself as it were from what is" (IM 185/GA 40, 194). In the Hölderlin lectures, he points out that the original language of a *Volk*, the poetic speaking that brings forth its genuine being, tends to deteriorate into common prose and, finally, into idle talk (*Gerede*) (H 63–64).

Uprootedness is a recurring theme in Spengler's writings as well. In *The Decline of the West* and *The Hour of Decision* (1933), Spengler writes of the destruction of the life of the *Volk* through the literal uprooting of peasants and the formation of giant cities. The life of these cities is said to be characterized by a constantly uprooted and groundless chattering and writing. This is "civilization," as opposed to "culture." Heidegger also condemns "the modern man of the city and ape of civilization" (*Fundamental Concepts of Metaphysics*, GA 29/30, 7) and, much like Spengler, he views this decline as "the emasculation of the spirit" through its misinterpretation as "intelligence," mere calculative and utilitarian cleverness (IM 48–50/GA 40, 51–53).

Heidegger's analysis is, however, more subtle and complex than Spengler's. For Heidegger, "uprootedness" is not merely a function of urbanization. This literal form of uprooting did trouble him, but "uprootedness" fundamentally names a progressive alienation from the real concerns of existence. This means the divorce of spirit or mind (*Geist*) from the experience of historical being-in-the-world, so that the former is no longer the expression of the latter. The uprootedness of cosmopolitan life, and of the form of knowledge belonging to it in the universities, is an instance of this divorce, and so is the uprooting of language. Poetry, the original language of a *Volk*, is historical and particular. The language of the cosmopolis and the university, by contrast, is supposed to be universal. Heidegger thinks, though, that this universality is achieved at the expense of a living language. It is achieved by killing the language, flattening the meaning of words into technical significations. The "truth" of the language is then no longer experienced; that to which the words were originally a response, and to which they therefore truly correspond, is no longer re-presented in the speaking of the words. Since, originally, that to which the words correspond is nothing other than the historical and particular existence of concern to human beings, it is predictable if one of the fundamental moods symptomatic of an age in which such uprooting occurs is boredom.[16]

When Heidegger claims that the Greek and German languages are "the most powerful and most spiritual of languages" (IM 57/GA 40, 61), his remark has to be situated in relation to this analysis of uprooting. We might compare his views with those of Fichte in the fourth of the *Addresses to the German Nation*, where Fichte proclaims the superiority of the German language above other European languages for abstract thought, and also compares it with Greek. The basis for this claim rests in the alleged "purity" of the German language, the fact that, because of its unbroken development, its abstract terms are built out of its own sensuous terms, as opposed to the other European languages, whose abstract vocabulary is constructed from, for instance, Latin. Because Latin is a foreign language belonging to a distant age and culture whose living realities have passed into oblivion, the sensuous basis of abstract terms derived from it is no longer immediately present (Fichte 1846, 311–27). Consequently, a present language constructed on the basis of Latin, or one that is historically discontinuous, may appear on the surface still to be living but it has "a dead constituent" further down, for it is "cut off from the living root" (Fichte 1846, 321). The foundation of its words cannot be experienced, and that means, in the terms of Heidegger's analysis, that the "truth" has become detached from these words. If, then, spiritual or intellectual activity – for example the activity of philosophizing – is conducted within these terms, without the terms being analyzed to their existential roots, that activity will be superficial. It will raise only pseudoproblems and yield only pseudoknowledge.

The claim that the metaphors behind abstract terms are less dead in German than in other European languages may in itself be doubtful. But these views,

[16] In *Fundamental Concepts of Metaphysics* (GA 29/30). Cf. Nietzsche: "everywhere language is sick" ("Richard Wagner in Bayreuth," Nietzsche 1983, 215).

I believe, underlie Heidegger's statement in *Introduction to Metaphysics* that "the organizations for the purification of the language and defense against its progressive barbarization are deserving of respect," although they "demonstrate the more clearly that we no longer know what is at stake in language" (IM 51/GA 40, 55) – even if such statements also demonstrate the more clearly that Heidegger does not know what is at stake in the actual events of his day. Heidegger's own attempts to use "rooted" language and to uncover the roots of philosophical terms seek to renew philosophy in response to the need of an age that is becoming progressively uprooted. Because German is supposedly the language preeminently suited to this task,[17] Heidegger's thinking, in spite of his withdrawal from any form of direct political engagement after the failure of his Rectorate, always remains committed in a way to "the historical mission of the Germans."

Volk and Destiny

Along with the ills of "megapolitan" (*großstädtisch*) life, a major theme in *The Decline of the West* is the triumph of "causality" over "destiny" (*Schicksal*). This, according to Spengler, is a triumph of "rigid being" (Spengler 1959, I, 49) over becoming, of "space" over "time," of the categories of dead nature – the nature of metaphysics as well as of physics – over those of lived history, life itself as "the form in which the actualizing of the possible is accomplished" (Spengler 1959, I, 54). The region of nature, as what is already fully accomplished and therefore static, has laws. The region of history, on the other hand, as what is constantly being accomplished and therefore evolving, "has destiny, but no laws" (Spengler 1959, I, 118). The idea of destiny expresses the sense of life as "directed, irrevocable, time-laden" (Spengler 1959, I, 117), where time is not the infinite set of points that physics and metaphysics wrongly conceive on the model of space, but the irreversible course of life in which each moment contains something unique and proper to it alone. " 'The proper' (*das Eigne*), 'destiny' and 'time' are interchangeable words," says Spengler, and "we ourselves are time, inasmuch as we live" (Spengler 1959, I, 122). The idea of destiny cannot be given a clear formulation, but "every higher language possesses a number of words such as fortune, doom, dispensation, vocation (*Geschick, Verhängnis, Fügung, Bestimmung*), about which there is, as it were, a veil" (Spengler 1959, I, 117).[18]

[17] I would therefore take issue with Julian Young's claim that "there is no valid derivation of linguistic chauvinism from Heidegger's thought" (Young 1997, 217).

[18] I have altered the translation; the original text is in Volume 1, p. 164 of *Der Untergang des Abendlandes* (1919).

These words occur repeatedly in Heidegger's writings. There is a ready match between Spengler's diagnosis and Heidegger's critique of categories as inappropriate to describe the being of Dasein in *Being and Time*, along with his reformulation of the structure of existence, which is historical and directed, in terms of existentials (BT 44). The impossibility of formulating laws for what is unique and constantly evolving raises problems for knowledge, not only for any attempt to draw conclusions about the totality of being (metaphysics), but also – and especially – for "knowing one's way around the world." It raises a problem for existence itself, for any thinking concerned with *how to be*, which is not confined to academic philosophy. Basically, if as Heraclitus says, *panta rhei*, commonly translated as "everything flows,"[19] then the question of existence concerns how to go with the flow, in an appropriately skillful (*er-eigenet, geschickt*) manner.

Heidegger's supposedly "antinormative" thinking, like that of many of his contemporaries, including Carl Schmitt, whose *Concept of the Political* was published in the same year as *Being and Time*, grapples with this question. It is not a matter of elevating the irrational but of attempting, not always successfully or commendably, to respond to the difficulty posed by the fact that the situation is constantly changing. Schmitt, in *The Concept of the Political*, is not antinormative in the sense of opposing all norms in favor of arbitrary decision based on personal preference. He is responding to what he sees as a fact, that "every norm presupposes a normal situation, and no norm can be valid in an entirely abnormal situation" (Schmitt 1976, 46). Such a situation, being abnormal, will require a decision that cannot appeal to established norms precisely. Therefore, "looked at normatively, the decision emanates from nothing" (*Political Theology*, Schmitt 1985, 31–32). Heidegger responds to the problem that, if everything flows, then every situation is to some degree a state of exception requiring decision, whereas acting purely according to norms, in a lawlike way, is equivalent to not having to make a decision. That does not make the decision purely arbitrary. For Heraclitus, after all, being is not merely flow; it is flow with a certain *logos*. Being in flow with *logos* is the essence of Heidegger's conception of "destiny," which helps to guide decision in the absence of constantly valid norms.

As I argued in Chapter 1, the charges of arbitrariness and fatalism against Heidegger's thought rest on a misunderstanding both of his notion of decision as a free resolve and of his conception of destiny. I pointed out parallels with Kant in Chapter 2, but the primary resolve at the basis of decision in *Being and Time* can also be compared with Fichte's account in *The Vocation of Man*, where it is described as a resolution (*Entschluß*) to listen and respond (*hören,*

[19] Admittedly in the popular chatter of which Heidegger is suspicious; see IM 133–34/GA 40, 141.

gehorchen), to pledge obedience (*Gehorsam*) to the private and particular voice of conscience. This voice commands, first and foremost, that a person become what he or she should be, and do so without fear or casuistry (Fichte 1981, 294, 278). Like Heidegger, Fichte describes the voice of conscience as bidding every person to his own *Bestimmung*, his own vocation, destiny, or place. The decision to follow this voice represents, Fichte maintains, the entry into moral life, which is the life of practical reason, of ends rather than causes. Only through this free decision is man truly capable of creating, of bringing something out of nothing (Fichte 1981, 254), and the same is true for Heidegger.

Heidegger describes authentic decision as the readiness to follow conscience which, we have seen, is also the resolve for destiny as vocation or calling. It is the resolve to fulfill one's "essence," which is always determinate and particular. There are, in a way, "essences" in *Being and Time*, but they are constituted by historical being-in-the-world rather than being fixed in a static nature or floating about in the mind of God. Accordingly, destiny is not a matter of causal necessity but of willingness to respond to a need or distress (*Not*), where "need is the basis of the necessary (*das Notwendige*)" (H 244). Resolve for destiny is then readiness to answer the needs of the present situation by drawing on the past (tradition) to create something new for the future. This is historical, as opposed to physical, necessity, and it is identical with freedom. There is again a parallel with Spengler, who says: "When we use the risky word 'freedom' we shall mean freedom to do, not this or that, but the necessary or nothing," and who, in response to the objection that this limits what may be done, observes that limitation is just a fact, and that "to lament it and blame it is not to alter it" (Spengler 1959, I, 37).

These points relate to individual decision, but Heidegger says in *Being and Time* that all historizing (*Geschehen*) is a co-historizing (*Mitgeschehen*) (BT 384), and destiny is therefore collective. The destiny of an individual participates in the destiny of a *Volk*, as it must if individuals are situated within the language, tradition, and concerns of a particular *Volk*. And Heidegger supposes that each *Volk*, like each individual, has a unique historical vocation, where the fulfillment of that vocation is also the fulfillment of its "essence." Thus, the "will to essence" of which Heidegger speaks in the Rectoral Address is the initial resolve of the German *Volk* to hear and obey its national conscience, to follow its "calling" as a *Volk*. That means following the summons bidding it to become what it should be, drawing on its own traditions in response to the need of a Europe that "lies today in a great pincers, squeezed between Russia on one side and America on the other" (IM 37/GA 40, 37). While every *Volk* is special, then, Heidegger thinks Germany is especially special, for on it rests responsibility for the salvation of Europe and the occidental world.

Because Hölderlin is the poet who suffers the need of these times and brings it to word for the German *Volk*, he is the "poet of the future German being"

(H 220), who gives the *Volk* its destiny by pointing out its present distress and, through this, showing it what it needs to become. The decision of the *Volk* to hear the poet's words then means its choosing itself, wanting to be itself. The choice requires, first, that the German people open themselves to the need/distress of the present age, calling upon them to respond in thought, word, and act. In the Rectoral Address, the association of this openness with exposure to uncertainty is one instance of the link Heidegger draws between destiny and mood. Since destiny is constituted as a response to need, the choice to fulfill a destiny requires, first, the resolve to experience the lack or distress of the time, which in turn requires willingness to suffer a certain mood. Early in the Hölderlin lectures, this mood, which Hölderlin brings to the *Volk* so that it may become a national mood, is sadness; in the *Contributions to Philosophy*, it is anxiety and terror; in the *Fundamental Principles of Metaphysics*, it is boredom. These moods reveal, and make possible the choice for, collective destiny, in the same way that anxiety makes possible the individual resolve for conscience in *Being and Time*.

The mood of Heidegger's later writings is sharply different from the aggressively agonistic tone of his speeches and writings during the early 1930s, but the sense of a special German mission remains. In essays such as "Poetically man dwells" (PLT 211–29/GA 7, 189–210), first given as a lecture in 1951, the mood is much milder than in some earlier works, but the need of the situation – the absence of the holy and the devastation of the world through the technological mode of being – is the same. The vocation of the poets and thinkers in this moment of German history, including Heidegger, is still formed in response to the voice of being as it speaks from this distress. The gentle, slightly fragile, and distinctly pious tone of "The Thinker as Poet" (PLT 1–14) is the mood of a convalescent, and expresses Heidegger's changed sense of the disposition truly appropriate to an experience of what is wrong and what is required. It also reflects, of course, the changed factual condition of Germany.

At play here is the shift from *Entschlossenheit* to *Gelassenheit*, from resoluteness to letting be, in the course of which the language of heroism and self-assertion drops away. Wolin sees Heidegger's switch to the mood of *Gelassenheit*, understood as a receptive accordance with the sending or destining (*Geschick, Schickung*) of being, as part of a "strategy of denial," in which Heidegger tries to evade responsibility for himself and for Germany through recourse to the "history of being" (Wolin 1993, 288). Heidegger does repeatedly suggest that Nazism is the function of a view of being that is happening everywhere as a characteristic of the modern age, and his story about the history or destiny of being arguably does enable him to evade a measure of moral culpability by seeing the happening of this view as destined. What he could not accept above all, I venture, was the idea that Germany's most memorable contribution to the century might consist in its being the locus of a retrogressive barbarism that the civilized powers of the West had battled and overcome. This perspective (and it does contain some questionable elements) was too bitter a pill to swallow for a philosopher who had maintained that the salvation of Europe depended upon its developing an ear for Hölderlin (GA 65, 401, 422). Heidegger naturally preferred to emphasize what he saw as the modern and pan-European aspects of Nazism: its elevation of the will, its grand designs, the cold rationality with which it planned its manufacture of corpses. Granting these points, it is nevertheless hard to imagine Heidegger (or anyone) making the kind of political commitment he made, in the way he made it, from out of the stance of "releasement," a way of being that stands in opposition to the heroic temperament associated with self-assertion and personal glory.

The twists and turns in Heidegger's reflections on the meaning of resoluteness, leading ultimately to his abandoning the term while insisting it never meant self-aggrandizing assertion, are mirrored in his attitude toward national selfhood and the foundation for its decisions. While, in the early 1930s, Heidegger uses the language of "will" for the nation as a whole, which apparently needs to assert itself in heroically assuming his destiny, in the years following the Rectorate he sees the contemporary idea of *Volk* as "the monster of a drive to life" (*das Monstrum eines Lebensdranges*) (GA 94, 497) and complains that modern nationalism is merely a form of egoism (GA 95, 250). Heidegger's understanding of a nation's choosing to follow its historical destiny had been modeled on the readiness for the call of conscience by an individual, who is embedded within a time and culture and is therefore part of a *Volk*. It involves the transcendence of the everyday drive to life, not its amplification into a national monster. But in addition to the problem of intra-national diversity and domination, this idea of national destiny presents the same difficulties as those pertaining to individual conscience as recalling one away from everyday absorption toward what is required. How can one be sure of truly knowing what is required? It is possible, too, that the worst excesses of the twentieth century came from zeal in accomplishing an alleged historical mission, and not from greed and will to power, although in practice these are not always so easy to distinguish.

To the extent that Heidegger's political decisions arose from his sense of having a privileged insight into the character and destiny of Germany as a whole, along with an impoverished sense of who composed this "Germany as a whole," they reflect a way of thinking that was far too sure of itself. It is not that all talk of national destiny, in no matter what context, *must* be morally suspect. Witness Jawaharlal Nehru's famous reference to India's "tryst with destiny" on the eve of its independence. Yet a national prophet is a potentially dangerous creature, especially when he was as politically unskilled and inattentive to reality as Heidegger was. Heidegger's commitment was the predictable result of his lack of skill and realism, affording as it does the spectacle of a philosopher emerging from the cave of his ideas to discover their reflection in a political movement that became a byword for the morally grotesque.

Heidegger retreated from politics, but he never abandoned his sense that German culture had something special to offer the world in the time of its great need. One thing *Entschlossenheit* and *Gelassenheit* have in common, in Heidegger's writings, is that they are both meant to be ways of responding to a Heraclitean understanding of being as always in process. In fact, in the 1935–36 Hölderlin lectures, Heidegger says that the beginning of German philosophy with Meister Eckhart, from whose works the term *Gelassenheit* is taken, stood under the power of Heraclitean thought, a power that reaches to Nietzsche (H 133–34). Heidegger's interpretation of Lao-tzu's *tao* as "way," against the possible translation of it as "reason, mind, *raison*, meaning *logos*" (OWL 92/GA 19, 198), is part of this pattern of thinking, and echoes Spengler's observation that both *tao* and *logos* went through the same transformation in the direction of mechanism (Spengler 1959, II, 307). Thus, although Heidegger withdraws from practical and political engagement after the failure of his Rectorate, Karsten Harris is wrong to see in his later thought "a despairing denial of a social mission" (Harris 1978, 327). It is only that Heidegger's sense of how he himself should participate in fulfilling this mission, his view of his own still very German vocation, changes. If fulfilling one's mission as *Geschick* ("destiny," "sending") means accomplishing that for which one is *geschikt* ("skillful"), then direct political involvement seems not to have been the way for Heidegger. His perseverance in thoughtful, and still hopeful,[20] questioning of the tradition, however, remained in his mind a "social mission," as well as a specifically German task in the midst of a Western crisis.

Volk and *Völker*

I noted earlier that in his addresses and lectures during the Rectorate, Heidegger affirms a model of nations as singular cultural and political entities that interact while respecting each other's autonomy. One problem arising for such models, according to which each culture is made unique by its language and traditions, is that of how dialogue between different cultures is possible. Spengler was much concerned with this problem, and his view on it is summed up in the statement: "nations understand one another as little as individuals do ... each understands merely a self-created picture of the other, and individuals with the insight to penetrate further are few and far between" (Spengler 1959, II, 171).

[20] As Thiele notes, Heidegger laments the current predicament but "also indicates hope," a hope that "rests on the possibility for a fundamental transformation" (Thiele 1995, 175). This is hope for the "turning" through which human beings may be established on the earth as shepherds rather than masters.

Herder, to whom such ideas about cultural uniqueness and incommensurability can be traced, had been centrally engaged with the themes of cultural bias and cross-cultural understanding. While he is most often remembered as a champion of the idea that each culture has its own uniquely valuable way of being, he was equally emphatic about the enrichment resulting from knowledge of other cultures. This requires, for Herder, the cultivation of *Einfühlung*, a sympathetic imagination that can "feel its way into" the world of people living in other, very different times and places (see Barnard 2003, 5–8). Herder also stresses the virtue of impartiality, of not having any "favorite people" (*Favoritvolk*) in forming one's picture of the various nations peopling the earth over its history (Herder 1991, 698).

There is little evidence that Heidegger cultivated this virtue, and numerous entries in his notebooks attest to the shallowness and partiality of his negative stereotypes about, for instance, America and England (e.g. GA 96, 114, 243, 263). One misses the fair-minded spirit that led Herder to try (not always successfully) to portray with an even hand both the vices and the virtues of every nation he considered (Sikka 2011, 16). At the level of principle rather than practice, though, Heidegger does affirm respect for the otherness of others, whether individuals or nations, as part of a broader respect for boundaries, always in danger of being transgressed through a tempting refusal to accept one's own limits. Again there is a debt to the German Idealist principle that the realization of definite possibilities requires the self-assertion of the particular, but that this assertion also opens the possibility of evil, the danger that the particular will assert itself at the expense of others. We have seen that, for Heidegger, such perverse assertion, or "erring," is the movement wherein a particular – whether an individual, a people, a tradition, or a form of thought – seeks to press its identity beyond the time and place allotted to it in virtue of its historical essence. Behaving in this manner represents failure to heed the calling that directs each individual to a definite, and therefore finite, vocation. It is then also failure to accord with the *logos* of *physis*. It means being out of sorts with being, a discordance that is the source of human discord. Because of this emphasis on accepting finitude, Heidegger's thought has been interpreted as fundamentally incompatible with totalitarianism (see Schwann 1989, 102). I demonstrated in Chapter 4, however, that in his conception of justice Heidegger does at times imagine there could be individuals with special insight into the good, who would then be in a position to determine the rightful place of individuals and estates within the overall design of things.

Harmonia, moreover, at least for the early, violently Heraclitean Heidegger, is not equivalent to a lack of strife. On the contrary, it is won through *polemos*, and *polemos* is constantly essential to it. It also includes hierarchical differentiation, an order of rank. The Rectoral Address expresses this sensibility, and although it does not counsel literal war, its view of the relation between *Völker*, peoples or nations, is not so far from Spengler's when Spengler says, himself drawing on Heraclitus, that "war is the primary politics of *everything* that lives" (Spengler 1959, II, 440).[21] Heidegger later claimed that he was convinced his position could be reconciled with the will of those in power, "especially following Hitler's May 1933 speech asking for peace,"[22] and I see no reason to disbelieve him. He was not the only German who failed to foresee the future that Hitler and his party really had in mind for their nation. But the "community of nations" he speaks of in the Rectoral Address is nonetheless a harmony arising through *polemos*, through *Kampf*, struggle or battle. Heidegger does tend to see "confrontation" (*Auseinandersetzung*) of some sort as necessary for development. He had said of the Greeks: "This *Volk* evolved into the brief course of its historical uniqueness and greatness only through the most severe, but creative, confrontation with the culture that was, for it, the most foreign and difficult – the Asiatic culture" (NH 262). Because such struggle is supposed to encourage the participating members to develop according to their own unique natures, the resulting international community will maintain the differences and unique identities of the various peoples it comprises.

The way of being toward the other in this community is therefore one that allows the essence of the other to unfold, a relation that in the early 1930s did not exclude aggressive confrontations. By the time of the Hölderlin lectures, though, the willing that wants the other to be as it is and to retain its essence is called love (*Liebe*) (H 82), in one of Heidegger's rare references to this affective disposition. If "love" is defined in this manner, then perhaps up until the gentler tone characterizing Heidegger's postwar writings, love and struggle, indeed love and violence, are in his mind not mutually exclusive. Where "love" means the granting of essence, the needfulness of being that wants a world in order to be disclosed, and so hurls man into the distress of homelessness and mortality, might be imagined as an act of love that is at the same time violent. Being so loved the world, one might say (poetically), that it fashioned for the sake of that world a being in its own image, whom it cast into exile to be shattered, ultimately, against death.

Whether the granting of essence occurs through violent struggle, or as in the later works through the composure that lets be, the problem remains of how interaction is supposed to take place, a problem endemic to the Romantic tradition with its quasi-Leibnizian conception of cultures as self-unfolding, organic unities. Heidegger in part retains this essentialist notion of cultures, explicated through his analyses of language and historicality. A historical tradition is bound together; it evolves properly not through foreign influences

[21] Contrast Herder: "Not war but peace is the natural condition of the human race when it is at liberty" (Herder 1989, 316).

[22] In his "Letter to the Rector of Freiburg University," November 4, 1945; Wolin 1993, 63.

but through a transformative repetition of the possibilities offered by its past. Overcoming a tradition that has grown old and is in a condition of decline requires understanding it in its roots, and drawing from those roots the power of the possible that may give rise to something new. Heidegger therefore sees a relation between creativity, rootedness, and *Heimat*. In his essay on Hölderlin's poem, "Remembrance" (*Andenken*), he writes: "Everything 'creative' must be at home in the ground from which it sprang. How else could it grow up into its 'greatness'?" (G 4, 91). In *Discourse on Thinking*, he quotes with approval the following sentence from Hebel: "We are plants which – whether we like to admit it to ourselves or not – must with our roots rise out of the earth in order to bloom in the ether and to bear fruit" (DT 47/G 15). Herder had also been fond of this botanical analogy, writing at one point, regarding different cultures, that "each should find its place, so that it may rise up from its roots on its own impulse, and bring forth its blossoming crown" (Herder 1989, 316).

Heidegger's sense of what is needed for the renewal of European thinking involves this idea that the solution must be drawn from the same source that generated the danger. The occidental tradition, that is, can only be transformed through an internal critique; its ailments cannot be cured by a flight to "the East." However, dialogue is not flight, and we know that Heidegger did engage in conversations with "the East" himself, through a project, eventually abandoned, to translate the *Tao Te Ching* into German, and through contact with Japanese scholars. In a conversation with one of these scholars, Hisamatsu Shinichi, Heidegger emphasizes the importance of East-West exchange, through a form of encounter that, he says, "must begin from a deeper place" than a concern with economics and politics, and "is more important than economic or political contacts."[23] The published text of "A Dialogue on Language" provides a model of how the later Heidegger conceives the possibility of a genuine dialogue between such different traditions. It is also an instance, for better or worse, of how he himself entered into such dialogue. Letting the other be is central to Heidegger's ideal, and because the essence of the other is bound up with the language that speaks his world, it requires above all that we not immediately translate that language into our own. To do so is not only to falsify the other's being, but in the same act to destroy the possibility of being informed by it. That is why Heidegger cautions his Japanese interlocutor in the dialogue against interpreting Japanese art through the categories of European aesthetics, which, he says "must ultimately remain alien to Eastasian thinking" (OWL 2/GA 12, 82). The caution is not meant to exclude the other from conversation. In asking him to resist the temptation reinforced by the process of "the complete Europeanization of the earth and man" (OWL 15/GA 12/98), it

[23] Cited in Ma 2008, 73.

suggests that he approach what is different from a position that is true to the world in which his thinking is rooted and to which it belongs.

If there were no identity within the difference, no such approach would be possible. But it remains possible, Heidegger proposes, although uncertain, that "European-Western saying and Eastasian saying will enter into dialogue such that in it there sings something that wells up from a single source" – only, this would have to be "a source that would then still remain concealed from both language worlds" (OWL 8/GA 12, 89). In other words, there is a sameness approaching both participants through the dialogue, but it can never be articulated in the language of either, precisely because it is common to both. The Japanese participant says he senses a "deeply concealed kinship" between the two traditions, "precisely because your path of thinking and its language are so wholly different." This admission, Heidegger responds, "agitates me in a way which I can control only because we remain in dialogue" (OWL 41/GA 12, 129). The agitation results, I think, from the insight, though no more than a shadowy glimmer, into the common unsayable source that approaches the two precisely because of their very different ways of beckoning to it.

This is Heidegger's model, then, of a "released" way of being toward the other. It is a long way from the aggressive rhetoric of earlier works emphasizing creative strife as *polemos*, but is still part of the same project of trying to find an appropriate model to combine identity with difference, particularity with harmony, self-determination with respect for others, and independence with interaction. Not only does violence drop out of the later works, but Heidegger no longer produces a formula for the state and this, combined with the transformation at times of *Volk* into "neighbourhood," leaves more space to ask whether the described communities must find their "being" in a monoethnic state, or whether they can be groups within a multicultural state. It also leaves the nature of the units themselves more fluid.

There is, however, the inconvenient fact that while "A Dialogue on Language" is based on an actual dialogue, the actual person with whom Heidegger spoke claimed it did not go as Heidegger says it did in the essay (May 1996, 12–13). The essay is a piece of fiction rather than an accurate record. It is still possible to appreciate the model of cross-cultural interaction it recommends, but one cannot escape the irony of a text that purports to depict an instance of genuine dialogue, and yet changes what was actually said in order to make its point. This is rather typical of Heidegger. The messiness and unpredictability of actual dialogue, in which the other may not faithfully accompany me on the path I had envisioned for us, was not Heidegger's forte. Visible in the "Dialogue on Language" is also a persisting essentialism about these grand blocs – "European-Western," "Eastasian" – in their assumed difference from one another. I suspect Heidegger would have been disappointed if it turned out that some European and Asian traditions are more alike than he thought, or different in ways less interesting than he hoped. What would he have made of metaphysical speculations in classical Indian philosophy, for instance, had he studied them carefully? He may have had to revise his view that ontotheology is specific to Western philosophy, along with his assumption that the traditions of the "East" speak wholly otherwise.

It is also not true that Heidegger entirely reversed his earlier thinking on the issue of *Volk*, for instance as expressed in the *Introduction to Metaphysics*. That he published this text unaltered in 1953 has reasonably been taken as evidence that no such reversal took place. The remark in the text concerning "the inner truth and greatness" of National Socialism (IM 199/GA 40, 208), around which there has been much controversy, is perfectly consistent with his disdain for actual or "vulgar" Nazism. It also consistent with what he says about the matter in "Reflections on the Rectorate":

> The Rectorate was an attempt to see something in the movement that had come to power, beyond all its failings and crudeness, that was much more far-reaching and that could perhaps one day bring a concentration on the Germans' Western historical essence. It will in no way be denied that at the time I believed in such possibilities and for that reason renounced the actual vocation of thinking in favor of being effective in an official capacity. In no way will what was caused by my own inadequacy in office be played down. But these points of view do not capture what is essential and what moved me to accept the Rectorate. (Neske and Kettering 1990, 29)

Heidegger simply never came to believe that the "essence" of the political movement he had supported consisted in brutality and genocidal totalitarianism. He always felt instead that "the Nazis" were the *Unwesen*, the monstrous dis-essence, of National Socialism. Perhaps a part of the reason Heidegger never apologized for having supported "the Nazis" is that, in his mind, he never did. All he needed to take responsibility for was the blunder of having mistaken these dim-witted criminals for something better. In short, for Heidegger, "National Socialism" never truly happened. It fell prey to the ever-present danger of perversion, of being pushed out of its essence. It therefore did not bring forth its positive possibilities, and that means it never came to presence at all, or at least not "authentically."

Culture, Space, and Time

I have intended in this chapter to give a balanced and forthright view of Heidegger's understanding of *Volk*, not downplaying the objectionable elements in his reflections on the topic and their intimate connection with his support for National Socialism, but at the same time communicating a sense of why someone might find aspects of his position attractive without being drawn to his political conclusions. Heidegger's harshest critics unfairly rule out the latter possibility, suggesting that those who continue to engage with Heidegger in a positive way are either covert fascists or somehow deluded about the true character of his thought. But one can reject the idea that states should be ethnically or culturally homogeneous, that peoples have grand historical destinies, and that liberal democracy is only subjectivism writ large, while still finding a measure of truth in Heidegger's reflections on these themes.

The political implications Heidegger drew in 1933 from his analysis of the relation between *Volk* and space, for example, are flawed due in part to an insufficiently complex analysis of cultural identity within the line of thinking about *Volk* that goes back to Herder. The result is a failure to conceptualize properly the identity of being, for instance, a Jewish German, and to welcome difference within national borders. Equally important is the fact that in Heidegger's case (though not, I think, in Herder's), there is a pronounced failure to balance concerns about cultural identity with care for all persons, and to think intelligently and sympathetically about which consideration needs to be given priority, in which context, and to what degree. Nonetheless, Heidegger's understanding of the uniquely human relation to spaces that are *places*, his analysis of the way we make ourselves at home somewhere on the earth through our ways of dwelling, captures something important about the attachment people feel to specific locales.[24] Individuals may feel this for more than one locale, even considering more than one place a home and native land, something that seems never to have occurred to Heidegger. Heidegger's rustic tendencies also blocked appreciation for the fact that cities can contain neighborhoods as well, genuine communities of shared concerns, to which inhabitants may be deeply attached.[25] Nonetheless, he is right to recognize that people *have* homes, that they are not equally at home everywhere on the planet.

This recognition does not, on its own, exclude the ethical demand that people be able to find refuge in other nations if there are threats to their freedom and well-being where they currently are. It also does not exclude the possibility – a simple empirical fact – that they can make themselves at home somewhere else. But attachment to a place, even to a homeland, a *Heimat*, is not *per se* evil. It becomes so only if it results in xenophobia, inhospitality, and a sense of superior right over others. These are not necessary consequences of love

[24] See also Jeff Malpas' analysis of the relation between world and space in Heidegger's thought: *Heidegger and the Thinking of Place* (Malpas 2012), especially Chapter 6, "Place, Space and World," and Chapter 7, "Geography, Biology and Politics." Malpas' topic is not centrally that of nationhood and cultural diversity, but he rightly points out that Heidegger's reflections on place as *Heimat* are complex, and should not be summarily dismissed as symptomatic of the reactionary politics of Nazism (Chapter 7, pp. 140–54).

[25] Compare Heidegger's remark: "Two isolated farmsteads – if any such are left – separated by an hour's walk across the fields, can be the best of neighbors, while two townhouses, facing each other across the street or even sharing a common wall, know no neighborhood" (OWL 103/GA 12, 199).

for the place(s) in which a person has dwelled, or for the things that carry significance within the world(s) she has known. Heidegger's rich account of the way language captures and expresses that significance, originally naming not neutral objects and processes but things and events within a meaningful world, is helpful for analyzing the role language plays in shaping and preserving cultural identity, and the more than pragmatic importance people often attach to their "native" tongues. His writings, both early and late, aid in imagining what it means to be in the world, to *have* a world in the way human beings do, and why it is important to respect the world of a people as a component of respect for them.

This is not to deny that Heidegger's own conceptions of being a people are overly essentialist, and that his view of the connections between culture, ethnicity, and state are dangerously wrong. On the latter point, judging by his political speeches, Heidegger supposed that the borders of states should correspond to the identity of peoples, as defined by culture and ethnicity. This political thesis can lead to terrible forms of injustice, as the dismal history of ethnonationalism reveals. However, political theories supporting multiculturalism also rest on the view that culture is in one way or another essential to selfhood, with the implication that cultural respect is a component of respect for individuals. While the idea of culture employed by multiculturalist theorists has been criticized for being overly essentialist, it remains a fact that human beings are culturally situated, and *some* suitably nuanced recognition of this fact is required for an appropriate politics. Putting aside Heidegger's own cultural partialities and biases, and acknowledging that his understanding of cultural identity and interaction tends to picture cultures as "unified, holistic, and self-consistent wholes," in Seyla Benhabib's words (Benhabib 2002, 86),[26] his writings nonetheless provide helpful resources for conceptualizing and appreciating the elements of culture.

Those elements are emphatically not static, within Heidegger's analysis. How could they be, given his account of the temporality of human existence and being as a whole? If Heidegger does have a tendency to picture cultures as bounded wholes, these wholes are nonetheless *evolving* ones, and their unity is not given by changelessness. In relation to ideas and patterns of life, Heidegger does not conceive of cultures as constituted by the permanent possession of beliefs and practices, as if they were substances whose definition consisted in having such and such properties. Picturing cultures in this manner would mean employing the very substantialist ontology Heidegger exposes as inappropriate to the being of Dasein. Culture is a feature of Dasein's existence as being-with, not a property of objects. In *Being and Time*, Dasein imagines its future by

[26] Compare, however, Nikolas Kompridis' defense of the idea of cultural identity against such anti-essentialist critiques (Kompridis 2005).

drawing on its past, in terms of the heritage that has been handed down to it, which it can appropriate and revise in multiple ways (BT 383). What binds a culture together, on this account, is not a set of stable characteristics but the commonality of a shared history, on the basis of which the members of that culture relate themselves to a common future. Thus, collective cultural identity, like the individual selfhood of which it is a component, involves recalling and imagining, a process that *builds* the identities of peoples over time. Although Heidegger does not take his analysis in this direction, understanding the temporality of cultural identity in such terms can even help to explicate the sense of community among groups that have been marginalized or oppressed, an identity formed in part through self-location within shared narratives of the past.[27]

Again, cultural identities are in virtually all cases more complex than Heidegger appreciated. Individuals may draw on a number of traditions handed down to them, and they may genuinely be located in more than one culture. At the same time, it would be naïve to suppose that we can be "citizens of the world" in the sense not of *caring* for all the peoples of the world (a species of cosmopolitanism that may be humanly possible), but being formed by and having equal access to all of the world's cultures. Individuals are shaped by at most a small subset of those cultures, to which they relate in negotiating their existence in the world. That is not a matter of individual choice. It belongs to the facticity of Dasein, Heidegger might say, for whether a person reverently accepts, creatively revises, or strongly opposes an element in the heritage handed down by the tradition(s) she receives, the fact of the matter is that it is *these* traditions with which she engages, and not *those*. It cannot be otherwise, given that persons are specific beings in the world, born in a particular place, following a definite path, and capable only of finite understanding. Nothing in this conception prevents cross-cultural dialogue, or supports cultural determination if that means individuals are "only" products of their culture and therefore incapable, let alone barred from, criticizing or rejecting some established practice or belief imposed upon them. Indeed, registering dissatisfaction and responding to it by envisioning alternatives is very much part of the historicity of culture, as Heidegger understands it, and plays a central role in his conception of destiny.

[27] It is a pity Heidegger did not see this with respect to Jewish identity, but doing so would have required a sensitivity to the realities of power and subordination that he did not possess. I have sometimes drawn on Heidegger's account of historicity in some of my own work on identity construction among oppressed groups, without always referring to him explicitly. See "'Learning to be Indian': Historical Narratives and the 'Choice' of a Cultural Identity" (Sikka 2004); "In What Sense Are Dalits Black?" (Sikka 2012a); and "Untouchable Cultures: Memory, Power and the Construction of Dalit Selfhood" (Sikka 2012b).

There are also humbler versions of the idea that cultures might have destinies, unique contributions to make to the course of world history through the kind of process Heidegger outlines. This is a process where we register in a variety of ways the needs, concerns, and points of distress in our current situation, drawing creatively on the (usually multiple) traditions we inherit, in interaction with others (who overlap with "us" in many ways) to imagine something different and better. In view of the increasingly global hegemony of a particular view of humanity and being, which Heidegger diagnoses with considerable astuteness, it is well worth emphasizing that there *are* different cultural traditions in the world, and that non-Western ones are not merely backwards or a barrier to progress but may have something exceptional to offer.[28] Such an affirmation is an essential component of fostering a genuine mutual respect between peoples, which we are still far from having achieved.

[28] Compare J. L. Mehta's Heidegger-inspired understanding of dialogue in the present age, where each of the world's various traditions "is reaching out to the others, each is in crisis, each capable of renewal and, only if we respond creatively, each assured of a future, each called upon to contribute, in its own way, to the task of meeting a common threat and a universal crisis" (Mehta 1992, 258).

6 Was Heidegger Racist?

Were it not for his connection with Nazism, one would assume Heidegger could only have been antagonistic toward any conception of human beings seeking to ground their nature in a biological characteristic such as race. As deployed within Nazi ideology, the idea of race is linked to a biologically based species of anthropology. Heidegger's thought is, in its fundamental principles, opposed to any such anthropology, insisting that everything proper to humanity must be understood through the structures of freedom and historicity. For Heidegger, nothing about us is "natural," if our concept of "nature" is derived exclusively from an orientation toward aspects of being that do not include the kind of existential structures he outlined as fundamental to Dasein in *Being and Time*. The biological concept of race is "natural" in precisely this reductive sense. Thus, one would not expect Heidegger to grant any validity to this concept, and that expectation is confirmed by a survey of his works. Nowhere does he give credence to any theory of racially distinct groups, let alone to a hierarchical ranking of such groups. George Steiner remarked in 1999 that "there is in Heidegger's voluminous writings no spoor of biological racism" (Steiner 1999, 4), and publications since then, including his notebooks, only confirm this claim. It would be reasonable to conclude that the idea of race, to the extent that it is present at all in Heidegger's thought, functions only in a negative way, as something he opposes.

Julian Young reaches this conclusion, arguing that "the Heidegger literature contains, unfortunately, a great deal of unhelpful and confusing talk about Heidegger's alleged 'metaphysical' or 'intellectual racism,' " but that "there is no such thing," as "biological racism is the only kind there is" (Young 1997, 36). However, if the term "racism" applies to prejudices against ethnic or cultural groups conceived as other, and held to be innately inferior, wicked, or dangerous – and we do often use the term this way – the matter is not so simple. As Tariq Modood points out, "it could indeed be said that in the long history of racism, it is nineteenth-century biologism that is the exception, and certainly Europe's oldest racisms, anti-Semitism and Islamophobia, are culturalist" (Modood 1997, 155). Heidegger is known to have held some anti-Semitic views (we knew this before the publication of his notebooks, in spite of sensational publicity suggesting otherwise), and he did support a political regime founded upon racist principles. Granting that he could not have endorsed any concept purporting to apply to the essential constitution of human beings based on the alleged findings of biology, he might nonetheless have affirmed some nonbiological notion of race, which would explain a part of his attraction to Nazi ideology. If so, that could justify describing him as "racist" after all.

This chapter examines Heidegger's relation to the idea of race in light of such questions. It explores, first, the nature and extent of Heidegger's sustained, sometimes covert, critique of race and associated ideas within Nazi ideology in his lectures and writings during the later 1930s, and over the course of the war. As would be expected, anti-biologism forms a staple component in this critique, but it functions as part of an opposition whose aim tends to be correction rather than destruction. Heidegger's critique of race, along with other elements in Nazi ideology, seeks to bring this movement back to its proper "essence," saving it from the corruption he thinks it has undergone as a result, in part, of contamination with biologistic ideas. I examine further this alleged "essence," extending my analysis in the previous two chapters to locate the Nazi views, revolving around the idea of race, that would have attracted Heidegger's sympathy in spite of his rejection of biologism, because he himself held non-biologistic versions of these views. The results of this analysis will suggest that the parallel notions Heidegger espoused belong to the sphere of what we have come to define as "culture" rather than "race," and that the prejudices he held against particular groups of people (including Jews) justify the charge of "cultural racism."[1] At the same time, "biology," in the form of lineage linked to history, does enter into Heidegger's conception of the identity of peoples. I propose, however, that, if one adds modifications and caveats, this conception of ethnicity is in some measure right. It acknowledges a dimension of the reality of "race," presenting one reason why categories such as "race," "culture," and ethnicity cannot be clearly distinguished. Finally, I consider the charge of cultural – or "metaphysical," or "ontohistorical" – racism against Heidegger's prejudices, and particularly his anti-Semitism, asking what implications we should draw about the status of Heidegger's works as a result, in light of the fact that so many major philosophers within the Western canon are guilty of one or another variety of racism.

[1] I apply this term broadly to negative stereotypes about Jews that trace their alleged shortcomings to history and culture, rather than biology. It therefore covers the panoply of descriptors that have been applied to Heidegger's anti-Semitism, such as "spiritual," "intellectual," "metaphysical," and "ontohistorical" (see Fagenblatt 2016, di Cesare 2016, Trawny 2014, 2016).

Heidegger's Anti-Biologism

In his interview with *Der Speigel* in 1966, Heidegger is asked whether his relation to the NSDAP changed after his resignation as rector. He responds:

> After my resignation from the Rectorate, I confined myself to my teaching responsibilities. In the summer semester of 1934, I delivered the lectures on "Logic." In the following semester, 1934/35, I held the first lecture course on Hölderlin. In 1936 began the lectures on Nietzsche. Everyone, who could hear, understood that these lectures were a confrontation with National Socialism. (Heidegger 1981a, 203–4)

The published texts of the courses Heidegger mentions in these statements do exhibit an increasingly critical relationship to Nazi ideology, including elements underpinning Nazi race theory. In the lecture course called *Logic*, Heidegger is evidently still hopeful about the future of Germany under Nazi rule. His choice to illustrate his analysis of history by presenting a meeting between "the Führer" and Mussolini as an example of a genuine historical happening (L 83) demonstrates that these two figures and what they represent still constitute, for Heidegger, a positive historical force. To be sure, the reference is made while drawing a contrast between the unfolding of events with human significance and mere sequences of occurrences, thereby distinguishing the realms of history and nature. In this context, a meeting between Hitler and Mussolini would count as genuinely historical, regardless of how it were judged, but Heidegger does at this juncture see the event as promising rather than threatening.

Heidegger's rare explicit remarks on race in the lectures on logic appear in the course of his analysis of history as definitive of being human and essential to membership in a *Volk.* On the surface, the remarks are neither positive nor negative in their attitude toward race, seeming merely to describe an aspect of what the term is held to mean. Heidegger claims at one point that " 'race,' like *Volk*, is ambiguous," because "it concerns that aspect of a people which is connected, in its genetically determined drive to life, with blood and with the physical," but can also connote rank (L 65). Considering the highly charged climate of ideas in which he is speaking, one could complain that even pointing out these features of the idea of race, particularly the connection between race and rank, without critical comment is problematic, as it implicitly lends credence to an idea that ought simply to be rejected. On the other hand, considering that same climate, including its lack of tolerance for dissent, what is *not* said, in this passage or anywhere else, is equally significant. Heidegger does not endorse any notion of "blood" as determining the character of a people, or any doctrine regarding the superiority of one biological race to another, or any idea of degenerate races. He does mention sickness and blood at one point, but maintains that these are actually historical rather than purely biological phenomena (L 153). Again, it could be objected that, at the time these lectures were delivered, affirming *any* notion of sickness and blood, however revised and transformed, could still be construed as supporting a hierarchical ranking of groups of people, along with the oppressive policies this ranking was employed to justify. This objection is valid, as is Bernasconi's suggestion that Heidegger is aiming for a revised understanding of biological categories, not a simple rejection of them (Bernasconi 2000). Still, Heidegger's intent is critical of what becomes the dominant ideology of race in Nazi Germany, which refers to an inherited biological basis that determines character. He rejects a biological construal of "blood," claiming instead that what is called "blood" is determined by disposition and character, not the other way around (L 153). In general, his analyses assert that the elements determining the character of a people, and presenting at the same time the possibility of superiority or degeneration, belong to the realm of history rather than nature. They concern historical rather than genetic inheritance, and decision rather than causation.

With respect to the constitution of individuals and peoples, Heidegger's basic thesis in these lectures is that history is essential to, and definitive of, being human. In arguing this thesis, he makes some statements seeming to support the notion that "negroes" have no history. These statements, recalling Hegel's claim that Africa "is no historical part of the world" (Hegel 1956, 99), occur as part of Heidegger's consideration of a possible counterexample to his thesis that history is the defining characteristic of being human. Heidegger imagines someone might point out that "there are human beings and human groups (negroes, for instance Xhosa) who have no history" (L 81). He goes on to say that a people without a history is still capable of entering history, so that "a *Volk* without a history, which then enters history, is without history in a totally different sense than the earth is without history" (L 84). Heidegger does not clarify where "negroes" finally fit in terms of this framework, nor does he give the matter much thought. But we should not assume he thinks the Xhosa, for instance, are without history (*geschichtslos*) (L 83) in the sense that they lack the structure of Dasein, and are therefore more natural than human, which would make them incapable of being historical.

"Racism" is not, though, limited to beliefs about biological capacities. It can also include vague classifications of human beings on the basis of color or geographical origin, and the association of the resulting categories with various marks of inferiority and lesser human development. From this perspective, Heidegger's remarks about "negroes" are racist in a number of ways. There is, first, the dubious supposition that some unitary and distinct group is named by the term "negroes," a group that would have to be identified by biological characteristics, by skin color and lineage perhaps, or by the same types of characteristics, whatever these may be, that distinguish biological species and subspecies. That is not at all how Heidegger would normally define a *Volk*, and he certainly never speaks of "Caucasians" when referring to Europeans. The very use of the term "negro" shows lack of sufficient awareness that there *are* African peoples who are properly *Völker* (even though he mentions one, the Xhosa), and Heidegger does not acknowledge any distinction between such peoples and people of African descent living elsewhere. In addition, the idea that "negroes" have no history is racist in its assertion that the people gathered under this category have no explicit historical consciousness or traditions, and in this sense belong (so far) more closely to nature than other people do, even if they are still people who are capable of entering history in a way non-human beings are not. Racism is, furthermore, culpable because it involves more than an honest intellectual mistake. People who hold ideas judged as racist are usually being taken to task for making denigrating generalizations about others of whom they know little or nothing, and an important aspect of racism consists in this unthinking, self-superior, often ill-willed manner of passing judgment. Heidegger's statements about "negroes" could be judged as racist in all of these ways. That does not provide evidence of a general biological racism, however, or of sympathy with the side of Nazi ideology that embraced this brand of racism. Sadly, among Western philosophers, Heidegger is hardly unusual in excluding Africans from full humanity at the cost of being inconsistent. In 1934, this exclusion was not limited to opponents of the liberal democratic "West."

By the time he delivers his first set of lectures on Hölderlin (winter semester, 1933/34), Heidegger's disillusionment with the actuality of Nazism is palpable. Whereas in the *Logic* lectures he had still tended to support this actuality, while wanting to help shape and purify it, by now he is harshly critical, which nonetheless does not mean he has withdrawn allegiance from the better form of National Socialism he continues to envision as a possibility. Heidegger's disenchantment with the popular rhetoric of Nazism is evident in overtly critical remarks in the Hölderlin lectures, suggesting that in its current form, Nazi ideology is not genuinely revolutionary but largely continuous with the decadent course of Western history, characterized by subjectivism and nihilism. Criticizing the conception of poetry as an "expression of experiences," for instance, Heidegger claims that all conceptions of this sort move within the same manner of thinking, regardless of whether the expressed experiences are interpreted as "the experiences of an individual – 'individualistically' – or as the expression of a collective soul (*Massenseele*) – 'collectivistically' – or with Spengler as the expression of a cultural soul, or with Rosenberg as the expression of the soul of a race or of a people" (H 26).

The same genre of disenchantment is evident in other critical remarks in these lectures:

> The author Kolbenheyer says: "Poetry is a biologically necessary function of the people." It does not take much intelligence to see that this is also true of digestion. (H 27)

> Not long ago, one searched for the hidden bases of poetry through psychoanalysis, now it is all about national character and blood and soil, but everything remains as it was. (H 254)

Heidegger's disgust with the reductive biologism that characterized so much Nazi ideology is evident in the remark about Kolbenheyer, whom he also criticizes at length in the 1933–34 lecture course, *Being and Truth* (BTr 159–64/ GA 36/37, 209–13). The second comment shows that Heidegger is no longer likely to speak positively, as he had in the Rectoral Address, about "the forces rooted in the soil and blood of a *Volk*" (SU 14), a shift registered in the notebook entries written during this period. The 1934–35 Hölderlin lectures are nonetheless thematically continuous with the lectures on logic in their focus on historicality, and in their interpretation as historical of phenomena constitutive of the character and identity of a people that Nazi ideology represented as physical. An example is Heidegger's claim that, in Hölderlin's poetry, *Heimat* is "not a mere place of birth, nor only a familiar landscape," but is "the power of the earth, on which a person 'dwells poetically' at any given time, in accordance with his historical existence" (H 88), and that "earth and homeland are meant historically" (H 196). Accordingly, "fatherland," has nothing to do with any "doubtful and noisy patriotism" but means "the land of the fathers, it means us, this people of this earth as historical, in its historical being" (H 120).

Max Müller is therefore wrong to claim that "Heidegger was not concerned with Hölderlin's conception of the fatherland, which was what especially interested the National Socialists about this poet," and that, after 1934, "as far as a nonparticipant can tell, not a single political word was spoken in [Heidegger's] courses" (Müller 1990, 190). The Hölderlin lectures are still deeply political, for their themes are directly related to the social and political ideologies of Nazi Germany. The shift occurring in 1934 is not a shift away from the realm of politics, but toward a more critical assessment of what is actually occurring there. Yet the substantive content of Heidegger's philosophy does not undergo a major change in 1934. His understanding of the nature of human existence, and of the role of national identity within that existence, remains fundamentally unaltered. What has changed radically is his view of the relation of central items of Nazi ideology to his own understanding of these issues, and to the "ideals" of National Socialism, as he sees them.

Heidegger remains critically concerned with biologistic ideas, along with other features of Nazi ideology in its effective actuality, throughout the lecture courses he gives in the late 1930s and early 1940s. In the 1942 summer semester lectures, *Hölderlins Hymne "Der Ister"* (GA 53), he still attempts at times to oppose such ideas by offering alternative non-biologistic interpretations. He again refers to the term "blood," for instance, construing it as a label for "physical life," and claiming that the connection between human beings and blood is "first determined by the relation of human beings to being itself" (GA 53, 147). "Blood," that is, names an aspect of being human that, precisely because it is an aspect of being *human*, cannot be analyzed in the terms appropriate to the investigation of nature. In that case, the concept has to be understood via the structure of being human. For Heidegger, the heart of that structure consists in a reflexive relation to being, articulated through the temporality of Dasein. Likewise, the relation to what is one's own, as opposed to what is foreign, is constituted by, and must be interpreted through, this structure. It "is never the merely self-assured affirmation of the so-called 'natural' and 'organic'" (GA 53, 179). Heidegger maintains that "all the simply 'organic' of nature is foreign to the law of history, as foreign as is the 'logical' of reason" (GA 53, 179). He thereby challenges a popular dichotomy exploited in Nazi propaganda, while guarding himself against the anticipated objection that anyone who criticizes one side of this dichotomy must be promoting, instead, the decadence of an abstract reason increasingly divorced from the realities of human existence.

This challenge is also visible in the *Contributions to Philosophy*, where Heidegger claims that the absolutization of spirit within German Idealism achieves a suppression of individuality and an alienation of being that actually expedite the fall into positivism and biologism. He adds that "the present 'confrontation' – if it at all deserves to be called such, with German Idealism is merely 're-active' and *absolutizes* 'life,' in all the indeterminateness and confusion that can lurk in that noun" (CP 249/GA 65, 315). By now, the contemporary emphasis on "life," with its accompanying biologism, belongs for Heidegger to the falling movement of Western thought, through which reality in the modern age has exclusively become that which the subject can place before itself and represent (*vor-stellen*) as an object. In opposition to the dominant public rhetoric of overcoming decadence by a return to life over spirit, Heidegger is proposing that this glorification of a vague notion of "life" is in fact a continuation of Western decadence. Any attempt to characterize a *Volk* on the basis of this notion must then also belong to the same decadence. Heidegger insists, instead, that the essence of a people resides in historicity, and that "'life' and the body, breeding (*Zeugung*) and lineage (*Geschlecht*), descent (*Stamm*), stated in a basic word: the earth, belong to history" (CP 316/GA 65, 399).

By this point in the development of his thought (the *Contributions* was composed from 1936–39), Heidegger sees Nietzsche's emphasis on life and biological forces as part of this merely reactive movement of decline (CP 249/GA 65, 315). In the text of his first lecture course on Nietzsche, by contrast, *The Will to Power as Art*, delivered in 1936, his interpretation is more charitable. He already sees in Nietzsche's thought a culmination rather than an overcoming of the declining movement of Western metaphysics. However, his dominant view in these lectures is that Nietzsche is fundamentally *not* a biological reductionist, if one takes care to understand properly what he means by "life" and related notions, but that unfortunately and to his discredit, he does sometimes, in his analysis of aesthetic phenomena, use a false and misleading reductive vocabulary drawn from physiology and biology (GA 43, 113–14).

It would be wrong to assume that any attempt to dissociate Nietzsche from biologism constitutes per se a critique of the Nazi appropriation of Nietzsche. Alfred Bäumler, whose *Nietzsche der Philosoph und Politiker* (1931) is part of that appropriation, also rejects the idea that Nietzsche's thought is biologistic and sees his attempt to root consciousness in life-functions as a hyperbolic reaction to the overvaluation of consciousness by other philosophers (Bäumler 1931, 28). Heidegger criticizes Bäumler's reading of Nietzsche for being guided by politics rather than metaphysics,[2] but praises him for being one of the few who go against "the psychological-biologistic interpretation of Nietzsche through Klages" (GA 43, 25). However, Bäumler's rejection of the biologistic understanding of Nietzsche does not prevent him from applauding Nietzsche for emphasizing the origin of the individual within the concrete unities of race, people, and class (Bäumler 1931, 179), and for the fact that "before his eyes stood again the old task of our race: the task, to become the leader of Europe" (Bäumler 1931, 182). Heidegger also emphasizes the role of cultural membership in shaping historical existence and he believes in a special mission for Germany within Europe, but he never speaks of these in terms of race, nor is the language of race present in what he sees as positive about Nietzsche.

A central component of the Nazified Nietzsche, moreover, did concern biologically based racial theory, and the distance between these views and the ones expressed in Heidegger's lecture courses should be emphasized. Consider the following statement from Heinrich Härtle's *Nietzsche und der Nationalsozialismus*: "Since the knowledge of race is fundamental for our political world, nothing distances us from, and binds us more strongly with, Nietzsche as those ideas whose truth or error is rooted in his understanding or misunderstanding of the problem of race, an understanding in which he is bound to his times" (Härtle 1937, 8). Heidegger sees the issue of race as central neither to politics nor to an interpretation of Nietzsche. Although he does speak positively of the idea of rank, understood in some fashion, one cannot imagine his making such a statement as, "Nietzsche shows the errors and dangers of a doctrine teaching the equality of all that bears a human face" (Härtle 1937, 24). Heidegger never promotes the view that Nietzsche was anti-Semitic, let alone rightly anti-Semitic (see Härtle 1937, 38, 44, 49, 50, 54), nor is there any mention of Jews

[2] He makes this point when criticizing Bäumler's attitude toward Nietzsche's doctrine of eternal recurrence. Heidegger feels that Bäumler rejects this aspect of Nietzsce's thought as unimportant only because "the doctrine of eternal recurrence does not fit with his politics, or at least he thinks it does not fit" (GA 43, 25).

in his own lectures on Nietzsche. One might also compare Heidegger's subtle interpretations of notions such as "life," "body," and "blood," with Härtle's claim that "as a thinker of life and of the body, Nietzsche had to run up against the race-question" (Härtle 1937, 55). For Härtle, Nietzsche adopts the right position on this question when he remarks, in *The Will to Power*, that "there is only nobility of birth, nobility of blood" (Härtle 1937, 55),[3] and the wrong position in believing that the character of a people is determined by "external" factors.

Härtle's description of the essential difference between Nietzsche and National Socialism on this point is worth quoting at length for the light it sheds on how Heidegger's notion of *Volk* compares with a contemporaneous racialist one:

> The National Socialist concept of a *Volk* is not only historical or intuitive, but has a scientific and biological basis.
>
> Nietzsche once attempted to explain the development of a *Volk* in this way: "When people have lived for a long time together under similar conditions (of climate, of soil, of danger, of needs, of work), then something arises, in which there is a certain 'agreement,' a *Volk*." Something is lacking here, which for us is central, *race*. Only because Nietzsche – in conformity with his times – does not understand the *Volk* racially as well could he distance himself to such an extent from the *Volk*.
>
> For us too is *Volk* not only race. We recognize the "steady modification" of our inherited condition through place and history, landscape and destiny. The accent, however, lies on the racial. A Jew may live for a thousand years in the German community, with its place and destiny, but he will never become a member of the *Volk* (*Volksgenosse*). But the Huguenots, who are classified as Nordic, would become full members of the *Volk*. (Härtle 1937, 82)

Given Heidegger's disagreement that any concept essential to a description of being human "has a scientific and biological basis," and given his insistence that all such concepts are in fact grounded in historicity, his thought on this subject also lacks what is central to "the National Socialist concept of a *Volk*" as defined by Härtle.

In a context where Härtle's picture of Nietzsche is an example of the authorized Nazi version – and the version consonant with the ideology of racial eugenics – Heidegger's claim, in the *Der Spiegel* interview, that there is a critical engagement with Nazism in his Nietzsche lectures is plausible, certainly with respect to the issue of race. In *The Nietzsche Legacy in Germany 1890–1990*, on the other hand, Steven Aschheim claims that even if their intent

[3] The full quotation in *The Will to Power* reads:

> There is only nobility of birth, only nobility of blood ... When one speaks of "aristocrats of the spirit," reasons are usually not lacking for concealing something; as is well known, it is a favorite term among ambitious Jews. For spirit alone does not make noble; rather, there must be something to ennoble the spirit. – What then is required? Blood. (WP 495–96)

was critical, many passages in Heidegger's Nietzsche lectures "could have been taken as validating the regime's self-conception and aims" (Aschheim 1992, 268). This may be true with respect to some aspects of the lectures, and Heidegger does not provide in these lectures any extended critique, as he might have done (though not without considerable personal risk), of the Nazi ideas from which he distances himself, including the idea of race (Aschheim 1992, 267). Aschheim's remarks are directed against interpretations that claim Heidegger's Nietzsche lectures intentionally do not contribute to the political reading of Nietzsche within the Nazi context. As an example of such an interpretation, Aschheim quotes David Krell's claim that what students in these lectures would have heard "was in fact totally out of context" (Aschheim 1992, 266). "But within the contours of the Third Reich and Nietzsche's authorized role," Aschheim contends, "the very use of Nietzschean categories and terminology formed part of an already-charged political context informing the audience's receptivity and predispositions" (Aschheim 1992, 267). Within that very context, though, taking into account the nature of the literature being published defining and promoting the Nazi Nietzsche, the critical force of Heidegger's Nietzsche lectures is also evident on the topic of race. Given what is generally being said, and said emphatically, about Nietzsche and race at this time, what Heidegger does *not* say is again significant and would have been perceived as such, as would his presentation of a view of Nietzsche incompatible with the Nazi racialist one.

Heidegger's notebooks largely confirm the content of his lectures during the Nazi period, as well as his claim that he did support the regime in the beginning but became critical of it after his resignation from the Rectorate. On the subject of race, the criticisms in the notebooks are much the same as in his lectures, but also as in the lectures, there is some evolution in his approach to prevailing Nazi ideas, from an attempt at revision to disillusioned rejection. Soon after his resignation from the Rectorate, Heidegger complains about the "bleak biologism" of "vulgar National Socialism," which supposes that "culture" simply grows like a plant from the "*Volk*" (GA 94, 142), as if this could happen without decision and knowledge (GA 94, 144). A few years later, he will reach the conclusion that this kind of "cultural politics" (*Kulturpolitik*) reduces humanity to a "rational animal," a conception involving the concepts of "race" and "reason" (GA 94, 370). Notebook entries from the later 1930s onwards criticize this conception in various ways, and one can see in them the development of Heidegger's critique of the modern view of humanity and being, as expressed in his public works. Race is an anthropological concept, and "anthropology," Heidegger suggests, is "the glorification and solidification of the human as *subject* – of the something present-at-hand which is the relational centre for everything present-at-hand" (GA 94, 491–92). This "subject character" of humanity is hardened by the preeminence of the "biological" interpretation of the essence of the *Volk* (GA 94, 521). The "unconditional subjectivism of the racial people (*Rassevolk*) and racial struggle (*Rassenkampf*)" is nothing creative but only a consequence of humanity's increasingly establishing itself as present-at-hand (GA 95, 41). Such movements reflect the "anthropological humanization of humanity" (*Vermenschung des Menschen*) (GA 95, 211); that is, the "humanization of humanity into animality" (GA 95, 422).

Attempts at racial engineering are part of this trend, where "humanity sets itself as an animal (race – blood) as its own goal and takes the planning of its history into its will" (GA 95, 361). The glorification of "blood" is only a foreground and pretext for "the unconditioned rule of such machination (*Mach-schaft*)" (GA 95, 381). The supposed "scientific" foundations for the "ethnic-political worldview" (*völkisch-politischen Weltanschauung*) are actually grounded metaphysically in the interpretation of what-is as "life" and of humanity as the "predatory animal" (*Raubtier*) (GA 95, 429), or more precisely as "the producing predator," Nietzsche's "super-man" (*Über-mensch*) being the pattern for the not yet fully established *animal* "man" (GA 95, 437). Thus, "all racial thinking is modern," being based on the modern conception of humanity as subject (GA 96, 46), and is "a *consequence* of the power of machination, which must force down every region of what-is into planning calculation" (GA 96, 56). Nietzsche's thought anticipated this wasteland, whose devastation is brought about by the unconditionality of machination, and finds its "success" in the exclusive subject-character of the animal, "man," as predator (GA 96, 14).

This understanding of Nietzsche, according to which he is the forerunner of the modern conception of humanity as a predatory producing and calculating animal, is one Heidegger arrives at gradually after the Rectorate year. Initially, he criticizes only what he regards as misappropriations of Nietzsche's thought, maintaining that Nietzsche is actually far from biologism, even though his manner of expression suggests otherwise (GA 94, 423). Heidegger's earlier remarks on race in the notebooks are also revisionary rather than outrightly critical:

> The many who now talk "about" race and rootedness (*Bodenständigkeit*), and mock themselves in every word, every action and omission, and prove that they not only "have" none of this, let alone that they *are* fundamentally classy (*rassig*) and rooted. (GA 94, 173)

> Race – that which is *one* necessary and indirectly expressed condition for historical Dasein (thrownness), is not only falsely made into the single and sufficient condition – but at the same time becomes that *about which* is spoken. The "intellectualism" of this approach, the incapacity to discriminate between racial breeding (*Erziehung*) and theorizing about race. *One* condition is elevated to the unconditional. (GA 94, 189)

It is difficult to render in English the precise sense of the German terms *rassig* and *Erziehung* in these remarks. The language of class – of behaving in a way that is "classy" or "well-bred" – probably captures the meaning best. Heidegger's point is that being classy, spirited, firmly rooted in the soil, well-bred are necessary conditions for genuinely being a people, and in this sense "race" is a necessary condition for *Volk*. But it is not sufficient for being a people, and also should not be interpreted biologically (GA 94, 351). For Heidegger, "race" is also historical, and "breeding," in relation to Dasein, means proper education or upbringing (the more common meaning of *Erziehung*).

Thus, Heidegger's critique of biologism does not entail an unambiguous rejection of the notion of race. Nor does it seem to have ruled out the belief that Jews could not quite become full members of the German nation. It also did not prevent Heidegger from holding appalling anti-Semitic views, evident in the notebooks (and elsewhere) in such remarks as: "the Jews, *with their pronounced talent for calculation*, 'live' already for the longest time according to the principle of race, which is why they also defend themselves the most strongly against its unlimited application" (GA 96, 56). Heidegger even occasionally granted credence to the possible existence of a global Jewish conspiracy.[4] And there is the plain fact that for a time he supported an openly racist regime, even if he did not offer public support for its specifically racist policies. Peter Trawny therefore suggests that Heidegger's thought exhibits what could be described as "ontohistorical anti-Semitism" (Trawny 2014, 11). This is an anti-Semitism rejecting race as a biological category but nonetheless viewing the Jews as a rootless, cosmopolitan, calculating type that furthers modern uprooting simply in being what it is, and that might even be doing so deliberately through international cooperation (Trawny 2014, 33, 45–46, 49). In that case, was Heidegger guilty of "cultural" anti-Semitism, as some have argued (e.g. Young 1997, 37–38, 42)? Is "culture" the best lens for understanding the ambiguities about race in his thought? If so, though, why does he emphasize *Bodenständigkeit*, rootedness or indigeneity, in a way that seems connected with lineage? What is the connection here between "race" and "culture"?

Race and Culture

In *Heidegger and Modernity*, Luc Ferry and Alain Renaut pose the following questions about Heidegger's support of Nazism:

[4] GA 96, 243, 262. Although Heidegger's remarks about *Weltjudentum* have come as a shock to many, the notebooks are not the only place where Heidegger expresses such views. Karl Jaspers reports in his autobiography that he had spoken to Heidegger "about the Jewish question, about the evil nonsense of the elders of Zion," and Heidegger had responded: "But there is a dangerous international organization of Jews." See Trawny 2014, 45–46.

Is it really credible that a sensible and responsible person who joined the National Socialist Party in 1933 could do so without at least "concealing" the anti-Semitic "component" and by being so naïve or blind as to imagine it "possible to separate the racism from the movement"? Who – above all, what intellectual who is in principle an attentive analyst of ideas and texts – could imagine that racism in the Germany of 1933 was merely one aspect of Nazism, one not consubstantially bound up with it and its constitutive principles? Rather than dreaming up an unlikely compromise, isn't it more plausible to suppose that Heidegger knew what he had to about Nazism and hence could recognize a *certain* anti-Semitism in himself? Certainly he never subscribed to a biological basis for it (nor to the exterminative fate), but in some of its fantasies, anti-Semitism readily linked up with the idea that a lack of rootedness, in whatever sense one understands rootedness, was not exactly a sign of authenticity. (Ferry and Renaut 1990, 24–25)

Nazi anti-Semitism did indeed frequently link Jews with a lack of rootedness. Härtle finds in Nietzsche a seed of the hypothesis that "the Jews are neither a *Volk* nor a race, but the human anti-race, the parasites of the human species" (Härtle 1937, 47). Alfred Rosenberg, in *The Myth of the Twentieth Century* (1930), also refers to the Jews as a parasitic anti-race (Rosenberg 1930, 437), seeing in Judaism a variety of "raceless universalism" (Rosenberg 1930, 39), which he in turn associates with Bolshevism, communism, Marxism, democracy, liberalism, and international finance. For Rosenberg, these are all instances of the same degenerate way of thinking, based on an idea of man that is simultaneously individualistic and universalistic. Supposedly, according to this idea, the species is composed of atomic individuals who are equal and alike, and who form no significant community except that of humanity itself. Within Rosenberg's anti-Semitism, then, the Jews are identified as a *Volk* by the very fact that they lack the features identifying a *Volk*, so that they are a sort of race/*Volk* that is not one.

Judging by his remarks in the notebooks, Heidegger shared this view that Jewish identity involves, as one of its features, a lack of rootedness, due to the fact that Jews in the diaspora do not clearly belong to and identify themselves with a single nation and locale. He also seems to think that this lack of simple belonging to one nation inclines Jews toward thinking of man as "man," toward universalism and cosmopolitism, and the politics allegedly associated with these, liberalism and Bolshevism, about which Heidegger frequently makes negative remarks. All of these are for Heidegger expressions of modern Western metaphysics. They rest on a conception of humanity as composed of atomic individuals interchangeable in time and space, whose competitions and solidarities are shaped exclusively by economic concerns. "Semitic nomads," in Heidegger's mind, will incline toward precisely this metaphysics because of their historical uprootedness from a homeland, an idea meshing neatly with typical European anti-Semitic prejudices.

Presumably, Heidegger only believed that these features of the Jewish spirit were rooted in history rather than biology. The biographical evidence concerning Heidegger's personal attitudes and behavior toward Jewish colleagues and students is mixed, but contains enough to render plausible Ferry and Renaut's suggestion that Heidegger recognized in himself "a certain anti-Semitism."[5] Anyway, Heidegger freely admits anti-Semitism "with regard to university matters" in a letter to Hannah Arendt, while adding that "this has nothing to do with personal relations to Jews (for example Husserl, Misch, Cassirer, and others," and that "most of all, this cannot affect the relation with you."[6] One might conclude, then, that there was a self-conscious nonbiological parallel in Heidegger's thought to the biologically based anti-Semitism of Nazi ideology. Following Trawny's suggestion that this is an "ontohistorical anti-Semitism," I want now to examine other elements, pertinent to the issue of race, within the expressed ideology of National Socialism that would have attracted Heidegger's sympathy because he himself held similar views, but ones grounded in "history" rather than biology.

First and foremost, as demonstrated in the previous chapter, Heidegger was attracted to ideas of the *Volk* as a cohesive unit, formed of bonds transcending economic interests, whether of individuals or classes. "There is only *one single* German 'estate' (*Lebensstand*)," he says in a speech on "Labor Service" delivered in 1934 (NH 181). Individuals are part of this estate insofar as they are part of the *Volk*, but to become a proper member of the Volk, one needs to know "how the *Volk* is structured and renews itself in this structure" (NH 199). Heidegger drops such specifically Nazi vocabulary as *Volksgemeinschaft* and *Volksgenosse* after his resignation as Rector, but he remains committed to the notion of the organized unity of the *Volk* as something desirable. In the *Logic* lectures, to the question of who "we" are, he answers, "We stand within the being of the *Volk*; we are ourselves the *Volk*" (L 57), where "the *Volk* is created by history" (L 85). He still supports a national brand of socialism, moreover, where all work together toward a common goal but the aim is not "an empty leveling." It involves, rather, "concern for the measure and essential structure of our historical being" and therefore wants "ranking according to calling and work" (L 165).

Although Ernst Krieck attacked Heidegger's thought as incompatible with National Socialism,[7] Heidegger could have agreed with the view, expressed in an article in the journal *Volk im Werden*, which Krieck edited, that "the liberal

[5] On this point, see Safranski 1998, 248–63: "Is Heidegger Anti-Semitic?"

[6] Cited by Ingo Farin in Farin 2016, 307.

[7] In a notebook entry, Heidegger remarks that he has been asked why he does not respond to Krieck, and says the answer is that "in a battle I only go against opponents, not loudmouths for mediocrity" (GA 94, 179).

theory of an industrial society does not recognize the *Volk*, but knows only the free being next to one another of producers, that is, capitalists, the owner of property and the worker" (Pfenning 1940, 28). He could have agreed, too, with Rosenberg that "this atomistic world-view was and is the precondition for the political doctrine of democracy" (Rosenberg 1930, 190). And against Marxism, or any brand of *international* socialism, Heidegger affirmed the belonging of the worker to a national identity in which he would play a central and defining role, and within which he would not be divided from or against other classes, a recurring theme within Nazi speeches and writings. In general, Heidegger's ideal *Volk* always possesses a single character and a single destiny; that is what makes it a *Volk*. *Being and Time* had already stressed that the historicality of Dasein is fundamentally bound up with the destiny of a *Volk* (BT 384), so Krieck is quite wrong to claim, in "Germanischer Mythos und Heideggersche Philosophie" (1934), that the concepts of *Volk* and destiny do not exist within Heidegger's philosophy (Krieck 1934a, 248–49). No one who had read the relevant sections of *Being and Time* could have believed this. In fact, Heidegger could in any period of his thought have supported Krieck's statement that "action, way of life, world-view, and poetry belong inextricably together and bring to expression the line of destiny of a *Volk*" (Krieck 1934b, 291), though he would have wanted to subject these ideas to a deeper scrutiny.

What Heidegger could not have supported was Krieck's view that the constant and basic character of any *Volk* is granted by race, as a biological category (Krieck 1934b, 289). For Heidegger, it is granted instead by history, to which place and landscape are intimately connected, as he suggests in the Hölderlin lectures. Heidegger would therefore also have been attracted to the Nazi emphasis on the link between national identity, particularly German identity, and landscape. He would, for instance, have been sympathetic to the notion that "landscape is the native ground from which each *Volk* takes its origin, as stated in another article in *Volk im Werden*, entitled "Landscape and National Community" (*Landschaft und Volksgemeinschaft*) (Sprengen 1934, 434). Initially, Heidegger likely saw such notions as naïve expressions of something that in a more sophisticated version was true, but he became increasingly exasperated with the reductive frameworks within which they were developed and debated. Within Nazi racist ideology, for example, reconciling a strictly biologistic understanding of the character of a people with this emphasis on landscape poses something a problem. How can one maintain, on the one hand, that race determines character in such a way that centuries of living in a certain milieu cannot change the cultural identity of an individual, while maintaining at the same time that there is a deep connection between relation to a particular landscape and that identity? An article in the Nazi daily, *Völkischer Beobachter*, called "Wirkt die Landschaft auf die Rasse ein?" ("Does Landscape Influence Race?"), offers an ingeniously absurd solution, suggesting that a race's "original landscape" (*Urlandschaft*) leaves irremediable biological traces in its "idioplasm," which is passed on from one generation to the next (Banse 1934). This is precisely the sort of foolish biologism, oblivious to concerns about the different modes of analysis proper to different regions of being, that elicits Heidegger's frustration and contempt, as his notebook entries reveal.

Yet, through his analysis of historicity, Heidegger produces at the same time an account of how the essential unity of a people is both present and achieved. The account includes an emphasis on decision and resolve in bringing about the unity of a people and in bringing that people into its destiny. This is *Heidegger's* understanding of being in the process of becoming a people – *Volk im Werden* – another frequently repeated theme in Nazi writings, which often appealed to the same German Romantic tradition by which Heidegger was influenced. Another 1934 article in the *Völkischer Beobachter* remarks: "When Novalis pronounces: 'The *Volk* is an idea – we must become a *Volk*,' he says a hundred years earlier that which today belongs to the firm content of our knowledge and will" (Hösel 1934). An article in *Volk im Werden* states: "In this sense the words of Novalis can still engage us today: 'We should become a *Volk*,' or, as Schlegel expressed it: 'Being German lies not behind, but before us'" (Eckhard 1941, 107). Heidegger is himself emphatic that the essence of a people, as of an individual, lies in a future that it must envision and struggle to achieve, but that is precisely why he thinks deterministic modes of causal explanation, whether mechanistic or biological, have no place here.

Eventually, Heidegger comes to the conclusion that the unity of the *Volk* he thought of as an ideal was the antithesis of the kind of unity being promoted so enthusiastically in his own nation:

> The most dangerous forms are those whereby a worldless "I" apparently gives itself up and submits to another which is "greater" than itself and to which it is assigned as a part or a member. The dissolution of the "I" in the "life" of the *Volk* – here an overcoming of the "I" is initiated without its first condition: namely, a reflection on being-a-self and its essence. (CP 254/GA 65, 321)

"The most dangerous" forms of nationhood are ones where the *Volk* is nothing more than a greater assertion of the "I"-subject, a calculating animal on a grand scale. But Heidegger retains a version of his belief in the unity and singular identity of a *Volk* whose selfhood would be conceived in a different manner.

His views on the specific character of the German people in relation to "becoming" also fit with commonly asserted Nazi ideas. In the 1934–35 Hölderlin lectures, he connects the character of German thought, as manifest in Hölderlin, Nietzsche, and Meister Eckhart, with Heraclitus, claiming that the latter stands for "the original power of occidental-Germanic historical existence, in its first confrontation with the Asiatic one" (H 133–34). Hölderlin is supposed to have overcome the Asiatic conception of fate, as the ancient Greeks first did in their development as a people (H 173). These statements echo ideas frequently expressed in Nazi discourses: the belief in a special link between Germany and Greece, the praise of Heraclitus against Parmenides as a thinker of becoming rather than being, and above all the description of the dynamic character of the German *Volk*: "The German is not, he *becomes*, he develops," says a 1934 article in the *Völkischer Beobachter*, citing Nietzsche, and "development is therefore the authentic German discovery and contribution within the great realm of philosophical formulations" (Rathje 1934). Rosenberg also claimed that "this continual 'becoming' (*werdende*) struggle for 'being' (*Sein*) is the Germanic religion, which is present even in those forms of mysticism that are most detached from the world" (Rosenberg 1930, 131).

We have seen that for Heidegger the identity of a people is bound up with the historical mission it is purportedly called upon to play in virtue of its character and situation. Although he becomes increasingly skeptical about the possibility of this being accomplished at the level of politics, at the time he supported Nazism he firmly believed that the state was the proper expression and vehicle of the singular historical character and mission of the *Volk*. Heidegger had developed this idea in *Nature, History, State*, and still maintains it at the time of the lectures on logic:

> The 'state,' not as an abstraction and not as derived from an invented right related to a timeless human nature, but the state as the essential law of historical being through whose structure the *Volk* first secures its historical continuity, and that means the preservation of its mission and the struggle to accomplish its task. The state is the historical being of the *Volk*. (L 165)

Like other National Socialists, then, Heidegger opposes the notion of the state as founded upon any conception of universal human rights in that, as another article in the *Völkischer Beobachter* puts it, "for National Socialism the state is not a mere external form, but simultaneously the expression of the essence and will of the *Volk*" ("Nationalsozialismus als Grundlage des neuen Deutschen Rechts," 1934). Heidegger agrees, and this idea of the state entails that it should be a monocultural one, whose ethics are tailored to suit the character of its cultural population.

Significantly, Heidegger maintains in the *Logic* lectures that "there is no absolute truth," since "we are for now only human beings and not gods," while insisting that "a truth is no less a truth just because it cannot be held by everyone" (L 79). He does not explicitly say here that ethical principles are expressions of a particular *Volk* rather than absolute truths binding upon all people. His statements nonetheless suggest this idea, since they are made against the backdrop of a political context in which Nazi spokesmen were in fact deriding claims to absoluteness with the intention of promoting the alternative view that moral principles are specific and variable, rooted in the characters of different peoples rather than in the nature of a universal humanity.

Contemporary interpretations of Nietzsche often focused on precisely this point. Härtle, for example, uses Nietzsche in support of the claim that "there is no meta-ethic ... morals spring from the conditions of life and the will to growth of estates, peoples, races" (Härtle 1937, 10). Kurt Kaßler, in *Nietzsche und das Recht*, claims that the Nietzschean point of departure maintains that "right is *immanent*, not transcendent" (Kaßler 1941, 32). Kaßler's claim that this right is "anthropocentric and biological" (Kaßler 1941, 32) would have been anathema to Heidegger, but in his first set of lectures on Nietzsche, Heidegger does point out that Nietzsche understands the "should" as immanent: "If what-is is conceived as will to power, then there is no need for a should which would first have to be imposed upon what-is, so that what-is could be measured against it. If life itself is will to power, then it is itself the foundation, the principle of any value-positing" (NI 38). Heidegger is explicating Nietzsche here, not agreeing with him, and by the time these lectures were delivered (1936–37), he has come to see Nietzsche as a representative of the modern constellation of ideas that he criticizes, which certainly includes the idea of value. But Heidegger was no friend to ideas of universal or transcendent "values," either, and given his own analyses of situatedness and destiny, he might have sympathized with some version of the notion that the ethics of a people is immanently rooted in its historical and cultural character.

Other elements in Heidegger's analysis of Dasein in *Being and Time* ought to have added the moral constraint that every person is to be treated as an end in itself, as I argued in Chapter 2. The following remarks in a notebook entry likely written around 1940 confirm that Heidegger did not abandon belief in the inestimable importance of the individual, which had been implicit in *Being and Time*:

> Whether the Bolshevists kill one person without any administration of justice or investigation, merely because he holds another conviction, or kill hundreds of thousands, counts for the *same*. Our age, being accustomed to the quantitative, thinks that here a hundred thousand are "more" than one, while in fact an individual is already the maximum, which cannot be captured by any number. In order not to confuse our German attitude, we should not, also not here, degenerate into an intoxication with numbers. (GA 96, 236)

I do not know whether, in his earlier support for Hitler, Heidegger thought the ideology he was supporting was compatible with this conviction about the "maximal" status of the individual; or whether he thought that status could be overridden by a "special" destiny, in agreement with Hegel's contention that the actions of "world-historical" individuals cannot be judged by ordinary moral norms (see Chapter 1); or whether he was just so unreflectively enthused by the historical moment that he did not ask himself such sober questions. Whatever was the case on this point, he did incline to the idea that different peoples have different ethical characters, a relativistic or pluralistic view that can in principle, however, be accompanied by a measure of universalism.[8]

Heidegger's sense of the appropriate relations between different peoples or nations also corresponds to some Nazi pronouncements – hypocritical and mendacious, to be sure – on this subject. I demonstrated in the last chapter that Heidegger's conception of the singular character and destiny of each people was accompanied by the idea that peoples should be independent of one another and should confront one another from this independent position. Such a relation between peoples is supposed to respect the different identity of each one, while promoting the fulfillment of its unique destiny, and this ideal is reflected in Heidegger's speech supporting Germany's withdrawal from the League of Nations (NH 144–46). Accordingly, in the second of his lecture courses on Nietzsche, Heidegger suggests that "the future mission of Europe," in which he believes Germany has a special role to play, "can only find its answer through the exemplary and decisive historical shaping of individual peoples in competition with each other" (GA 44 107).

Although questionable in itself, this notion of a creative and respectful competition between peoples who are different but not unequal may seem far removed from the reality of Nazism. But it is not so far removed from the claims Nazi officials and supporters sometimes made, at least in the earlier years of the regime. For instance, in an October 1933 article in *Wille und Macht*, Friedrich Lange writes,

> Hitler-Germany, which places the *Volk* at the centre of thinking, feeling and acting, also respects the character of other peoples. "In that we adhere to our own character with unlimited love and faithfulness," explains the *Führer* in his well-known speech of May 17, 1933, "we also, on the basis of the same consideration, respect the national rights of other peoples, and wish from the depths of our hearts to live with them in peace and friendship." (Lange 1933, 11).

On February 17, 1934, an article in *Völkischer Beobachter* proclaimed that "the German racial laws do not wish to pass any judgement on the worth and value of other peoples and races," and that Hitler himself says this in *Mein Kampf* ("Der Sinn der Rassegesetzgebung des Dritten Reiches," 1934). A few days later, another article supported Nazi policy toward the Jews by stating, "it is self-evident that the Jewish race is not of lesser value (*minderwertiger*) than many other races … but one thing is clear, that it

[8] "Relativism" and "universalism" admit of degrees and combinations, and are not simply and starkly opposed to one another. I argue in Sikka 2011 that Herder's position blends the two; cf. Parekh 2006; Wong 2006.

possesses a different value (*anderswertig ist*) and ... is therefore completely unsuitable for a cultural cross-breeding with the German people" (Fischer 1934). And although Ernst Kriek dismissed Heidegger's thought, his own stated vision for Europe is in 1935 much like Heidegger's one year earlier. "The new Germany," he writes, "is built upon *Volksgemeinschaft*, Europe will be built upon the *Gemeinschaft* of individual European peoples (*Volksindividualitäten*)" (Krieck 1935, 330).

In sum, Ferry and Renaut are right to suggest that Heidegger "knew what he had to about Nazism" when he lent his support to the party in 1933. While he rejected biologically based conceptions of race, he held a strong view of the unity and identity of every particular *Volk* that fit well with some Nazi racial ideas. This view included the idea that each people has a single, unique character and destiny and a set of corresponding obligations. At one time, he also believed that the nature of a people, with its will to achieve its proper historical mission, was ideally expressed in the form of the state (and perhaps he never gave up on this idea but only on the Nazis as embodying it). These essentialistic beliefs do form a kind of "cultural" parallel to the equally essentialistic beliefs that underlay biologically based Nazi race ideology. Heidegger combines these beliefs with the idea that different nations can and should respect one another in their unique identities, where an important part of that respect consists in the possibility of creative confrontation. His understanding of the nature and mission of the German people, however, does suggest that it has a particularly important role to play in shaping the future of Europe. In addition, his views about *völkisch* identity position the Jews as not belonging fully to the German *Volk* and suggest that they may not be able to be full members of any Eruopean *Volk*. In the last chapter, I focused on the philosophical background of Heidegger's idea of *Volk*; in this chapter I have tried to show why he would have thought he saw this idea reflected in contemporary Nazi discourses.

Should we conclude from these observations that Heidegger is a "cultural" racist? That he personally entertained negative stereotypes about Jews, and about England and America, is attested by his notebook entries, and there is no denying the crudeness of these views. In addition, he at times affirmed views suggesting the cultural inferiority of African peoples, and there is some cultural bigotry in his privileging of the German language and "mission" over that of every other Western nation. Heidegger does not say the German language is superior to all other European languages in every respect, and his view of Germany's mission is combined with the idea that every *Volk* has a unique destiny. Not every positive appraisal of some element in one's own culture amounts to cultural bigotry, moreover, nor does every criticism of an element in another culture. Yet it is starkly apparent that Heidegger does not form his impressions of the character of other European nations through anything like the favorable gaze he directs toward his own.

What, though, of his analyses of the identities of peoples in general? Do they also fundamentally involve bigotry or cultural racism? Essentialism about cultural groups does not by itself entail racism, since it need not be accompanied by belief in the superiority of one group over another. It is problematic for other reasons, assuming a higher degree of internal homogeneity than actually exists, and misrepresenting the nature of cross-cultural interaction by interpreting it as an exchange between radically distinct and independent entities. Cultural essentialism is often attacked for these flaws, since policies adopting or promoting this mistaken view of peoples and their appropriate interaction will be oppressive whether or not they involve racism. A liberal analysis will naturally want to add the moral necessity of respecting universal basic rights and to insist on the dangers of ignoring individual rights in the name of any group-identity, a danger made immeasurably greater by the presence of a strongly authoritarian state with the power to enforce that identity. I pointed out in the last chapter that it is not only political theories endorsing ethnic or monocultural nationalism that raise such worries but multicultural ones as well, especially in light of the problem of cultural essentialism.

I have also argued, however, that these criticisms can be accepted while acknowledging that *Volk* nonetheless names something real, that cultural identity is not purely a fiction, and that political theory and practice need to recognize this genre of identity. In *Heidegger's Crisis: Philosophy and Politics in Nazi Germany*, Hans Sluga claims that German philosophers who raised questions about German identity in the 1920s and 1930s "failed to consider the possibility that nations are fortuitous and their boundaries shift, that they are discursive constructs with no reality outside the speech that defines them" (Sluga 1993, 84). If by "nation" Sluga means not only a state but also a *Volk*, however, this complaint ignores the possibility that a people can have a genuinely distinct identity without it being the case that one could specify that identity clearly through some list of necessary and sufficient conditions. There are hardly any types of things that meet such stringent criteria, which are clearly not suitable for all kinds of identification and sorting. Fuzzy borders are still borders, and one should not posit false alternatives here. It is perfectly possible to affirm the reality of cultural identity and still reject the "binary logic" whereby one simply "is a member of a particular nation or not," and to agree that "the social reality that such political distinctions are meant to regulate consists of an infinitely complex web of relations with all kinds of gradations and variable degrees of closeness and distance" (Sluga 1993, 123).

From my argument, it would seem, then, that Heidegger embraces a strong view of cultural identity, where that identity belongs to the realm of "history" and has nothing to do with biological descent. However, this does not fully account for the idea that Jews are not quite "rooted" in the German *Volk*, or any *Volk*. If, as Heidegger thinks, identity is determined by history rather than descent, why *would* a German Jew have a different manner of thinking than any other German? And should Heidegger's views not entail that within a couple of generations any people from anywhere could become members of any given *Volk*? Yet such a supposition does not seen consonant with Heidegger's descriptions of *völkish* identity, with its emphasis on *Bodenständigkeit*. In the final part of this chapter, I ask whether there might not be a "biological" component in Heidegger's view of *Volk*, after all.

Roots

In March of 1934, Heidegger gave a broadcast lecture, "Creative Landscape: Why Do We Stay in the Provinces?" in which he explained his refusal of a second offer from Berlin University. The lecture celebrates the simple existence of Black Forest farmers, and it does so in a highly romanticizing language. In it, Heidegger says, "The inner belonging of my own work to the Black Forest and its people comes from a centuries-long and irreplaceable rootedness (*Bodenständigkeit*) in the Alemannian-Swabian soil" (NH 216–18). In one of his early notebook entries, dating from about 1931, Heidegger writes:

> Rooted (*Boden-ständig*) can mean, one who comes from the soil (*Boden*), who is nourished from and stands on the soil – this is the original sense – the one that often sweeps through me in body and mood – as if I were going over the field in a plow, over lonely field-paths between ripening corn, through the wind and clouds, sun and snow, which in their turning and waving held mother's blood and that of her ancestors ...
>
> The other rooted ones (*Boden-ständigen*) – those for whom these roots (*Wurzeln*) have died, but who nonetheless persist through returning to the soil (*Boden*) and valuing it. (GA 94, 38)

Remarks like these pose a problem for the claim that Heidegger's concept of *Volk* has nothing to do with biology in any sense. It has nothing to with *genetics*, as a field of inquiry within the modern discipline of biology, and its popular uses and abuses, but it does not exclude the idea of lineage, of biological descent from parents and ancestors. Within Heidegger's thought there is no sense in which the character of a people is transmitted by means that the discipline of biology could describe in terms appropriate to the region of reality it studies. And yet, when speaking of *Volk* and related matters, Heidegger always writes under the assumption that the members of the *Volk* possess a *Bodenständigkeit* acquired through their having dwelled in the same place over generations. He always assumes that the members of the *Volk* are *eingeboren*, native. Thus, although I have been speaking mainly of cultural identity, the identity of the *Volk* is for Heidegger also an ethnic identity. A *Volk* is constituted by history, but the possession of that history by its members is linked to descent, to hundreds of years of *Bodenständigkeit* in a particular place.[9]

In *Nature, History, State*, Heidegger writes that, by *Volk*, "we mean something even more strongly binding than race and a community of the same stock: namely, the nation, and that means a kind of being that has grown under a common fate and taken distinctive shape within a *single* state" (NHS 43). This statement suggests that a *Volk* is more than race, but it does not deny that it is, to begin with, "a community of the same stock." In the *Logic* lectures, when considering the important role of decision in forming the "we" of the *Volk*, Heidegger adds:

> Yet it is not up to us whether we belong to a *Volk* or not. For that has already been decided, independently of our will, on the basis of our descent (*Abstammung*), which we did not ourselves choose. One can perhaps will citizenship but never membership in a *Volk*. (L 60)

The point seems to be that we can resolve upon the essence, the highest potential, of the *Volk* to which we belong and can win that essence, thereby becoming the genuine "self" of that *Volk*, just as Dasein in *Being and Time* can choose itself authentically or lose itself in the "they." But membership in the *Volk* whose essence can be won or lost is not itself a product of decision. In the language of *Being and Time*, it is part of the facticity of Dasein, a condition into which it is thrown. "Race," therefore, defined in terms of lineage, is also a component of "thrownness" (cf. Trawny 39). This aspect of "cultural" identity is given, and Heidegger always supposes it is given by descent. The supposition is usually not explicit – the above-cited remark from *Logic* is a rare instance – but a German resident who did not identify herself with a long line of German descent is unlikely to be comfortable with the language of *Erde* and *Heimat* and *Vaterland* in the Hölderlin lectures. And in the place of which Heidegger writes in "The Pathway" – where, he says, "more frequently through the years, the oak by the wayside carries me off to memories of childhood games and early choices," where at times "the east wind is blowing up a storm where mother's home village lies," where "behind the castle, rises the tower of St. Martin's Church" (Heidegger 1981b, 69–71) – in this place, there is not much room for a latecomer, an immigrant. The language in which the village is described does not welcome the presence of anyone who could not unambiguously locate herself in that place, in virtue of a past extending well beyond her arrival here.

[9] In *Heidegger's Roots*, Bambach discusses at length Heidegger's emphasis on *Bodenständigkeit*, relating it to myths of autocthony, especially as these intersected with Heidegger's sense of an intimate connection to the Greeks (Bambach 2003, 46–50, 180–246). Bambach does not, however, provide any analysis of how this notion fits with Heidegger's understanding of the structures of being human, most centrally, historicity.

The question then is, how can Heidegger's thoroughgoing anti-biologism be reconciled with his assumption that the members of a *Volk* are defined by descent, which is a given aspect of who they are? Heidegger does not confront this question directly, but the most plausible hypothesis consistent with his views is that descent becomes a determining factor through the way "biology" enters history; that is, through the inevitable role it plays in *self*-identification. Let me rehearse the problem a little further to show why this solution is needed. To Heidegger it seems obvious that we do not choose the *Volk* to which we belong, even though we may be able to choose our citizenship in a nation. Heidegger did not choose to be born where he was, to have the mother he had, to be formed through the language of Meister Eckhart and Angelus Silesius, Hölderlin and Rilke. This is part of his "past," the history into which he was thrown, and it would remain so if he had emigrated, as so many German intellectuals did during the Nazi period. He could be read as meaning simply that people are born into one culture or another, and that is just a fact. The question, though, is why should membership in a cultural identity, rather than only citizenship in a nation, not be open to anyone who was either born in that same place, or who chose to move there and did in the end assimilate herself to its traditions? If culture is the determining factor, why does Heidegger take it for granted that descent is essential to membership in a *Volk*, an idea that helps make sense of his assertions, in the early notebooks, that "race" is a necessary but not sufficient condition of being a *Volk*?

The answer, I am suggesting, lies in the conditions for the act of self-identification, given the framework of Heidegger's analysis. Heidegger may have supposed that anyone who is not located within a particular line of descent will not identify himself completely with the history of the *Volk* whose intergenerational continuity is bound up with certain lines of descent. This claim could justify the belief (assuming Heidegger did hold this belief) that German Jews are never full members of the German *Volk* and that they think somewhat differently than those who are, without attributing this difference to any straightforwardly biological factor. The difference would occur because, due to their awareness of their own descent, Jews locate themselves within the history of a different community, whose origins lie elsewhere and which has been in a condition of wandering for millennia. They then would never identify fully with the history of those who do identify themselves unambiguously with a certain place in Europe and the "destiny" unfolding there.

But if this is Heidegger's implicit supposition (and I admit I am here articulating a point that remains unthought by Heidegger himself), he is in a way right, in spite of being very wrong in many of the social and political implications he draws from this view. For some purposes, people *do* identify themselves with a history tied to their descent, to their family and ancestors. It is even true that, regardless of language, nation, or culture, a Jew may still remain a Jew. Heidegger may have been anti-Semitic but this claim is not itself so. Levinas (who was not an anti-Semite) indicates the possibility of a Jew remaining a Jew by suggesting, with Heidegger and Nazi *völkisch* ideology very much in mind, that the identity of being Jewish is linked to the consciousness of the face beyond any homeland, the face that is "absolute" and "without any cultural ornament" (Levinas 1987, 95–96).[10] For Levinas, this culturally non-specific face forbids all violence. Levinas seems to agree, then, that there is a universalizing tendency in the Jewish mind, linked to a lack of *völkisch* rootedness, an awareness of belonging to a people without a homeland, and it inclines Jews to maintain precisely the "error" Härtle sees Nietzsche as exposing – namely, "the equality of all that wears a human face" (Härtle 1937, 24).

It would also need to be recognized that this is not the *only* location for an individual who happens to be Jewish, that such an individual can also at the same time truly "be" German, for instance, situated within German history as his *own* history and identifying with the same traditions Heidegger saw as building the "we" of this *Volk*. I have already underlined the problem of essentialism in Heidegger's conception of *Volk*, and its inadequacy for analyzing the complexity of cultural identity. But I am arguing that there is nonetheless some truth in the idea that an individual identifies with a *Volk* in part through self-identification with a line of descent and that this idea is not by itself racist.[11] Nor is it *per se* necessarily politically noxious. It does not entail that states should be monoethnic, as it can just as readily serve to advance one dimension of the recognition of various identities required for harmonious and just relations within a multiethnic state. It might be countered that identifying people in terms of their ancestry in any way, or legitimating this kind of self-identification, is dangerous simply because it provides a framework for distinguishing between "races," a necessary condition for racism. However, respect for others requires recognizing the way they identify themselves rather than covertly attempting to absorb and assimilate. Refusing to admit the reality of any dimension of race cannot be the only way to defeat racism, as if it were impossible to respect others while acknowledging difference.

Another possible objection is that if the reality of race is established only by contingent psychological and social facts – self-identification by descent being among these – then the best strategy is to work to eliminate those facts rather than granting them some permanent or semi-permanent status. Self-identification by descent is a *stubborn* fact, though, common in determining

10 On the tension this sets up for Levinas' relation to Israel, see Fabenblatt 2016, 159–60.

11 This thesis helps to explain and analyze the phenomenon of cultural revivalism among individuals and communities who have "lost" their cultural roots and seek to "rediscover" them. See Sikka 2004.

our sense of who we are, and moral and political theories must take such stubborn facts about human psychology into account. If the stubbornness of this fact is invisible to many people, that is because those who locate themselves within the historical lines predominating in a given society have a tendency to fall into the illusion that they are not locating themselves anywhere, that race, culture, and ethnicity are not important features of their identities or therefore of anyone else's. But they fall into this illusion only because their own historical identity is reflected so broadly in the cultures and institutions of their society that it seems not to be there at all. As Linda Alcoff writes, "when your own particular and specific attributes are dominant *and* valorized, they can be taken for granted and ignored" (Alcoff 1995, 271). It is dislocation that makes a person aware of location. Individuals actually have no choice but to locate themselves somewhere in history, and if that is so, then self-identification by descent, within some though not all contexts, is inevitable. Consider the psychological unfeasibility, as well as undesirability, of an African American identifying herself entirely with the history of a majority European population, where that history includes slavery. To quote Alcoff again:

> Systems of oppression, segregated communities, and practices of discrimination create a collective experience and a shared history for a racialized grouping. It is that shared experience and history, more than any physiological or morphological features, that cements the community and creates connections with others along racial lines. And that history cannot be deconstructed by new scientific accounts that dispute the characterization of race as a natural kind. (Alcoff 1995, 272)

I would add that, given the "historicity of Dasen" – the fundamentally narrative character of being human – we naturally situate ourselves among stories extending beyond our birth and telling us who we are. In so doing, we cannot help but place ourselves within racially defined historical communities, even when the conditions that brought those communities into being have changed substantially. Furthermore, the existence of a few people, if there are some, who do not in any circumstances identify themselves in terms of descent, it does not disprove the generalization that most people do, and social ideals need to take account of this. The existence of a few people who do not have the usual needs and desires does not invalidate the generalizations about those needs and desires on which moral and political theories are based, nor does it suggest that the unusual psychology is the one that should form the foundation of moral and political reasoning.

I realize that considerations about racial identity arising in the context of anti-racist reflections may seem a long way from Heidegger, given that they represent the antithesis of the movement he supported. But the conception of historicity providing the framework for Heidegger's understanding of cultural and ethnic identity is useful for such considerations. Heidegger has a strong view of cultural identity being determined by history rather than nature, and is therefore not a biological racist, yet he does suppose that descent plays a role in determining membership in a *Volk.* And indeed it does, for not only is it true that we are born into a place and time, but descent intersects with history through forms of self-identification which are, for most people, inevitable. I stress that one cannot derive from these facts alone the conclusion that states should be monoethnic, or that there is no basis for universal rights, or that cultures and/or races are homogeneous units clearly distinguishable from one another. All of these claims require further premises that may not (and I believe do not) hold up under examination.

However, the claim that people do, as a matter of stubborn psychological fact, identify themselves in terms of descent explicates one dimension of the reality of race, linked to physical facts but not describable in physicalist terms. It also indicates one reason among several why, in practice, a clear line cannot always be drawn between "race" and "culture." In *Multicultural Citizenship*, Will Kymlicka uses the term "a culture" in a sense synonymous with "a people" and "a nation," providing for this form of group identity the following definition: "An intergenerational community, more or less institutionally complete, occupying a given territory or homeland, sharing a distinct language and history" (Kymlicka 1995, 18). A few pages later, he distinguishes cultural groups, thus defined, from "racial and descent groups" (Kymlicka 1995, 23). If people identify themselves partly on the basis of descent, though, and if this self-identification plays a role in their location of themselves within a certain intergenerational community and history, the distinction cannot be neatly drawn. With respect to the categories of "history" or "nature," it might be that this aspect of culture/race could be reabsorbed into the sphere of history since, although it is linked to biological facts, it fundamentally has to do with a human form of awareness and self-understanding. Perhaps, however, it would be better just to say that some phenomena resist being classified under one of these two domains.

Acknowledging these points, there remains the forensic issue of Heidegger's culpability for his racist views (and anti-Semitism *is* a form of racism), along with the serious question of how knowledge of a philosopher's having held such views should determine our attitude toward his writings. The problem here, though, is that Heidegger is not exactly alone, among the illustrious members of the Western philosophical canon, in having expressed racism of some variety toward some group of people. There is, for instance, the following footnote in Hume's essay, "Of National Characters" (1753):

> I am apt to suspect the negroes and in general all other species of men (for there are four or five different kinds) to be naturally inferior to the whites. There never was a civilized nation of any other complexion than white, nor even any individual eminent either in

action or speculation. No ingenious manufactures amongst them, no arts, no sciences. (Hume 1882, 253)[12]

Kant also maintained the superiority of the white race above all others, in addition to supposing that Christianity's supersession of Judaism constituted, for the latter, a good death (Larrimore 1999; Bernasconi 2001; Mack 2003, 23–41). Hegel echoes these ideas about the inferiority of Jews and Judaism (Mack 2003, 42–62). Additionally, his philosophy of history relegates India and China to lowly positions, excludes Africa altogether,[13] and represents native Americans as having "gradually vanished at the breath of European activity," apparently due to their natural inferiority rather than the terrible violence inflicted upon them (Hegel 1958, 98).[14] John Stuart Mill defended British colonial rule in India and elsewhere as a form of justified benevolent despotism, claiming "to suppose that the same international customs, and the same rules of international morality, can obtain between one civilized nation and another, and between civilized nations and barbarians, is a grave error" (Mill 1984, 118).

Consider also, in the twentieth century, Husserl's assertion of the superiority of European man "which all other human groups, too, feel with regard to us, something that apart from, all considerations of expediency, becomes a motivation for them – despite their determination to retain their spiritual autonomy – constantly to Europeanize themselves, whereas we, if we understand ourselves properly, will never, for example, Indianize ourselves" (Husserl 1965, 157). And then there is the strange case of Levinas, who complains of philosophy's neglect of the ethical moment and the imperative imposed by the face of the other, but denigrates African culture (while knowing next to nothing about it), speaks of the "yellow peril" of Asia, and proclaims: "I often say, though it's a dangerous thing to say publicly, that humanity consists of the Bible and Greeks. All the rest can be translated; all the rest – all the exotic – is dance" (Levinas 1991, 18; see Sikka 1999, McGettigan 2006, Ma 2008a). Apparently, "the generosity of Western thought" extends only so far (Bernasconi 1992).

Historically, such racist views have been connected with very grave moral wrongs. They have formed the basis of ideologies whose historical deployment has justified such horrors as the Atlantic slave trade and Leopold's Congo, the dispossession and slaughter of Native Americans, the subjugation of countless Africans and Asians under colonial rule, the Opium Wars in China – to name a few highlights from a history that provides far too many examples from which to choose. Somehow, though, the complicity of the prejudices of philosophers in these events does not generate quite the same level of scrutiny

[12] On the history of this footnote and its revisions, see Immerwahr 1992.

[13] See Bernasconi 1998.

[14] See Park 2013, 113–32.

as Heidegger's moral failure. Regarding the latter, Trawny writes: "It does not need to be said that the Shoah is of such significance that philosophy too cannot avoid it" (Trawny 2016, 169). Unfortunately, it *does* need to be said that this is also true of a number of other events within the history of Western racism, although philosophy has on the whole managed to avoid them rather well. But then, if we were to dismiss from the canon as entirely unworthy of attention all the eminent modern philosophers whose views reflected or helped to support Eurosupremacist racism, there might be little left.

7 The Status of Reason

"The Word of Nietzsche: God is Dead," one of numerous essays where Heidegger diagnoses the critical condition of humanity and being in the modern age, ends with the sentence: "Thinking begins only when we have come to know that reason, glorified for centuries, is the most stiff-necked adversary of thought" (QCT 112/GA 5, 267). This sentence expresses an attitude toward reason that many commentators have seen as a – perhaps *the* – crucial problem with Heidegger, both the man and his works. Richard Wolin places Heidegger among a coterie of dangerous irrationalists that includes Nietzsche and Foucault, alluding, in the title of one of his books, to *The Seduction of Unreason* (Wolin 2004). Elsewhere, discussing Karl Löwith's criticisms of the methodology and style of Heidegger's later thought in particular, he remarks:

> Heideggerian "thinking" intentionally flirts with a prophetic-oracular rhetorical mode – to wit, the oft-cited claim from the 1966 *Der Spiegel* interview that "only a god can save us" ... His later philosophy tends to provoke either fascination or repulsion; rarely does it elicit the type of sober and measured evaluation conducive to appraising its genuine intellectual worth. (Wolin 2001, 95).

Repulsion evidently characterizes Habermas's response to the methodology and style of Heidegger's later thought, which contrasts so sharply with his own commitment to a communicative rationality whose success depends upon giving mutually intelligible evidence and reasons. Heidegger's radical critique of modern reason, as Habermas complains in "The Undermining of Western Rationalism," renounces conceptual clarity and argumentation, devalues all scientific thinking and methodical research, and dismisses as inauthentic chatter the everyday practice of mutual understanding in favor of cryptic pronouncements about "being" whose "practical political side consists in the perlocutionary effect of a diffuse readiness to obey in relation to an auratic but indeterminate authority" (Habermas 1993b, 140). While the problem becomes especially acute in Heidegger's later writings, it stems, Habermas thinks, from "an apophantic concept of truth" already present in *Being and Time* (Habermas 1993b, 145). This concept, criticized by Ernst Tugendhat as actually passing over the problem of truth, "reserves the title of truth for the so-called truth-occurrence, which no longer has anything to do with a validity-claim transcending space and time" (Habermas 1993b, 154). Heidegger thereby reduces truth to historically conditioned meaningfulness, making it a function of "the luminous force of world-disclosing language," raised above any critical forum (Habermas 1993b, 154).

Elsewhere, Habermas argues that this kind of move effaces the distinction between philosophy and poetry,[1] leaving the thinker with no grounds for justification besides the mystical intuition of his own insight. "While mystical contemplation is speechless," however, "privileging a mode of intuition or recollection that repudiates the reasonableness of discursive thought, dialectical thought always criticizes the intellectual intuition, the intuitive access to the (supposedly) immediate" (Habermas 2002, 157). Habermas protests against the rise of such a radical critique of reason, "one which does not simply protest against the inflation of the understanding (*Verstand*) into instrumental reason, but which equates reason as a whole with repression – and then fatalistically or ecstatically seeks refuge in something wholly Other" (Habermas 1992, 8). In Heidegger's case, he claims, this wholesale abandonment of reason, "lacking the corrective of pragmatic rationalism," led to a "nurturing of anti-Christian and anti-Western effects" promoting "the psychosis of irrationalism," even if that is not what Heidegger wanted (Habermas 1993a, 196). It is this irrationalism, with its basis in a notion of truth as what is disclosed in an epoch, that led Heidegger to support Hitler, Habermas thinks, and to refuse to accept responsibility for his guilt afterwards (Habermas 1993b, 156–57).

It is not, moreover, only philosophers generally unsympathetic to Heidegger's philosophy who have been worried by the apparently uncommunicative character of his thinking. This was also a serious concern for Karl Jaspers, Heidegger's one-time friend and philosophical ally. The 1945 letter Jaspers wrote to Friedrich Oehlkers, a member of the de-Nazification commission investigating Heidegger's political activities during the Nazi period,[2] acknowledges the importance of Heidegger's philosophy but also states that his way of thinking is essentially "unfree, dictatorial, uncommunicative" (H:J 271). In his notes, Jaspers complains about the "morass-like nature" of the ground of Heidegger's thought beneath the "impurity" and "magic" in which it is clothed, describing Heidegger's philosophy as "prophetic" and "without responsibility."[3] In a 1952 letter to Heidegger himself, he responds with alarm

[1] In "Philosophy and Science as Literature?" Habermas remarks: "The later Heidegger still distinguishes between thinkers and poets. But he treats texts by Anaximander and Aristotle no differently than texts by Hölderlin and Trakl." He sees both the early and the later Heidegger as important to the genealogy of thought that ends in "the leveling of the distinction between the genres of philosophy and science on the one hand and that of literature on the other hand" (Habermas 1992, 206).

[2] The letter was written at the request of both Oehlkers and Heidegger himself, and the full German text is printed in *Martin Heidegger/Karl Jaspers: Briefwechsel, 1920–1963* (H:J 270–73).

[3] Notes 127 (1954/55) and 130 (1956/60), in Jaspers 1986, 503–5.

to Heidegger's talk of an "advent" hidden in the contemporary "homelessness" (*Heimatlosigkeit*),[4] expressing the worry that a philosophy containing such fantastic visions might, in its separation from reality, once again prepare for a victory of totalitarianism (H:J 215).

Heidegger does have a tendency toward oracular excess, and an insufficient critical distance from the illuminating quality of his own insights. He was also, to put it mildly, not terribly good at dialogue, meaning real exchanges with existing others rather than fictional conversations between invented personae. As witnessed by his exchange of letters with Jaspers, as well as his rewriting of the conversation with a Japanese scholar in "On the Way to Language," in actual dialogues, Heidegger finds it difficult to listen to what the other person is saying and to put himself in question when responding. Although he does engage in conversation, he seems able to speak at length only to those who are willing to follow him along the winding ways of his own paths of thinking and quickly parts company, in one fashion or another, with those who want to go in another direction.

Leonard Ehrlich suggests that this tendency results in "a vision without exposure to those who are not like-minded" (Ehrlich 1994, 39). That is in my view an overstatement, but it is true that in practice Heidegger does not display the commitment to intersubjective communication that both Habermas and Jaspers, thinkers who are very different in other respects, see as essential to the common pursuit of truth and to ensuring the preservation of human liberty against the temptations of dictatorship. There does seem to be a totalizing tendency in the movement of Heidegger's thought, in spite of his emphasis on finitude. It is rooted perhaps in an authoritarian or self-enclosed streak in his personal character, which Jaspers points to when he accuses Heidegger of the linked vices of being dictatorial and uncommunicative. Although they agreed on many philosophical points, Jaspers saw Heidegger's postwar descriptions of what is wrong with the times as leaning away from comprehensible analyses of concrete realities toward obscure prophecies about arrivals and destinies, eschewing any attempt to justify these claims according to common measures of evidence.

In this final chapter, I revisit Heidegger's critique of reason in light of these problems, assessing its range and justice, while asking whether it really does eschew all argumentation and evidence, and reduce truth to the feeling of illumination. I will argue that, while readers should keep a critical distance from the insularity and high-handedness of Heidegger's manner of thinking and speaking, we should also be wary of limiting discourse to what can be justified

[4] Jaspers is responding, in this letter, to a previous letter from Heidegger in which he uses this terminology; see H:J 203.

before the tribunal of a "reason" that, precisely in its pragmatic and communicative deployment, insists on agreement within the terms of what is generally held to be true at the time, ruling out speech that seeks to challenge the justice of those terms themselves. Although it errs in its own ways, Heidegger's alleged "irrationalism" is legitimately suspicious of such demands for immediate clarity and justification. His own more inventive and unruly way of proceeding, which indeed blurs, though without effacing, the distinction between philosophy and poetry, carries risks and uncertainties but also harbors the possibility of formulating new responses to new problems, which the established language of a publicly accountable reason cannot anticipate in advance. This way of proceeding is grounded, moreover, in a recognition of the temporality of being and the finitude of human understanding that are, on Heidegger's (reasonable) analysis, the truth about how things are. His struggles to sketch a way of thinking and acting that would accord with this truth do not constitute "relativism," understood as a despairing renunciation of the possibility of any right knowing. Instead, they seek a middle way between such a nihilistic abandonment of truth, on the one hand, and, on the other, insistence on grasping the ultimate truth about all things, once and for all, through a method that pretends to establish a permanent foundation for certainty.

Heidegger's Critique of Modern Reason

At a philosophical level, Heidegger's critique of modernity, targeting what Heidegger sees as the central metaphysical presuppositions of the age, is a "critique" in the Kantian sense of an analysis that seeks to understand the fundamental nature of something, thereby also determining its proper applications and its limits. That was the aim of the inquiry into reason undertaken by Kant in his *Critique of Pure Reason*, and it is also the aim of Heidegger's account of modern reason, so central to his critical evaluation of modernity as a whole. Heidegger sees the elements of modernity he confronts in his writings as historically and culturally specific, belonging to a positive picture of the world and of ourselves that emerges at a certain juncture in Western history. He also thinks that this picture has come to assume a universality and global truth to which it is not entitled.

Thus, Heidegger espouses what Charles Taylor describes as a "cultural" view of modernity, according to which modernity involves the rise of a "new culture … with its own specific understandings of, for example, person, nature, and the good" (Taylor 1999, 153). Taylor distinguishes this kind of theory from the "acultural" view, which understands modernity as a culture-neutral development. On an acultural view, "we moderns behave as we do because we have 'come to see' that certain claims were false – or, on the negative reading, because we have lost sight of certain perennial truths" (Taylor 1999,

157). A paradigm case of such a theory, Taylor suggests, "would be one that conceives of modernity as the growth of reason, defined in various ways: for example, as the growth of scientific consciousness, or the development of a secular outlook, or the rise of instrumental rationality, or an ever-clearer distinction between fact-finding and evaluation" (Taylor 1999, 154). Heidegger does view modernity as "the growth of reason," however, defined in exactly the ways Taylor lists here. Only, he interprets this "reason" as itself a culturally specific phenomenon, with some legitimate claims to truth but also some that are vastly overextended, and others that rest on doubtful presuppositions. Like Taylor himself, Heidegger tries in his writings to identify what he sees as the basic concepts and metaphysical theses underlying the modern world-picture – its views about humanity and reality, and about knowledge, truth, and goodness – as well as to trace the historical development of these ideas. He also offers reflections that serve to undermine the legitimacy of the modernist premises he examines. At first glance, these reflections may not look like traditional philosophical arguments. But they *are* arguments, based on a blend of phenomenological observation and critical analysis that does not eschew "reasoning," interpreted as thinking in accord with evidence, broadly understood, and willingness to be corrected.

Consider Heidegger's critique of subjectivism, the view of the relation between humanity and being that he sees as defining the metaphysics of the modern Western world. Subjectivism involves the supposition that the human subject is the measure of a reality to which it opposes itself, and which it constitutes as an objective field to be known. Increasingly, in the modern age, that objective field is constructed as material to be ordered and reordered in the service of technological projects. Heidegger uses the term "enframing" (*Gestell*) to describe this way of approaching reality, and the term "standing-reserve" or "stock" (*Bestand*) to describe reality as encountered through this mode. We can see in these terms, and in the basic structure of analysis supporting them, a historicized adaptation of a central element within Husserlian phenomenology: the idea that there are different kinds of intentional states or ways of being directed toward things, correlated with different kinds of intentional objects.

Husserl's own technical terms for these – *noeses* for intentional states, and *noemata* for intentional objects, both located within the space of "pure consciousness" – reflect his primary orientation toward forms of *knowing*. In *Being and Time*, Heidegger adopts from Husserl the idea of intentional states constituting their objects but rejects the assumption that "knowing" forms either our primary mode of engaging with the world or our initial means of coming to understand it. He also rejects the "bracketing" of external existence and reduction to "pure consciousness" essential to phenomenological method as Husserl developed it, seeing this move as untrue to Husserl's own best insight about intentionality as already involving a directedness toward *things*, within the world (where else would things be?). Accordingly, the revisions to phenomenological method in *Being and Time* result in an analysis of Dasein as being already in the world and directed toward innerworldly entities rather than mental objects. Intentionality is retained but now consists of ways of being toward what there is within the world, correlated with different ways that entities within the world may be encountered or discovered. Heidegger's analysis also emphasizes that human beings are not primarily theoretical observers but engaged agents, discovering the world through pragmatic activity and other forms of caring for their own existence.

Heidegger's later works can no longer be described strictly as phenomenological because they are based on increasing recognition that the "matters themselves," to which phenomenology seeks to return in its analyses, are presented to us historically. Yet Heidegger's method in his later works still includes elements of phenomenology and radicalizes his revisions to phenomenological method in *Being and Time*. His move away from what he saw as the subjectivism of Husserlian phenomenology is now confirmed and developed further, but Husserl's thesis of a correlation between *noeses* and *noemata* is revised in light of a clearer understanding of the historical "relativity" of our views of ourselves and reality, in a sense that does not abolish truth. Heidegger's thesis in his later works is that different aspects of being are revealed (and they are truly *revealed*) to different, historically constituted ways of being on the part of what Heidegger had earlier called Dasein, and now refers to more simply as humanity.

Thus, the later works employ a historicized analogue to the structure and method of analysis Heidegger had developed earlier. In *Being and Time*, Heidegger begins with the question of the meaning of being *tout court*, takes the being of Dasein as the preeminent topic of investigation, and turns to examine not consciousness but the things within the world that Dasein encounters in the first instance and for the most part: equipment or tools. The nature of these entities is analyzed to reveal something fundamental about the being of Dasein, who can encounter equipment only through a projection of ends. In later works, such as "The Question Concerning Technology," the question is about the meaning of being in the *modern* age; the entity to be analyzed is *modern* man; and the focus is on the things the *modern* way of being encounters within the correspondingly modern world: the objects of technology. These objects in turn reveal the fundamental nature of human existence in the modern world. The essence of reality and the essence of humanity are still determined correlatively, but now in a process of "epochal" disclosure. In the modern epoch, humanity has become the subject, the center of all relations, to whom being as a totality is delivered over as something to be mastered, controlled, and harnessed to increasingly large-scale projects of engineering, both of material and social reality. A particular approach to the world is at play here, Heidegger suggests, where we position ourselves in a certain manner toward the being of beings, which correspondingly shows up for us as standing-reserve or resource, a field for ordering, classification, management, and manipulation. This is modern calculative reason, and if Heidegger's critique of it were only directed toward its objectifying and instrumentalizing approach to reality, Habermas and Jaspers would be right to complain that it only touches on one aspect of the specifically modern idea of reason.

But there is more to Heidegger's dismantling of the basic assumptions upon which the modern Western world-picture is based than a critique of instrumental rationality. That dismantling has two interrelated dimensions, a historical and a conceptual one. Heidegger engages, on the one hand, in a kind of historical deconstruction of the modern view of the relation between humanity and being by tracing the path through which it emerged and pointing to alternative conceptions in the distant past, particularly among ancient Greek thinkers. In so doing, he seeks to dissolve the self-evidence this view has come to acquire and open up the possibility of thinking otherwise. This allows him to challenge modern Western suppositions about the naiveté of earlier understandings of being, including those that did not distinguish between the "is" and the "ought." At the same time, Heidegger offers some more straightforward arguments, drawing on phenomenological observation, against the subject-object picture and the relations of separation and dominance it implies.

With respect to the historical trajectory through which subjectivism emerges, the story Heidegger tells often names Descartes as a seminal figure, signaling an important turn. With Descartes, Heidegger proposes, the subject first becomes the ground of knowledge and the foundation of certainty. Indeed, it is at this juncture that humanity first *becomes* a "subject," meaning, Heidegger says in "The Age of the World-Picture": "Man becomes the being upon which all that is, is grounded as regards the manner of its being and its truth ... Man becomes the relational center of that which is as such" (QCT 128/GA 5, 88). Correspondingly, within this conception, the world becomes for the first time an "object," divided into regions constituted as subjects of knowledge for the various natural and human sciences. Only at this point can it properly be said that we have a "world-view," a picture of the world, because only in thinking of ourselves as subjects over against the world as object do we project the latter as something from which we stand at a distance, of which we form a "picture."

Given the nature of Heidegger's descriptions of the subjectivist paradigm, both early and late, it is clear that a confrontation with Kant also played an important role in the development of his critique. Heidegger tends not to offer extended and explicit criticisms of Kant on this score, preferring, in such works as *Kant and the Problem of Metaphysics* (Heidegger1997; first published1929), to interpret Kant as an ontologist rather than a thinker who ushered in full-blown subjectivism. But as early as *Being and Time*, Heidegger had challenged on phenomenological grounds the idea that the world we encounter consists of phenomena understood as *mere* appearances, and thus as possibly false or illusory, and this criticism is tacitly oriented toward Kant's distinction between phenomena and noumena (see BT 27–31). Although *Being and Time* looks for the organizing principles of the world we encounter and locates them in the projecting activity of human existence, it does not interpret this existence in terms of a subject separated from and imposing its own structures upon the world. It also directly challenges philosophical skepticism, and the idea that, for all we know, the character of *all* that appears to us may be a product of subjective projection and so not "true."

From the perspective of the modern paradigm Heidegger is criticizing, it might seem natural to see in his later works a premodern mythological and anthropomorphizing thinking that we have surpassed, but, as I have pointed out, Heidegger's reflections ask us to consider what would justify such an objection. Is there not something odd in thinking of ourselves as radically separated from the nature that gives rise to us? This conception of ourselves does not even accord best with a rigorous naturalism, and a *truly* rigorous naturalism would have to be premised on a broad enough conception of nature to include all the kinds of being that we encounter. It would have to be able, for instance, to accommodate teleology, intentionality, awareness, and agency – the whole host of phenomena that continue to trouble contemporary philosophers of mind. We are a long way from that, and it is Heidegger's contention that the mathematical projection of nature upon which modern natural science, and particularly physics, rests cannot possibly do the job.

This does not amount to a wholesale rejection of scientific method, as Habermas seems to think, nor is it an abandonment of "objectivity" within its appropriate sphere. At a certain point in its analysis (¶69), *Being and Time* provides a phenomenological description of how the objects of science come to be constituted. This is, on Heidegger's account, a process whereby the world we encounter through our everyday concerns and projects is emptied of significance, flattened out, in a way, to become a collection of mere things, objects present before us. These, "the aggregate of the present-at-hand," are then divided into various regions, which are in turn investigated by the different sciences, employing concepts appropriate to the kind of being these entities manifest. In scientific investigation, we do not understand things on the basis of a projection of practical ends, as tools suitable to accomplish this or that goal, as we do in our everyday being in the world. Science still involves projection, but of a different kind. The condition for the possibility of the emergence of the kinds of objects studied by the natural sciences, Heidegger says, is the mathematical projection of nature. "Only 'in the light' of a Nature which has been projected in this fashion can anything like a 'fact' be found and set up for an experiment regulated and delimited in terms of this projection" (BT 362). Entities are always, for Heidegger, discovered through a prior projection of their being, through some set of concepts or some understanding that anticipates what is to be encountered. Science projects, "frees," or illumines the being or character of what-is in a particular manner. And natural science, with the model being physics, does so by projecting in advance a mathematical conception of "nature," involving one among many possible ways of revealing the "being of beings," the nature, in a broader sense, of things, in the broadest sense of whatever is in any way.

After *Being and Time*, Heidegger increasingly examines "projections" historically rather than phenomenologically and comes to see modern science as involving not only mathematization, which was known to the Greeks, but a specific conception of the field of nature, inaugurated by Newton and Galileo. Galileo, Heidegger maintains in his 1933/34 lecture course, *Being and Truth*, "first laid down what *should belong to the essence of nature*, in that he approached it as *the spatiotemporal totality of the motion of mass-points*" (BTr 126/GA 36/37/, 162). This is a "*reaching ahead* into actuality" prior to experimentation and mathematics (BTr 126/GA 36/37, 162). Considerably later, in "Modern Science, Metaphysics, and Mathematics," Heidegger traces the shift from the Aristotelian conception of nature to the modern one projected by Galileo and Newton, describing the latter as follows:

> All bodies are alike. No motion is special. Every place is like every other, each moment like any other. Every force becomes determinable only by the change of motion which it causes – this change in motion being understood as a change of place. All determinations of bodies have one basic blueprint, according to which the natural process is nothing but the space-time determination of the motion of points of mass. (BW 291/GA 41, 92)

Heidegger thinks that this projection of nature – which is not a view from nowhere but is grounded in a thematization of present-at-hand objects and their motions – is not suited to capture every dimension of being. Above all, it cannot properly describe the spatiality and temporality of Dasein's own being-in-the-world. There is no implication that the modern scientific way of constituting the being of beings is *per se* a falsification, however, as long as it is not overextended to cover regions of being to which it is inappropriate.

Heidegger's analysis of projection is indebted to Kant, but because he rejects Kant's distinction between phenomena and noumena, his account does not assume that the projections on the basis of which entities are understood in one way or another are merely subjective, nor does he relegate the entities thereby constituted to the realm of phenomena bearing we know not what relation to things in themselves. Rather, *Being and Time* consistently uses, in relation to various forms of human understanding (including scientific understanding), language suggesting illumination, uncovering, discovering, and revealing. The implicit critique in *Being and Time* of the projection of the being of beings proper to physics in particular does not seek to undermine the legitimacy and claims to truth within this province of knowledge, but only to provide an analysis setting those claims and the methodology by which they are derived within what Heidegger believes are their proper limits. On Heidegger's analysis, the mathematical projection of nature, in its specifically modern variation, involves a particular way of disclosing what things are. There is no warrant for the supposition that the projection of nature forming the foundation of modern science is privileged in capturing the whole truth about what-is, such that every other interpretation must either be reducible to its terms or be considered merely subjective, and therefore not really real. Heidegger's point, then, concerns the metaphysics of modern natural science, not the truth, in an ordinary sense, of well-founded scientific claims, which he does not dispute.

This point, first raised in *Being and Time*, forms the main theme of later essays, such as "The Question Concerning Technology" and "Science and Reflection," which argue that modern science is based on a certain decision about the being of beings, a theory of the real, if you like, that decides in advance what will count as real on the basis of specific criteria. Those criteria are embedded in the idea of nature as a "calculable coherence of forces" (QCT 21), and what is real is taken to be what can be mathematically described in terms of this model. In "Science and Reflection," Heidegger writes:

> An oft-cited statement of Max Planck reads: "That is real which can be measured." This means that the decision about what may pass in science, in this case in physics, for assured knowledge rests with the measurability supplied in the objectness of nature and, in keeping with that measurability, in the possibilities inherent in the measuring procedure. (QCT 169/GA 7, 52)

Heidegger connects this reliance on measurability with the achievement of certainty and control. His account of technicity suggests that the aims guiding its projection of nature – calculation, control, and management, grounded in the desire to secure our own existence – are implicit within the cognitive values of modern science and play a foundational role in determining its methodology as well as the nature of its objects. "Technicity," in that case, is not merely applied science but the essence of modern science, and in a way prior to it.

This is an instrumentalist notion of science, although not of a crude sort. Heidegger is not claiming that modern scientific research aims primarily at the production of useful technologies, but that an orientation toward control, prediction, and certainty always determines what it counts as real and true. Joseph Rouse and Cathryn Carson raise some fair objections against this claim, which is rooted in a Baconian view of scientific aspirations and a Newtonian conception of the objects of science, both of which have been at least partially superseded within modern physics.[5] What remains relevant in Heidegger's critique, though, is the fundamental metaphysical question he poses about why the specific forms of experimentation that modern science involves, and, crucially, why measurability in the precise quantitative language of mathematics, should provide the exclusive criteria for admission into being.

On this point, Heidegger's analysis is in important respects continuous with Husserl's critique of "naturalism" and "objectivism" as providing the framework for all knowledge, although he is very far from sharing Husserl's view that philosophy should be a "rigorous science" in some other sense.[6] Thomas Nenon offers the following summary of Husserl's critique of "naturalistic objectivism":

> [Husserl] notes that the successes of modern natural science have led many to assume that "to be true" means "to be objectively true" and that the language and methods of natural science provide the standard for objectivity. Following this assumption, all there is, is a nexus of temporally and spatially located causally determined objects whose properties are just those measured by natural science. Hence everything there is, is measurable and whatever is not measurable, does not exist. Correspondingly, all real truths can be reduced to the truths of natural science expressed in the language of mathematics. This specific form of naturalism, taken to its furthest extreme, Husserl calls 'objectivism.' (Nenon 2008, 66)

Heidegger's analysis leads one to ask whether any noncircular argument can be given for the claim that the real is *only* what can be measured, or that being is exclusively what can be represented as object. He accepts that we can obtain a particular kind of understanding, what we have come to think of purely as "knowledge," only through such representation and through the methodology of science. But this is virtually a tautological claim. Only through the methods

[5] Rouse criticizes "Heidegger's rendition of the history of modern science as a relentless expansion of calculative control," presenting examples of shifts in scientific research that do not seem to fit Heidegger's account. "Far from invariably seeking greater mastery," Rouse notes, such shifts may *sacrifice* calculative precision and laboratory control to advance different concerns" (Rouse 2007, 186). Cathryn Carson makes a similar point, drawing attention to the consensus among modern German intellectuals that modern science is "instrumental at its core," where:

> That character is supposed to be anchored in its nomological orientation, its experimental method, and its unreflexive constitution of nature as object. Then lawful regularity obtained through scientific investigation opens the door to prediction – and thus to control. In this view, instrumentality is simply in the nature of science: the 'I' of its investigator, the subject facing its objects is intrinsically in search of mastery over its world. (Carson 2010, 484)

Carson argues that Heidegger's commitment to this questionable instrumentalist view of modern science is reflected in his exchanges with Heisenberg. For example, Heidegger "persisted in asserting, against Heisenberg's explications, that modern physics traced space-time trajectories of material bodies ... Then causal accounting was still supposed to make objects calculable and governable, no less when absolute was weakened to statistical causality" (Carson 2010, 495).

[6] See "Philosophy as a Rigorous Science" and "Philosophy and the Crisis of European Man" in Husserl 1965.

and concepts of science can we, for instance, perform repeatable experiments under controlled conditions and obtain precise mathematical results, which sometimes enable us to re-order and re-organize the objective world through technology. Heidegger denies, however, that forms of disclosure, ways of experiencing the world, which do not enable us to do precisely that, or do not enable us to represent as an object what we have experienced, are necessarily false or subjective and so merely apparent as opposed to true. Again, his analysis raises the question of what argument can be given in favor of this view that does not already presuppose what it needs to demonstrate.

In relation to technicity, I have already outlined how Heidegger, adapting Husserl's idea of a correlation between intentional acts of consciousness and their objects, argues for a similar correlation between different ways of being toward what-is and different ways in which it discloses itself to us. Technicity comports itself toward nature in the mode of enframing, disclosing it as standing-reserve, and Heidegger often describes this relation in terms suggesting violence. Nature is here challenged and set upon: "Everywhere everything is ordered to stand by, to be on call for a further ordering" (QCT 17/GA 7, 17). The deeper epistemological and metaphysical point is that we have come to assume, without good grounds, that this is what nature is, what being "is," full stop.[7] And at the same time we have come to assume that what *we* are, in our essence, is the being who is capable of such measuring calculation, that this is what defines us as human and gives us our pre-eminence. Heidegger contends that this definition of ourselves determines how we understand rationality. That the human being, *anthropos*, is the "rational animal" now means that it is the animal capable of bringing reality to a stand before itself in order to serve its self-projected ends. Nietzsche's thought, in spite of its own questioning of reason, and his metaphysics of becoming, is the culmination of this view of what we are.

Thus, Heidegger is offering a critique not only of instrumental rationality but of a certain conception of ourselves in relation to the really real, a definite metaphysical view of subjects and objects. This critique challenges common-sense, modern dismissals of certain modes of thinking and saying as "mythological," "subjective," "primitive," "anthropothorphic," or at best "merely"

[7] Cf. Kim 2005:

> Heidegger's critique of the essence of modern technology and science rests upon his view that the world need not appear to us as real and true only by being brought to a standstill. *Gestell* reflects a metaphysical commitment to being-as-presence, either theoretically as *vorhanden* or technologically as *zuhanden*. (211)

Heidegger connects the desire for security with this quest to bring reality to a "standstill" by representing it as present before us. However, the relation between the later analysis of technology, and the categories of being *vorhanden* or *zuhanden* in *Being and Time* is complex, as argued in Chapter 4. In *Being and Time*, *Zuhandenheit* is not a variety of "being-as-presence," but is constituted through an orientation toward the *future*, through purposive projects in light of which entities are grasped as ready-to-hand.

poetic, premodern, and by that fact alone not "rational," or "objective." It does not move, moreover, within the philosophical discourse of modernity, which demands that speech about moral and political matters be ordered in terms of the needs and priorities of human subjects, while the truth about objects is given by science. Instead, Heidegger subjects that very discourse to critical scrutiny, seeking to expose its assumptions as possessing only a limited validity that comes to be overextended within a particular phase of Western history.

The Concept of Truth as Disclosure

Tugendhat complains that Heidegger's definition of truth as unconcealment in *Being and Time* ends up reducing truth to the immediacy of the given, because it fails to differentiate adequately between the mere unconcealment of an entity and the unconcealment of it as it is *in itself*. Through this equation of truth with disclosedness, Tugendhat contends, the specific meaning of truth in opposition to falsity is lost (Tugendhat 1967, 329).[8] In the later works, Heidegger conceives of truth as unhiddenness, and Tugendhat acknowledges that truth is not then simply equated with what is immediately open, since the truth relation involves a questioning beyond the open into the hidden (Tugendhat 1967, 395). But, according to Tugendhat, this only deepens the problem, because such questioning does not mean a critical surpassing of what is immediately open toward another, truer view. It means only a recognition of the hidden that preserves it in its hiddenness, as what Heidegger names "the mystery" (Tugendhat 1967, 397). On the basis of such concepts of truth, it cannot be properly distinguished from its opposites, from falsity, error, disguise, and appearance.

In fact, however, Heidegger never equates truth with the immediately given, not even in *Being and Time*. He does claim there that the disclosedness of being-in-the-world (which includes entities uncovered within the world) reaches "the primordial phenomenon of truth" (BT 221), but he means only that the disclosedness of the world, presupposed with the very being of Dasein, is the "origin" of truth as correspondence, in the sense that a proposition can only be judged as "true" or adequate to the way entities are if those entities are already apparent to us in some fashion. As Wrathall says, for Heidegger, "propositional truth … is grounded in the truth of entities, because a true assertion can only correspond or fail to correspond with the way things are if entities are available as the standard against which the assertion or proposition can be measured" (Wrathall 2011, 13). Truth, in the sense of correspondence with the way things are, is therefore dependent upon a more basic "clearing" within which entities are discovered and become accessible. Dasein is itself this clearing, so it has an inescapable relation to truth. Yet truth is not immediately given; it must be

[8] A summary of Tugendhat's critique, translated into English, can be found in Tugendhat 1993.

wrested from entities and defended against semblance and disguise, a process involving struggle (BT 222–23). Heidegger's point is that this struggle takes place, and can only take place, on a foundation already presupposing the simultaneous and equally basic disclosedness of Dasein and the world.

Tugendhat claims that this is not what "truth" means, and that to identify truth with disclosure is to lose the critical and normative implications of the term, essential to its sense. William Smith argues that explaining Heidegger's understanding of disclosure as prior to correctness does not answer this part of Tugendhat's objection, which asks by what right one can call such disclosure "truth" (Smith 2007). That is what primarily worries Tugendhat, because he thinks that by dropping the "in itself," Heidegger in effect reduces truth to appearance, letting drop the crucial component of truth as *adequacy* to the way things are. Heidegger later acknowledges himself that there was something misleading in his use of the term "truth" to name the primordial openness of the world, on the basis of which we can pick out entities and make judgments about them (BW 447/GA 14, 87). That in relating to truth we attempt to formulate *adequate* accounts of the way things are was always, however, a feature of Heidegger's understanding of truth. *Being and Time* itself seeks to give appropriate descriptions of the genuine being of phenomena, understood as entities in their self-showing (and we have no other mode of access to them), criticizing what Heidegger sees as the obfuscations and falsifications of mistaken interpretations within the tradition he inherits. Our ordinary understanding of truth as adequacy to the being of things is not undermined by this analysis, which also preserves the possibility that our assertions may be contradicted by the presentation of contrary evidence, including statements demonstrating that things are not as we say they are.

The reason *Being and Time* drops the "in itself" when speaking of truth, I believe, is that this mimetic idea of correspondence is only phenomenologically appropriate to the objects of knowledge, to propositions about entities discovered as present-at-hand, and fails to capture dimensions of truth central to Heidegger's account of Dasein. One of these is the association of truth with a *manner* of appropriating a content, harking back to Kierkegaard's notion of truth as subjectivity (see *Concluding Unscientific Postscript*, Kierkegaard 1941, 178, 181–82). Truth is also, for Heidegger, linked to a way of being, such that, when "falling," Dasein is in "untruth." When it is in that way, Dasein's engagement with entities is uprooted in such a manner that it does not genuinely appropriate what has already been uncovered (BT 222). As I suspect most academics in the humanities (and surely in philosophy) know, one can talk, assert, even argue, while having little or no relation to what is being talked about, to the "matters themselves" truly at stake in the talk. Genuine discourse can become mere empty talk, a juggling of signifiers with no referent in sight. One can also "know" certain facts about one's own existence: that all human beings are mortal, for example, and that they are free and responsible. And yet, one can live in denial of these facts, fleeing into the illusion that there will always be time, avoiding any deep responsibility for shaping the course of one's life through immersion, instead, in daily preoccupations and superficial socializing. The definition of truth as correspondence, or as unconcealing the way things are "in themselves," cannot make sense of these kinds of untruth, which, Heidegger's analysis suggests, are the kinds that matter when it is a question of the "truth of existence" (BT 221). They certainly matter to the "ought" of existence, both practical and moral. Dasein can be more or less transparent to itself, more or less clear about the truth of its condition, and this transparency or lack thereof affects its thinking and acting (cf. Duits 2007). In this sphere of truth, the objective content of my assertions may be correct (e.g. "all men are mortal"), but if that content has not been deeply grasped (Kierkegaard would say "become inward"), then I am not "in the truth."

Furthermore, as I sought to demonstrate in Chapter 4, Heidegger's analysis of "values" suggests that the mimetic conception of truth as correspondence with objects cannot generate a coherent account of normative claims, those that relate in some manner to an idea of the good. We do not formulate, comprehend, or criticize such claims by comparing them with the "in itself" of "ideal objects," nor can any sense be made of the existence of such objects. If comprehending the form of the good is understood as accordance with such an object, then this is a bad picture, and insistence on maintaining it will not yield the "objective" truth on questions of what ought to be done. Nor can rightness on such questions be guaranteed by insistence on a single principle to which we could appeal with certainty, as to the fundamental axioms of mathematics, if such a procedure is alien to the sphere of existence in which we try to determine what is wrong and what needs to be done. In these respects, Heidegger is a critic of Platonism regarding the good. What he retrieves from Plato's account, though, is an analysis of being according to which the truth of entities, in their appearance to us, is a function of our projection of the good, where we are related to being in such a way that this projection is nothing merely "subjective" but a form of unconcealing – precisely, of truth.

The unconcealing is, for Heidegger, historical and finite, a revision of the tradition that will seem strange and unsettling to those who rely on the foundationalist pictures Heidegger seeks to dismantle, and who cannot imagine any alternative to these pictures besides "relativism" or "anarchy." I have tried to show in the preceding chapters, however, that Heidegger's criticisms of approaches he sees as phenomenologically inapt, untrue to the character of being and being human, do not prevent him from struggling to uncover and articulate the truth about the being of beings – of humans, animals, society, nature, and art, for instance – and to be guided by that truth in acting. At the same time, Heidegger advocates a stance that holds itself open for discovering the limitations of a given view, even the view that human beings are ends in themselves, in response to new disclosures and unanticipated forms of distress. This is a Hegelian conception of historical change insofar as it roots the possibility of transformation in the power of the negative; that is, in the perception of distress and the simultaneously responsive and creative envisioning of what is needed to heal the distress.

But it is decidedly un-Hegelian in its view of the place of "reason." Heidegger's conception of truth allows for forms of disclosure other than propositions, such as affects and works of art, within a history of being that never surpasses the need for such disclosure in the establishment of a final rational understanding. For Heidegger, affective response and artistic creativity play an essential role in identifying what is wrong and what is needed at a given time, and can lay the basis for radical critique. In *Being and Time*, the "clearing" of Dasein is constituted by emotion and mood, along with understanding, and affects are not "inner" psychic occurrences. They are linked to the world and help to disclose how things are in that world. Fear, for example, discloses something as a threat to Dasein and in so doing has a relation to truth. There is also in *Being and Time* the special mood of *Angst*, which is supposed to reveal Dasein's being to itself in a preeminent way, bringing it before the truth of its mortality, freedom, and responsibility. Some years later, in "The Origin of the Work of Art," Heidegger will locate the essence of the work of art not in "aesthetic" properties but in its also being a mode of revealing truth. The peasant shoes in van Gogh's painting reveal the truth of the peasant's world in its relation to the earth. The ancient Greek temple reveals the world of this people as it intersects with the natural elements of their environment. These works reveal truth not by corresponding to anything but by establishing and presenting what is essential to those who are in the world at a specific place and time. Thus, art is not necessarily mimetic and yet can be "true." While these are examples of works that establish and lay open the world of a people's concerns and ideals, Heidegger often suggests as well that poetic works may register dissatisfaction, distress, and loss, hinting at what is needed for wholesome change in a manner that challenges convention. These kinds of works are not "rational" but neither are they merely subjective or arbitrary. Rather, their disclosive potential lies in their following the measure of being in a manner that follows no preestablished rules, but nonetheless has its own rigor.

Those who connect Heidegger's moral and political flaws with irrationalism might well be suspicious of this attribution of disclosive power to affects and art. It would be easy enough to point to similar sensibilities at work in Nazi anti-intellectualism and glorification of "life," or to Nazi propaganda strategies employing stirring symbols and grand displays to heighten emotion and override sober reflection. Heidegger's notebooks reveal how critical he was, though, of such glorifications of the "irrational" in his contemporary context. In one place, he describes the rush toward the "counter-rational" as a *Versumpfung* – literally, "swampification" – of philosophy which, for all its pretensions of "closeness to life," and "depth," is in fact merely reactive, the flip side of the modern worldview rather than an overcoming of it (GA 95, 60). The rejection of intellect is, Heidegger thinks, part of the contemporary idle talk that supposes there is no longer any need for thinking: "One says, National Socialism is made not through thoughts but through deeds; granted – does it follow that now thinking should be disparaged and held suspect – or does the opposite follow, that therefore thinking must first be heightened to an unaccustomed greatness and certainty?" (GA 94, 188). For this to happen, it must be possible to *question*, the task of philosophy.

Because questioning is essential to philosophy, Heidegger writes, there can in principle be no such thing as a "National Socialist philosophy," for the same reason that there can be no such thing as a "Catholic philosophy" (GA 94, 509). To say that a "philosophy" is "National Socialist" or not is as meaningful as describing a triangle as courageous or cowardly (GA 94, 348).[9] In fact, the lack of questioning is more extreme under National Socialism than within Christian-Catholic apologetics, Heidegger maintains. He gives as an example the current "nonsense about 'decision'," which he describes as "the echo of the *equally* superficial 'National Socialist philosophy' that, with the help of tarted up ways of talking and slogans, pretends to have overcome 'Christianity' and allegedly undertakes 'decisions' after it has first offered for these a 'sacrifice of thinking' in comparison with which the 'thinking' of a Catholic vicar could still be called freedom of spirit" (GA 95, 338). This is not thinking. It is dogmatism, and like every dogmatism it regards all challengers as enemies, "be that heathens or the godless or Jews and communists" (GA 95, 324).

Thus, Heidegger's various critiques of "reason" do not mean that instead he endorses either unquestioning obedience or unthinking enthusiasm. His criticisms of "ratio" have a specific target. "Reason" is in any case not a magic word whose mere utterance grants protection from error and injustice. Racism, colonialism, and the subordination of women have all found their rational defenders, and philosophers have done their share in contributing to injustice in the name of the progress of reason and the civilization that allegedly exemplifies it. Emotions, moreover, can register aspects of a situation that cool calculation on its own may too easily allow a person to ignore. Hannah Arendt remarks, in *Eichmann in Jerusalem*, that for Nazi leaders training their subordinates to carry out mass murder, "the problem was how to overcome not so

[9] Cf. Richard Polt: "If critical reflection is lacking neither an individual person nor the people as a whole can truly *be*. In order to be someone, one must pose to oneself the question of who one is" (Polt 2009, 160). In the notebooks, Heidegger suggests that if the German seeks his goal, he has already found it, for it lies in *seeking*, itself (GA 94, 345).

much their conscience as the animal pity by which all normal men are affected in the presence of physical suffering" (Arendt 2006, 106). The choice of the descriptor "animal pity" reflects Arendt's own views about moral judgment, but drawing on Heidegger's general analysis of affect, it would be equally possible to speak instead of sympathetic imagination, which can inform and shape conscience, even if Heidegger does not himself pay attention to this particular phenomenon. And Heidegger's accounts of art and poetry suggest that, while aesthetic forms can be used to falsify and distort, they can also reveal ideals, as well as the distance of actuality from them, speaking truth in especially powerful ways. In short, dismissing all non-propositional forms of thought and expression as hostile to a "reason" whose moral excellence is beyond doubt is a highly questionable move.[10]

The most important element in the critique of Heidegger on truth advanced by Tugendhat, however, is not that it expands truth beyond propositions, but that Heidegger's understanding of truth as unconcealing results in a relativistic historicism. In *Being and Time*, all understanding requires interpretation, and interpretation proceeds through a fore-structure shaped by preconceptions inherited from one's tradition. The basis of truth as correspondence seems to become, in this context, the historically constituted horizon against which entities are understood and judgments made about them. Tugendhat complains that, in that case, one cannot criticize the horizon itself. As William Smith notes:

> While Tugendhat allows that the question of whether a world-horizon as such is 'true' is a meaningful – and even desirable – question, it is precisely this question that Heidegger makes untenable by equating 'truth' with the disclosedness of every world horizon ... What is troubling for Tugendhat is that this disclosure retains the name 'truth', yet has no obvious recourse to a critical norm that determines the success and failure of this disclosure. (Smith 2007, 162)

I have already demonstrated that Heidegger decidedly does not maintain that no criticism can be made of the basic concepts of an age. He would be involved in an egregious self-contradiction if he did, since his own critiques of subjectivism and technicity have as their target precisely the basic understanding of humanity and being that dominates in his own age. It is just that these critiques also do not aim to establish a single correct view of ourselves and of what-is as a whole, a finally complete theory, whether in the sphere of science or politics,

[10] Wolin's one-sided characterization of all "postmodern" philosophy as seduced by "unreason" and therefore inclined to fascism is a case in point. Wolin mentions Foucault's misguided support for Iran's Islamic Revolution (Wolin 2004, 6), but he never asks himself what the Nazis would have done with someone like Foucault and what that tells us about them, and him. Nor does he bother with troubling questions about the dark side of the Enlightenment raised by critics like Adorno and Dussel (see Dallmayr 2004) or consider the monstrosity of the "cunning of reason" as articulated within Hegel's philosophy of history, whose course looks suspiciously like the triumph of Western man (white and male) over all the rest.

whose basic terms would not be subject to revision. An important element in Heidegger's understanding of the relation between humanity and being is the acceptance that we cannot have such a view, because human understanding is intrinsically finite and subject to error, and because the process of history can be captured by no logic that could anticipate its end. His conception of the simultaneity of truth and error, and of concealment and unconcealment, is connected with this position on the finitude of human understanding and the unforeseeability of the shapes of future being in the world, but in conjunction with the interpretation of understanding as a site of disclosure rather than as a subjectivization of a reality to which it never has true access.

This understanding of finitude underlies Heidegger's criticisms of the history of metaphysics as a whole, in its quest for absolute knowledge, as well as his objections to particular metaphysical moves, such as the equation of true being with substantiality, or its reduction to what is calculable within the language of mathematics, or the attempt to capture it in a single name, such as "subject," "spirit," or "will to power." Heidegger deliberately offers no such name himself. While he has critical and insightful things to say on metaphysical topics, he offers no solution to the puzzle of how all the disparate and seemingly contradictory regions of being we encounter – particular and universal, matter and mind, freedom and causation, mechanism and teleology – fit together within some overarching theory of the real. Nor is any such overarching theory required for us to engage in conversational practices, including confrontational ones, that aim at discovering the truth. Recognizing finitude and historicality, while recognizing at the same time the special relationship to being that makes humanity what it is, means giving up metaphysics in one sense as the quest to secure the final truth about a stable reality. But it also affirms a metaphysics in another sense, for it takes up a realist position on the relation between humanity and truth.

In Heidegger's later works, the claim is that man is indeed the measure of all things,[11] not because human subjects impose their designs on the world but because they are *not* "subjects." They are sites at which nature breaks through in the form of an understanding of being. It does so over the course of human history by realizing different possibilities of human existence, all of which in their partiality conceal at the same time as they reveal the world. This conception of the simultaneity of truth and error in history underwrites Heidegger's critique of science and technology as reflecting how we are, and what we take ourselves and the world to be, in the modern age. The problem is not the existence of science and technology, nor even their means of securing truth and wellness within their limited spheres. The problem is a metaphysical picture

[11] See Heidegger's reading of Protagoras's famous saying in "The Age of the World Picture," QCT 143–47/GA5, 102–6.

insisting on defining all truth and purpose in terms of these modern aspects of Western culture. There are parallels here between Hegel and Heidegger in their conceptions of history, but whereas Hegel tells the story of the progress of reason, Heidegger tells the story of its exhaustion. For both, the climax involves a realization in which finite forms of human existence are explicitly related to a source that enables them and offers an inexhaustible wealth of possibility. For Hegel, at least on one common reading, the end of the story, determining the meaning of the entire narrative, is a seeing clearly in which all obscurity is overcome and freedom coincides perfectly with necessity. For Heidegger, on the other hand, the end is an understanding and acceptance of *always* seeing through a glass darkly and, as a consequence, always having to make decisions in the half-light of uncertainty. Releasement, *Gelassenheit*, is Heidegger's suggestion for a way of being, a mood and a comportment, appropriate to this situation. It requires giving up the quest for absolute certainty in a manner that is not nihilism but a path out of nihilism. It involves a vision in which humanity is essentially related to being and therefore to truth, but never possesses the whole of it without remainder, and errs in presuming otherwise.

Heidegger's later thought offers a critique of the "history of being" through which we come to conceive ourselves as subjects imposing the products of our own thought, feeling, and will upon a reality whose "in itself" is totally beyond us. It seeks to overcome both this subjectivism and the claims to perfect objectivity on the part of the metaphysics of natural science, which, in its extreme form, would eliminate most of the world in which we live and dwell by denying it admission into true being.[12]

Yet the telling of this history does also reflect a tendency, perhaps typical of a certain stripe of philosopher, to believe the narrator possesses some special insight into the essential truth lying behind the appearances, the really real as opposed to the merely superficial. For all his focus on concrete being-in-the-world in *Being and Time*, Heidegger's writings during the Nazi period are curiously removed from the reality of what is happening around him, as his notebooks demonstrate. Apart from a brief period of enthusiasm in the months immediately preceding and during his Rectorate, the entries are decidedly critical of the times and of the actual ideology of Nazism, but they are critical in a strange way. They do not target the straightforward violence against individuals that this ideology served to legitimate – discrimination, persecution, confinement, murder. Such events seem to be, in Heidegger's mind, symptoms of the *real* malady, the forgetting of being that defines the destiny of the West.

[12] See *What is Called Thinking?* WCT 41–44/WhD, 16–18.

Zaborowsky states the matter well:

> … through engagement with the question of Heidegger's relation to National Socialism we see again how, in spite of his hermeneutic starting point in questions of concrete life – concrete politics or concrete history – Heidegger did not belong to the most sensitive of contemporaries. Too important to him was the ontological-philosophical perspective, too quickly did he accept that perspective, for him to engage in detail with the lowly marshes of concrete life: The question of being which had occupied him since his philosophical beginnings and his struggle against the forgetting of being led Heidegger to another forgetting. For he often did not pose other questions at all, or at least not in an appropriate manner: the question about what-is in its concreteness, about the human being in his concrete mortality, about the happening of "real history" or about events in the political realm and their moral evaluation. (Zaborowsky 2009, 266–67)

Some notebook entries dating from 1938–39 exemplify this other forgetting. Heidegger complains at this critical historical juncture that the mutually destructive friction and hostility between states and peoples indicates "that genuine battles (*Kämpfe*) over beyng (*Seyn*) are increasingly disappearing as possibilities, and that offenses among entities alone have the upper hand and claim for themselves the right to define the essence of 'battle' " (GA 95, 39). On "decision" (*Entscheidung*), no doubt a pressing issue for many Germans at the brink of a literal war, he writes: "Now the de-cision that faces us is not the will of a generation against that of a former one, nor the "spirit" of a century against one that is passing away, nor the essence of an age against a coming one, nor 2000 years of occidental history against a foreign one, but the decision between the all too familiar and mastered *entities* and the hiddenness of *beyng*" (GA 95, 117). Regarding political options in this historical situation, Heidegger's judgment is: "If now occasionally the second world war comes into our sights, then it seems as if once again the authentic decision could not be calculated; for it does not read: war or peace, democracy or authority, Bolshevism or Christian culture – but rather: *reflection* and the search for the initiating appropriation through beyng, or the madness of a final humanization (*Vermenschung*) of an uprooted humanity" (GA 95, 192).

Although much has been made about Heidegger's remarks on Jews and Judaism in his published notebooks, it is, as Karsten Harries observes, more disturbing that he mentions Jews so rarely (Harries 2016, 210), in several lengthy volumes of reflection from years during which the persecution of Jews in his homeland could not have escaped his notice or anyone else's (even supposing it to be true, as he claimed, that he and others did not know the worst of it).[13] Instead of registering the horror of lives shattered by inhumanity, the

[13] Heidegger claimed in a letter to Marcuse that "the bloody terror of the Nazis in point of fact had been kept a secret from the German people" (translated in *The Heidegger Controversy*, Wolin 1993, 163).

notebooks, like other works during the 1930s, such as the *Contributions to Philosophy*, position these phenomena as a kind of shadow play, pointing to but also disguising what is truly happening. This aspect of Heidegger's style of thinking is linked to a peculiar way of negotiating the relation between the realm of ideas and the actual world. Arendt alludes to it in comparing Heidegger's misguided political ambitions with Plato's failed attempt to guide the tyrant of Syracuse. Aristotle, Arendt notes, had the latter example in mind when advising philosophers against dreaming of philosopher kings ruling the realm of pragmatic human affairs (Murray 1978, 301) (though Arendt does not mention as equally troubling Aristotle's tutorship of Alexander, which involved giving lessons to an imperialist on the superiority of his own people over the barbarians he allegedly had the right conquer). The "escape from reality" visible in Heidegger's basing his view of National Socialism on ideas culled from literary sources rather than the horrors that were actually taking place around him is reprehensible, Arendt thinks (Murray 1978, 302), but fortunately Heidegger did learn quickly from his mistake and drew back into his proper residence "to settle in his thinking what he had experienced" (Murray 1978, 303).[14]

Arendt is all too right about Heidegger's distance from actuality, and the resulting failure of his thinking in relation to real politics. And although Heidegger retreated from direct political involvement after 1934, this feature of the manner of thinking that led to his support for Nazism is still present in his later philosophy of history and critical reflections on the modern age. It is not best described as *detached* from reality, since Heidegger's thinking is, for most of his philosophical career, a reflection *on* what is actually happening. But analyses seeking to understand his thought entirely or mainly through proximate context and contemporary interlocutors also seem to be missing something,[15] for Heidegger's reflections on what is actually happening involve a sustained dialogue with the philosophical tradition he inherits and an application of that tradition to understand events whose truth is veiled. There is here a kind of Platonic Hegelianism that continues to look for the surfacing of the idea in the destined coming to presence of what-is. In a way, Heidegger remains too much a philosopher of a traditional sort in his attempts to discern the overarching pattern of history, the "big picture" in which there is a single drama taking place on a grand stage with nations and epochs as the actors. His own task in relation to this drama becomes that of understanding where the story is going and where we stand in relation to it – "we" Germans, or "we" in the West.

[14] See Villa 1996 for a fuller account of the relation between Heidegger and Arendt; especially pp. 230–40 on Arendt's assessment of "The Unworldliness of the Philosopher."

[15] The example I have in mind is the account Charles Bambach gives in *Heidegger's Roots* (Bambach 2003).

Heidegger is not the sort of thinker who could have entertained the possibility of there being many overlapping stages, and complex sets of particulars that could be divided into many unities from different points of view. To suggest this does not entail dissolving into a nihilistic meaninglessness, or holding that there are in truth no patterns or units and everything is only multiple and shifting. Nations are real; events follow a course; world-views do exist and change; and the modern age does have a dominant character with some particular features. Heidegger's inclination to situate these insights within the telling of a single grand narrative, however, leads him astray. He does not consider other possible ways of telling the story, from alternative points of view, nor is he adequately aware of the limitations and biases in his own perspective. These are lessons Heidegger could have learned from another Nietzsche, the one he ignores in casting this philosopher exclusively as the culmination of Western metaphysics, whose essential thought is supposed to be found not in the works he actually published during his lifetime but in the set of fragments posthumously compiled as *The Will to Power*. Heidegger might have paid more heed to the Nietzsche who calls for seeing with many eyes and who casts doubt on the human, all-too-human character of the pictures we construct. In spite of Heidegger's emphasis on finitude, this Nietzsche is significantly more alien to him than the one who announces will to power as the essence of being.

Acknowledging this flaw, and it is a serious one, Tugendhat is nonetheless wrong to claim that Heidegger's concept of truth reduces truth to self-certainty. Yes, there is something in Heidegger's moral and intellectual character that inclines him to have more faith in his insights than he ought to have, an unself-reflective spirit as well an undialogical one, as Jaspers complained. Nonetheless, as we have seen, his philosophical position does not rule out the possibility of criticizing the basic framework of an age, as Tugendhat claims, for Heidegger undertakes to do precisely that himself, hoping to prepare the way for a radical revolution in the Western understanding of humanity and being. At the same time, he draws attention to what he takes to be the necessarily situated character of all critique. No one can, on Heidegger's analysis, jump out of the network of inherited suppositions to a pure intuition of the truth. They can only turn toward their sources of dissatisfaction, sometimes first registered in moods and expressed in poetry and art, and in light of these try to imagine a different future by dismantling and creatively adapting the past. To think that this analysis of the conditions of human understanding fosters an uncritical attitude is to confuse different levels of analysis. As a phenomenologist trying to lay bare the structure of understanding, Heidegger points out its situated character, noting that judgments are made on the basis of what is already revealed as that to which they are supposed to "correspond," and that what is revealed is necessarily historically conditioned. An individual struggling to understand a matter, on the other hand, is of course oriented toward the matter itself, attempting to wrest free the truth about it in light of how it presents itself, in conversation with what has been said and is being said by others. This gives us no sure guidelines for knowing the truth, but that is the wrong thing to demand from a concept of truth. No philosophical analysis of the concept of truth will tell us how it is actually to be discovered in all the domains to which it pertains.

It does follow from Heidegger's account that we are never in a position to know the whole truth and nothing but the truth about being, and he tries to convey this truth about the human condition in his reflections on the nature and flaws of his own age. Heidegger's evaluation of this epoch is certainly blind to many of its positive dimensions, not least to the achievements of its ethics and politics in "freeing" the essence of many groups who were previously dominated by false representations.[16] But aspects of Heidegger's critique of the times, including precisely the ones Habermas sees as mystifying and contrary to the demands of communicative rationality, also identify difficulties that "humanistic" paradigms of thought are unable to capture.

Among these is the analysis of technicity as a form of comportment and a way of constituting the being of beings that blocks access to the dimension of the holy. Charles Taylor notes the link between this element in Heidegger's thought and "deep" ecology, meaning forms of ecological thought and practice that do not accept a purely instrumental conception of man's relation to nature (Taylor 1992). For many who find their lives impoverished by that relation (and not only materially), the problems posed by technology and environmental degradation may not be best framed in terms of a failure to manage nature effectively, or to use our technological tools for good rather than evil, or to factor into our calculations of utility the human need for natural beauty. And the problem with reliance on the justificatory practices of public reason is that they tend to exclude from the conversation discourses that do not easily fit with prevailing suppositions about what it is "reasonable" to say.

The Dark Side of Clarity

For Heidegger, the problem with demands for clarity is that what can be clearly stated at a given time and readily agreed to by a plurality of competent speakers is only what moves within the basic assumptions embedded in a given language. In the age of technicity, those assumptions are "humanistic" ones, involving a specifically modern Western interpretation of Protagoras's saying

[16] Wolin misrepresents Heidegger's position on democracy, however. In the *Der Spiegel* interview, Heidegger does not say, as Wolin maintains, that "whatever the solution is, 'it is not democracy'" (Wolin 1993, 296). He says that he does not know what sort of political system would be appropriate to the technological age, and that he is not convinced it is democracy (Heidegger 1981a, 55).

that man is the "measure of all things." According to this interpretation (which Heidegger claims is actually the reverse of what Protagoras was saying), the values posited by the human will define what is good, and do so in terms of the needs and wants of the human subject. "Nature" is accordingly understood as what opposes this will, needing to be mastered in order to secure the "freedom" of human beings, which is itself interpreted in terms of willing. "Reason" is the means for achieving such mastery.

As Fred Dallmayr points out, this reading of the modern Western picture of self and world, and of the place of reason within this picture, finds a parallel in Adorno's critique of "enlightenment," in spite of Adorno's antipathy toward Heidegger (Dallmayr 2004). An important difference is that Adorno – like Jaspers and, later, Foucault – emphasizes the violence, oppression, and suffering inflicted on human beings by this picture and the drives that propel it, whereas the language of Heidegger's reflections barely registers these realities and even tends to divert attention from them. This is part of the explanation for why critiques of reason, such as the one presented by Adorno and Horkheimer in *The Dialectic of Enlightenment*, do not provoke the same level of suspicion and hostility as Heidegger's does. They nonetheless do make some similar points, and are then equally open to the objection that they construe reason too narrowly, setting aside its positive potential and leaving us, in the end, without a reliable basis for critical reflection.

That is Habermas's criticism of Adorno and Horkheimer (see Hohendahl 1985), and it is continuous with his criticisms of Heidegger's abandonment of reason (although Habermas is much more averse to Heidegger than to members of the Frankfurt School, as is to be expected). The problem, as Habermas sees it, is that without some form of reason to constrain and guide critique, we have no way out of oppression. There is then only the Nietzschean will to overpower, which can perhaps be spotted at work here and there, but without any possibility of being superseded through the establishment of relations that would be free of domination. Habermas offers the ideal of communicative reason as an antidote to this negative postmodern condition, in which reason is endlessly criticized as a mask of ideology but there are no grounds for positive advancement and also no defense against irrationalism.

Jaspers was also concerned about the dangers of irrationalism, and therefore draws a distinction, as Habermas does, between "understanding" (*Verstand*) and "reason" (*Vernunft*). For Jaspers, the calculating planning that belongs to technicity is a function only of the understanding and is to be overcome not through a renunciation of rationality as a whole, but through a turn to a higher, more encompassing, form of it (FM 188). In contrast with Heidegger's claim that technicity is an outcome of Western metaphysics, Jaspers connects reason with the "philosophical thinking that is innate in all men" (FM 188), which can challenge the understanding's pretensions to totality, while guarding against a plunge into irrationality (FM 206). This "new – and age-old – thinking" (FM 2) is not a technique, but "a life-carrying basic mood" (FM 218) that keeps itself open to communication and thus to being tested against what others may have to say, while ensuring that its thinking is upheld by the "earnestness of existential responsibility" (FM 218).[17]

Openness to what others have to say and existential responsibility are laudable virtues that Heidegger would have done well to cultivate better in his own thinking and acting. However, political ideals of rational discourse usually involve more than trying to maintain a mood or an "open" way of being. Habermas's conception of reason in its practical political deployment does not merely endorse respectful listening and speaking. It involves a definite view about what kinds of speech count as rational and what the aims of that speech are supposed to be, placing special constraints on speech admissible within the arena of public political reason (see Sikka 2016). The aim of rational speech, for Habermas, is consensus, arrived at through a process of intersubjective communication in which the winner is supposed to be determined not by power but by "the unforced force of the better argument." Heidegger would object, though, that this argumentative contest is rigged, as from his perspective the terms of debate forming the framework of modern Western liberalism reflect the subjectivistic paradigm he wants to question. The problem is not the general requirement to give reasons of some sort, but the fact that only certain kinds of saying will count as proper reasons within a public forum structured by liberal principles.

Ruled out *a priori* are forms of speech that, for instance, make reference to the holy or sacred, that are poetic, or that are construed as relying on myth. These are some of the "others" against which Western reason has historically distinguished itself, and they remain the others of the form of reason Habermas wants to defend. His complaints about Heidegger's later writings target their mythic and poetic style, and the "neopagan turn" he sees in Heidegger's thought after *Being and Time*. But these elements are essential to Heidegger's critique of (modern Western) reason, because they articulate the alternatives toward which he is trying to gesture. It is, again, not a matter of preferring obscurity over clarity, or poetry over reason, as a general rule. It is that obscure

17 Admittedly there are points at which Jaspers' descriptions of "reason" are broad enough to encompass what Heidegger means by "thinking," but they stretch the meaning of the word so far that one wonders if it is being retained only for its rhetorical force. For example, Jaspers writes that reason "goes beyond the intellect to the source of thinking itself" (FM 217), where that includes not only speculative thought but "may have its full, real force in meditation and natural piety as well" (FM 217). He even claims that the understanding, when confronted by such modes of reason, throws out such "defensive classifications" as "visionary talk," "daydreaming," and "romanticism" (FM 205), classifications reminiscent of his own complaints against Heidegger.

and poetic sayings are required to challenge the dominant presuppositions of the age, which pass themselves off as authoritatively self-evident under the aegis of reason.

A recognition of these points underlies the Heidegger-inspired but still friendly critique of Habermas by Nicholas Kompridis in *Critique and Disclosure: Critical Theory Between Past and Future* (2006). Kompridis suggests that Habermas's critique of Heidegger, "whose apparent cogency owes more to Heidegger's flirtation with Nazism that it does with the content of Heidegger's philosophical views" (199–200), reflects "the ever-reappearing worry that whatever is not rule-conforming or rule-governed (because unfamiliar and uncontrollable) must be inherently unruly; if not irrational, then, definitely nonrational, and, hence, nonmoral" (235). The reason we need, however, to remain open to unfamiliar and therefore seemingly "irrational" ways of thinking and speaking is that "given our permanent dependence on the conditions of intelligibility supplied by our pre-reflective understanding of the world, the reflective disclosure of world presents itself as unending challenge and task, for what is in need of redisclosure cannot be known in advance of the particular historical contexts in which that need arises" (Kompridis 2006, 35).

In other words, no rules or set of procedures can substitute for "need-responsive cultural change and innovation" (Kompridis 2006, 137). The ever-changing context in which we confront the difficulties and crises of our being in the world, criticizing what is wrong and envisioning possible solutions, requires admitting into our reflections "meanings, perspectives, interpretive and evaluative vocabularies, modes of perception, and action possibilities that stand in strikingly dissonant relations to already available meanings and familiar possibilities, to already existing ways of speaking, hearing, seeing, interpreting, and acting" (Kompridis 2006, 104). Such dissonant discourses, precisely because they are innovative, cannot be tested or justified in terms of the settled vocabulary of our current understanding. Because the constraints of Habermas's model of critical theory would in practice limit social and political conversations to discourses that can be thus justified, Kompridis concludes that "it is conservative about possibility" (Kompridis 2006,197).

Maeve Cooke likewise draws on the idea of "world-disclosure" to question Habermas's sharp distinction between religion and reason, arguing that "both philosophical and religious arguments appeal to 'dogmas' in the sense of core convictions, which constitute riverbeds of thought (and experience); these change over time, sometimes almost imperceptibly and sometimes more obviously, due to more or less intentional human intervention" (Cooke 2013, 255). Habermas, Cooke suggests, exhibits an "insufficient appreciation of the ways in which the rational acceptability of practical validity claims *in general* is tied to non-argumentative 'world-disclosure' or 'revelation' " (256), such that coming to accept the validity of a particular perspective or position "may require us to come to see the world in a new way." And "coming to see the world in a new way involves *disclosure*," which "in this sense is not very different from revelation" (257).

Heidegger's appeals to the sacred in such works as "What are Poets for?" are not "religious" on Heidegger's own understanding of the term, which ties religion to "revelation" in a different sense, to faith in what has been revealed and is held to as certain by the believer. For Heidegger, such faith has its own sphere of validity, but it is fundamentally opposed to the spirit of open questioning essential to philosophy.[18] Only, that spirit does not exclude thoughtful meditations on poetry singing of the "default" of God and the loss of the holy. Nor, it seems, does it exclude the use of poetic and even pious language on the part of the philosopher engaging in such meditation, to point, obscurely, toward what he thinks is wrong and what is needed:

> Not only have the gods and the god fled, but the divine radiance has become extinguished in the world's history. The time of the world's night is the destitute time, because it becomes ever more destitute. It has already grown so destitute, it can no longer discern the default of God as a default ... Assuming that a turn still remains open for this destitute time at all, it can come some day only if the world turns about fundamentally – and that now means, unequivocally: if it turns away from the abyss ... The turning of the age does not take place by some new god, or the old one renewed, bursting into the world from ambush at some time or other. Where would he turn on his return if men had not first prepared an abode for him? How could there ever be for the god an abode fit for a god, if a divine radiance did not first begin to shine in everything that is? (PLT 91/GA 5, 269)

These lines from "What are Poets for?" would not, I believe, fit Habermas's conception of rational discourse, and they are typical of the "mystical" and "prophetic" tone that some readers of Heidegger's later works find off-putting. They recall Max Weber's claims about the disenchantment of the world; one might hear in them a nostalgia for childhood fantasies we have outgrown with the progress of knowledge. Heidegger's aim is to challenge the premises on which this genre of judgment would be based, though, and that cannot be done by stating, as a person easily might, that its premises are wrong – that God *does* exist, or that nature is in fact animated by spirits rather than being governed by the laws of physics. Heidegger does not want to say what these opposing propositions, whose meaning could readily be understood, would assert. That is not

[18] Commenting on the fundamental question of metaphysics, Heidegger remarks:

> Anyone for whom the Bible is divine revelation and truth has the answer to the question "Why is there something rather than nothing?' even before it is asked: everything that is, except God himself, has been created by Him. God himself, the increate creator, "is." One who holds to such faith can in a way participate in the asking of our question, but he cannot really question without ceasing to be a believer and taking all the consequences of such a step. (IM 6–7/GA 40, 8–9)

because he seeks to disguise his true intent in order to render it less vulnerable to "rational" objections. It is because the view of ourselves and being to which Western reason adheres in the modern age is one that leaves no space for ideas that neither agree nor disagree with it, for forms of critique that cannot move one way or the other within the confines of its basic assumptions.

Among those assumptions is the view that the truth about "nature" is what can be captured by the methodology of the natural sciences, all other sayings about nature being "merely" poetic or mythical. Another is that human beings either somehow fit entirely within the conception of nature on which these sciences are grounded, or they must stand outside it, positing a "supernatural" source for the faculties allegedly distinguishing them from nature, such as reason and morality. An evaluative judgment, driven by the desire for certainty and security, guides such assumptions, Heidegger's account suggests. It positions the "nature" that resists our understanding and material transformations (what Heidegger calls "earth" in "The Origin of the Work of Art") either as remaining yet in need of penetration by human understanding and labor, or as absurd and hostile if it refuses to yield to its advances. Heidegger reaches for other possibilities, finding resources for thinking differently in a variety of places that will necessarily seem strange to modern Western philosophers: the poetry of Hölderlin, Rilke, and Trakl; the sayings of Anaximander and Parmenides; "mystics" such as Meister Eckhart; and forms of "Eastern" thinking such as Taoism, with its evocation of a mysterious "way" of nature that continually forms and transforms the myriad things. Heidegger engages with these and other unfamiliar sources of thinking in unfamiliar ways, in order to address appropriately what he sees as the distress of the historical moment, while struggling to accomplish the turning required to heal this distress. His understanding of the need and what it requires links his later thought to broader intellectual movements over the last century, to criticisms of the dominating relation to nature that has led to the current environmental crisis, for example, as well as philosophical and theological options seeking ways beyond theism and atheism. It is because Heidegger speaks to the contemporary crises and aporias that have generated these movements that his thought finds resonance among many of their participants.

Heidegger's unruly methodology is also making a deeper point about the nature of reason generally, in relation to modes of thinking and speaking commonly contrasted with it. While he does not collapse the distinction between philosophy, poetry, and art, he does see the rational procedures of philosophy as *always* standing in need of the kinds of disclosure that form the province of these other spheres. Heidegger proposes that poetry and art – and one might add religion, if it is not exhaustively defined by faith as a mode of believing – may also serve the discovery of the true and the good, both negatively and positively. They may register that things are awry and in danger, thereby activating the power of the negative. They may also point to possibilities of healing, through works that gleam with the radiance of the beautiful and the holy. Gleams are only that, and Heidegger does not call for abandoning the struggle to speak the truth of being, which he sees as the task of the thinker rather than the poet. But he does not see the clarity of conceptual thought as ever able to establish a permanent daylight through the discovery of a set of ideas that will need no more radical revision, and therefore no more teaching from less clear modes of disclosure. That applies even to the fundamental concepts of modern Western political philosophy: its views about the status of the human subject in relation to other animate and inanimate beings; its conception of human freedom; and the divide it posits between the secular and the sacred. These ideas are the product of a particular history and culture, reflecting particular decisions in response to particular problems. They are not "just" relative in the sense of being no better or worse than anything else that might be said by anyone anywhere at any time. But they may have their dark sides, appearing over time, and they may also not be well-suited to address the new problems that likewise appear over time. That unsuitability is only to be expected if these ideas were never formulated in response to the problems we come to face, such as the possibility of creating technologies that undermine the natural environment on which we depend, or ones that set up human nature as something to be engineered.

Heidegger's understanding of the historical "relativity" of truth in a certain sense preserves a commitment to formulating an adequate account of how things are, fundamental to the idea of truth as correspondence. However, it simultaneously recognizes that genuine "correspondence" is not merely a reproduction of objects standing before us. Even the natural sciences do not reveal the truth about the entities standing within their provinces through this model of simple mirroring; the model is certainly not appropriate for thinking what needs to be thought within moral and political spheres at a given time and place. Because we are dependent upon language for thinking, new problems require new shapes of language, but we cannot simply hammer these out in view of our goals, as that is not how language works. We have to pay attention to how things stand with being (in the world) and try to speak accordingly. We also have to unearth the experiences and interpretations that lie below the customary meanings of the words we speak. And we have to allow into the conversation traditions of thinking from regions that have for centuries been dismissed as out of order without being given a fair hearing.

Heidegger's peculiar locutions about language itself suggest that, in undertaking all of these tasks, we need to understand as well that the language we inherit is not a tool we can use for whatever we want to think, because it shapes the thinking itself. This implies that the goal of "communication" needs to be approached with a measure of caution. In the third volume of his *Philosophie*, first published in 1932, Jaspers says:

> Communicative expression, as distinct from the mere expression of being, intends to convey something. This sort of expression alone is language in the proper sense of the word, in the sense that allows all other expression to be termed "language" only metaphorically. In this expression lies an intended meaning with transferable contents. (Jaspers 1971, 126)

Presumably, the uncommunicativeness of Heidegger's thought is due, in Jaspers' mind, to the fact that its form of expression cannot be reduced to "language" in this sense. Given that Jaspers agrees with Heidegger that thinking is bound to language, though, how does he think the currently existing "transferable contents" of language can enable us to think differently than we now do, if that is needed? Rejecting Heidegger's notion that modern technology has the character of an attack that must be overcome,[19] Jaspers claims that "fundamentally, the liberation occurs through our becoming aware of our 'thought-techniques' … We must become masters of our thoughts and our thinking" (H:J 184). But how is this supposed to occur, since how we are thinking will surely shape the reflection on how we are thinking?

Heidegger attempts to indicate alternative possibilities by gesturing toward them through his various reflections on language, through etymological investigations, historical deconstructions of meaning, and original poetic inventions and resignifications. The assumption guiding these attempts is that more is required to challenge and limit a predominant totalizing picture of human existence and the world than merely saying there are other possibilities. The latter also have to be *shown*, opened up, and made present against the compelling force and obviousness of the one that holds sway in the present age, laying claim to capture being in all of its dimensions. Heidegger attempts to do just that, through historical deconstructions intended to delimit and thereby relativize the predominant assumptions behind technicity, and through evocative language drawing on unfamiliar sources and demanding an unaccustomed following along in the direction of something that is often only half thought by Heidegger himself. This language does intend and mean, and it reaches for truth, but it remains unclear because it is trying to say something *else*, and on Heidegger's analysis one can only say clearly what has already been said, and said many times.

[19] Cf. Heidegger's response in H:J 187.

Conclusion

I have sought in this book to present and evaluate Heidegger's reflections on a range of interconnected moral and political topics, while making explicit the position on the character of humanity and being, and the relation between the two, underlying these reflections. Because of his emphasis on the temporality of being, which carries the implication that human thinking and acting are always "timely," many readers, both sympathetic and unsympathetic, have concluded that Heidegger is a "postmodern" or "postmetaphysical" thinker. Heidegger does challenge aspects of modernity, centrally its conception of the human subject as the seat of all value. He also does aim to overcome metaphysics understood as the quest to provide a solid and immutable foundation for knowledge. However, I have tried to demonstrate that these features of Heidegger's position are accompanied by a form of realism that contradicts historicism, constructivism, or relativism about either fact or value, a distinction he in any case rejects.

Thus, the interpretation I have offered in this book speaks against such relativist readings of Heidegger as that of Lee Braver, who rejects the claim, advanced critically by Richard Rorty, that Heidegger retains a sense of humility or gratitude toward "something which transcends humanity." It is true, as Braver contends, that being "isn't something beyond us; in fact, it isn't any kind of thing at all," but it does not follow that the phrases to which Rorty alludes only seek to capture "our thrownness into and utter dependence on our particular culture" (Braver 2011, 249). This kind of reading is false to the language Heidegger uses in relation to human understanding, and overlooks a crucial element of his anti-subjectivism. Heidegger always insists that our understanding, when adequate, involves a *disclosure* of being, not a fabrication, and it can do so because we are intrinsically related to being. Consequently, Iain Thomson is closer to the mark in writing that "ontologically, Heidegger is more of a realist than a constructivist; our understanding of the being of entities is something to which we are fundamentally receptive, something … we discover rather than create" (Thomson 2005, 63). Or perhaps it would be better to say that Heidegger's understanding of the relation between "discovery" and "creation" cannot easily be slotted into contemporary epistemological dichotomies. It links him, rather, to some very un-modern ways of understanding our relation to being, while inviting us to rethink assumptions that such ways are primitive, naïve, or sinister.

Currently, philosophical debates about realism and anti-realism have little relevance for morality and politics except where they focus specifically on meta-ethical considerations about the objectivity of values. For Heidegger, though, the division between fact and value, linked to a way of conceiving the distinction between human subjectivity and objective reality, is itself the result of a particular decision about being. Within the modern Western self-conception, this decision is typically seen as having liberated human beings from naively anthropomorphic understandings of nature and their place within it, which in premodern societies were frequently employed as metaphysical or theological justifications for maintaining hierarchical social orders. These justifications, we know, have very often (perhaps always) been a mask for ideologies protecting the interests of the powerful and privileged. We have therefore learned to be wary of appeals to a "natural" order of things to which human societies are supposed to conform, or a god who has in one way or another assigned each individual to a given place. Many of the tropes I have isolated in Heidegger's thought might seem to resurrect such backward ways of thinking, reflecting a reactionary conservatism and hidden theology of which he is sometimes suspected, even though he has also been interpreted as a relativist, postmodernist, and atheist.

The position I have been attributing to Heidegger is neither premodern nor postmodern, but involves a peculiar brand of realism that does in a way affirm a natural order of things, and even suggests taking seriously notions of destiny and of the sacred, but without subscribing to the static ontologies on which such ideas have been grounded in the past. For example, Heidegger analyzes human freedom not as the exercise of individual choice but as the ability to follow a "calling." In *Being and Time*, the destiny or vocation transmitted by this calling is understood in terms of authentic self-realization and respect for others who are likewise called. In the later works, it is a capacity for respecting not only the proper nature of other human beings but of *all* beings, within a well-ordered design that we may help to bring about. These destinies and designs are not determined by a god nor are they a reflection of the status quo, but neither are they invented by human subjects choosing to value this or that. They are, rather, discerned through careful attention to the constantly unfolding character of entities, both those that are like ourselves and those that are not. In the case of human beings, the character in question is historical, and the destined vocation is a matter of finding an appropriate fit between past, present, and future, between what a person concretely is and what she is called upon to be within the historical and cultural definiteness of the situation into which she is thrown. This conception allows for an understanding of "freedom" as response and discovery rather than self-invention, while indicating the imperative to respect the responsible decisions of others regarding their own vocations. The imperative follows, within Heidegger's account, from truly understanding the being of others and holding myself to that truth. It does not require adding a value to a fact, since the true nature of a being cannot be understood in the first place except by reference to the good of its projected future.

It is always we who project that good, in a way. But Heidegger proposes that if we do so by paying self-restrained and conscientious attention to the way beings present themselves to us, rather than by imposing our fixed and self-securing designs upon them, our projections do not distort but help to "free," entities into their essential natures. Thus, Heidegger does not identify discovering the truth with pure receptivity, such that any active projection on the part of human beings would necessarily involve subjectivization. It depends upon the nature of the projection, whether it comes about through an insistence on ordering things to serve one's own ends or whether it is genuinely open to the ends of others.

In Heidegger's later thought, the ends that make up the good for human beings cannot be separated from the establishment of right relations to what is as a whole, where that means giving up the quest for mastery over nature and accepting instead a humble position as the shepherd of being. This is a kind of anti-humanism, and it renounces the centrality of the human subject in two respects. First, it gives up the aim of absolute knowing, which Heidegger sees as an exceedingly unfitting project for a finite being. Second, it lets go of the idea that the human subject is the end of all things, to which whatever is considered as not itself (and that may include even "human nature") is delivered over as stock to be rearranged and utilized. For Heidegger, these two assertions of human subjectivity are related, and they diminish rather than exalt the dignity of humanity. That dignity consists not in being an especially clever animal but in the capacity for a watchful keeping-safe of the being of all things: ourselves, other living beings, even mountains and rivers. Heidegger suggests, too, that this tending of what is as a whole is ultimately essential to human well-being.

On this model, justice means granting to every entity its appropriate place, which requires a self-restrained holding to the truth that, if we are honest, is disclosed to us when we genuinely pay heed to the being of others. Heidegger analyzes the self as capable of such responsibility for and to others, and indicates the possibility of a responsible self being released from the self-securing assertions of its will to become, instead, a sheltering open space. This possibility, as Heidegger envisions it, is not world-renouncing. On the contrary, it establishes the world in which human beings dwell but seeks to do so in a way that saves the earth. With respect to nature, Heidegger understands such saving in terms of harmonious accordance rather than separation. This accordance does not abjure productive transformation but seeks a mode of human production that understands itself as included within the origination of things, rather than being their exclusive source. Human making, interpreted in this manner, is a kind of disclosure. Its essence is especially revealed in art, whose beautiful forms arise from and reflect a struggle with elements that both resist its poetic power and are the necessary condition for its existence, and for human existence as a whole. On Heidegger's approach to them, these elements are mysterious but not therefore hostile, as letting go of the desire for total mastery has the consequence that what is mysterious may evoke awe and wonder rather than anxiety.

The world in which human beings dwell on the earth is, for Heidegger, a shared one but at the same time always local, since the way of being with others that constitutes community takes shape in a particular place over time. Heidegger is a communitarian of sorts, as he underlines the meaningfulness of place and tradition articulated within the shared vocabulary, especially the art and poetry, of a given cultural community. However, his understanding of the temporality of human existence entails that these communities are not to be imagined as static. Like the individual self, their identity does not consist in the constant presentation of a steady collection of traits. Rather, it is an ongoing process of projection and retrieval, through which the being of the "we" is continually reformed. That being is more complex and varied than Heidegger understood, but individuals do situate themselves among its narratives in their conceptions of who they are, a fact of identity deserving recognition.

Finally, Heidegger questions the self-evidence of what are presented as the truths of reason, while questioning also the character of this faculty, which is far from self-evident. On Heidegger's analysis, the being of "reason" is, like the being of all things, historical. The term does not innocently name a universal human capacity, nor is it synonymous with all rigorous thinking that aims for truth, although that is what its usage within Western metaphysics has asserted. Heidegger seeks to deconstruct those assertions by tracing the specific trajectory of reason in the West. In so doing, he offers a history of the present, of the shape of reason that defines Western modernity. This is not an abandonment of truth, but a call for openness to other forms of thinking and speaking, which might reveal new and salutary possibilities for being in the world in response to the lacks we experience at the moment.

I deliberately left the subject of reason for last so that my observations on this point would be illustrated by the preceding chapters. Judging by his own reflections on various themes, Heidegger's recognition of the time-bound character of thinking does not rule out attempts to speak the truth about how things are and how we ought to be if we understand them rightly. It did not lead Heidegger to abandon the effort to produce an adequate ontology of ourselves in our individual and social being, or of other kinds of entities in their relation to us, or of the appropriate ordering of entities that constitutes justice. This ontology not only implicates an ethics but *is* an ethics, for Heidegger's refusal of the distinction between fact and value means that the being of entities is always understood in the light of the good, whose truth we struggle to discern. That the quest for such discernment is an ongoing historical process, that thinking what needs to be thought at the moment requires retrieving the resources of the past while envisioning new possibilities, hardly means that we can no longer reach for the truth of being and hold ourselves and one another accountable in doing so. It does not mean we cannot continue to reason in *this* sense, which does not equate thinking with the goal of producing a final account of a perfected reality, or conceive truth as a mirroring of things as they "are" in themselves. Heidegger is only drawing attention to the dynamic character of being and the finitude of human thinking, and his claims about these fundamental truths are themselves reasonable, in a modest sense of that term.

I have in these concluding remarks highlighted what seems to me best in Heidegger's approach to moral and political topics, but I have also attempted throughout the book to keep a critical distance and not lose sight of Heidegger's shortcomings. These are considerable and should not be minimized, not least because the goal of achieving a proper appreciation of Heidegger's thought is ill-served by apologetics. It is enough if an analysis can demonstrate, as I hope mine has done, that Heidegger at least sometimes managed to think (erringly) what needed to be thought in his times, and that his path of thinking continues to point out directions worth following in ours.

Bibliography

Works by Heidegger

Works in German

1954. *Vorträge und Aufsätze.* Pfullingen: Günther Neske.
1959. *Gelassenheit.* Pfullingen: Günther Neske.
1962a. *Die Technik und die Kehre.* Pfullingen: Günther Neske.
1962b. *Nachlese zu Heidegger.* Ed. Guido Schneeberger. Bern: Suhr.
1975–. *Gesamtausgabe.* Frankfurt: Klostermann.
1983a. *Technik und Gelassenheit.* Ed. Wolfgang Schirmacher. Freiburg: Alber.
1983b. *Die Selbstbehauptung der deutschen Universität: Das Rektorat 1933/34.* Frankfurt: Klostermann.
1984. *Was heißt Denken?* Tübingen: Max Niemeyer.
1986. *Sein und Zeit.* 17th ed. Tübingen: Max Niemeyer.
1990. *Martin Heidegger/Karl Jaspers: Briefwechsel, 1920–1963.* Ed. Walter Biemel & Hans Saner. Frankfurt: Klostermann.

English Translations

1962c. *Being and Time*, trans. John Macquarrie & Edward Robinson. New York: Harper & Row.
1966. *Discourse on Thinking.* Trans. John M. Anderson & E. Hans Freund. New York: Harper & Row.
1968a. *Existence and Being*, 3rd edition. Contains: "Remembrance of the Poet" and "Hölderlin and the Essence of Poetry," trans. Douglas Scott; "On the Essence of Truth," and "What is Metaphysics?" trans. R. F. C. Hull & Alan Crick. London: Vision Press.
1968b. *What Is Called Thinking?* Trans. J. Glenn Gray. New York: Harper & Row.
1971a. *Poetry, Language, Thought.* Trans. Albert Hofstadter. New York: Harper & Row.
1971b. *On the Way to Language.* Trans. Peter D. Hertz. New York: Harper & Row.
1973. *The End of Philosophy.* Trans. Joan Stambaugh. New York: Harper & Row.
1977. *The Question Concerning Technology and Other Essays.* Trans. William Lovitt. New York: Harper & Row.
1981a. "Only a God Can Save Us." Trans. William Richardson in Sheehan 1981, 45–67.
1981b. "The Pathway." Trans. Thomas O'Meara in Sheehan 1981, 69–94.
1982. *The Basic Problems of Phenomenology*, revised edition. Trans. Albert Hofstadter. Bloomington: Indiana University Press.

1984a. *Metaphysical Foundations of Logic*. Trans. Michael Heim. Bloomington: Indiana University Press.

1984b. *Early Greek Thinking*. Trans. David Farrell Krell. New York: Harper & Row.

1985. *Schelling's Treatise on the Essence of Human Freedom*. Trans. Joan Stambaugh. Athens: Ohio University Press.

1987. *An Introduction to Metaphysics*. Trans. Ralph Mannheim. New Haven: Yale University Press.

1989. *Contributions to Philosophy (Of the Event)*. Trans. Richard Rjcewicz & Daniela Vallega-Neu. Bloomington: Indiana University Press.

1993. *Basic Writings*. Trans. J. Glenn Gray and Frank A. Capuzzi; ed. David Farrell Krell. New York: HarperCollins.

1995. *The Fundamental Concepts of Metaphysics*. Trans. Will McNeill and Nicholas Walker. Bloomington: Indiana University Press.

1996. *Nietzsche: Volumes One and Two*. Trans. David Farrell Krell. New York: Harper & Row.

1997. *Kant and the Problem of Metaphysics*. 5th edition. Trans. Richard Taft. Bloomington: Indiana University Press.

1998. *Pathmarks*. Ed. and trans. William McNeil. Cambridge: Cambridge University Press.

2002a. *The Essence of Human Freedom: An Introduction to Philosophy*. Trans. Ted Sadler. New York: Continuum.

2002b. *The Essence of Truth*. Trans. Ted Sadler. New York: Continuum.

2010. *Being and Truth*. Trans. Gregory Fried & Richard Polt. Bloomington: Indiana University Press.

2013. *Nature, History, State*. Trans. and ed. Gregory Fried & Richard Polt. London: Bloomsbury.

Primary Works by Other Authors

Alcoff, Linda. 1995. "Mestizo Identity." In *American Mixed Race*, trans. Naomi Zack. Lanham, MD: Rowman and Littlefield.

Arendt, Hannah. 1946. "What is Existenz Philosophy?" *Partisan Review*, 13/1, 34–56.

2006. *Eichmann in Jerusalem: A Report on the Banality of Evil*. New York: Penguin.

Banse, Ewald. 1935. "Wirkt die Landschaft auf die Rasse ein?" *Völkischer Beobachter*, November 24.

Bauman, Zygmunt. 1989. *Modernity and the Holocaust*. Cambridge: Polity Press.

Benhabib, Seyla. 2002. *The Claims of Culture: Equality and Diversity in the Global Era*. Princeton, NJ: Princeton University Press.

Brosnan, Sarah F. 2013. "Justice and Fairness-Related Behaviors in Nonhuman Primates," *PNAS*, 110 (Suppl 2), 10416–10423. www.ncbi.nlm.nih.gov/pmc/articles/PMC3690609/. Accessed February 15, 2016.

Bultmann, Rudolf. 1984. *The New Testament and Mythology and Other Basic Writings*. Ed. and trans. Schubert M. Ogden. Philadelphia: Fortress Press.

Cooke, Maeve. 2013. "Violating Neutrality? Religious Validity Claims and Democratic Legitimacy." In *Habermas and Religion*, ed. Craig Calhoun, Eduoardo Mendieta & Jonathan VanAntwerpen. Cambridge, MA: Polity Press. Pp. 249–76.

Donaldson, Sue & Will Kymlicka. 2011. *Zoopolis: A Political Theory of Animal Rights*. Oxford: Oxford University Press.

Douglas-Hamilton, Iain, Shivani Bhalla, George Wittemyer & Fritz Vollrath. 2006. "Behavioural Reactions of Elephants Towards a Dying and Deceased Matriarch," *Applied Animal Behaviour Science*, 100/1–2, 87–102.
Dworkin, Ronald. 2013. *Religion Without God*. Cambridge, MA: Harvard University Press.
Eckhard, Waldtraut. 1941. "Novalis als Urheber der organischen Staatstheorie." *Volk im Werden*, 9/4–5, 100–107.
Eckhart, Meister. 1986. *Meister Eckhart: Teacher and Preacher*. Trans. Frank Tobin. Classics of Western Spirituality. New York: Paulist Press.
Fichte, J. G. 1846. *Reden an die deutsche Nation. Sämmtliche Werke*, ed. I. H. Fichte. Berlin: Veit und Comp.
1847. *The Characteristics of the Present Age*. Trans. William Smith. London: John Chapman.
1970. *Grundlage des Naturrechts nach Principien der Wissenschaftslehre. Gesamtausgabe*, I, Vol. 4. Ed. Reinhard Lauth & Hans Gliwitzky. Stuttgart–Bad Cannstatt: Friedrich Frommann.
1981. *Die Bestimmung Des Menschen. Gesamtausgabe*, I, 6. Ed. Reinhard Lauth & Hans Gliwitzky. Stuttgart–Bad Cannstatt: Friedrich Frommann.
2012. *The Closed Commercial State*. Trans. Anthony Curtis Adler. Albany: SUNY Press.
Fischer, Eugen. 1934. "Rasse und Kultur." *Völkischer Beobachter*, February 23.
Gandhi, Mohandas Karamchand. 2002. *The Essential Gandhi: An Anthology of His Writings on His Life, Work and Ideas*. Ed. Louis Fischer. New York: Vintage Books.
Habermas, Jürgen. 1992. *Postmetaphysical Thinking*. Trans. William Mark Hohengarten. Cambridge, MA: MIT Press.
2002. *On Religion and Rationality: Essays on Reason, God, and Modernity*. Ed. Eduoardo Mendieta. Cambridge, MA: MIT Press.
Hegel, Georg Wilhelm Friedrich. 1956. *The Philosophy of History*. Trans. J. Sibree. New York: Dover.
Herder, J. G. 1989. *Ideen zur Philosophie der Geschichte der Menschheit*. Ed. Martin Bollacher. Frankfurt: Deutscher Klassiker Verlag.
1991. *Briefe zu Beförderung der Humanität. Werke in 10. Bänden*, vol. 10. Frankfurt: Deutscher Klassiker Verlag.
Hösel, Adolf. 1934. "Der romantische Seher." *Völkischer Beobachter*, July 17.
Hume, David. 1882. *The Philosophical Works*, ed. T. H. Green & T. H. Grose, vol. 3 (*Essays, Moral, Political and Literary*). London: Longmans.
Husserl, Edmund. 1965. *Phenomenology and the Crisis of Philosophy*. Trans. Quentin Lauer. New York: Harper & Row.
Jaspers, Karl. 1961. *The Future of Mankind*. Trans. E. B. Ashton. Chicago: University of Chicago Press.
1971. *Philosophy*. Vol. III. Trans. E. B. Ashton. Chicago: University of Chicago Press.
1978. *Notizen zu Martin Heidegger*. Ed. Hans Saner. Munich: R. Pipers & Co.
1986. *Basic Philosophical Writings*. Ed. and trans. Edith Ehrlich, Leonard H. Ehrlich & George B. Pepper. Atlantic Highlands, NJ: Highlands Press.
Kant, Immanuel. 1902–. *Kants Werke*, Akademie Ausgabe. Berlin: Walter de Gruyter.
1983a. *Metaphysical Principles of Virtue*. In Immanuel Kant, *Ethical Philosophy*, trans. James W. Ellington. Indianapolis, IN: Hackett.
1983b. *Perpetual Peace and Other Essays*. Trans. Ted. Humphrey. Indianapolis, IN: Hackett.

1992. *The Conflict of the Faculties.* Trans. Mary J. Gregor. Lincoln: University of Nebraska Press.

1996. *The Metaphysic of Morals.* Trans. Mary J. Gregor. In *Immanuel Kant: Practical Philosophy*. Cambridge: Cambridge University Press. Pp. 363–603

1997. *Critique of Practical Reason.* Trans. Mary Gregor. Cambridge: Cambridge University Press.

1998. *Groundwork of the Metaphysic of Morals.* Trans. Mary Gregor. Cambridge: Cambridge University Press.

Kierkegaard, Søren. 1941. *Concluding Unscientific Postscript.* Trans. F. Swenson & Walter Lowrie. Princeton, NJ: Princeton University Press.

1971. *Either/Or*, Vol. 2. Trans. Walter Lowrie. Princeton, NJ: Princeton University Press.

Kompridis, Nikolas. 1999. "Heidegger's challenge and the Future of Critical Theory." In *Habermas: A Critical Reader*, ed. Peter Dews. Oxford: Blackwell. Pp. 118–52.

2005. "Normativizing Hybridity/Neutralizing Culture." *Political Theory*, 33/3, 318–43.

2006. *Critique and Disclosure: Critical Theory between Past and Future.* Cambridge, MA: MIT Press.

Krieck, Ernst. 1934b. "Das rassisch-völkisch-politische Geschichtsbild," *Volk im Werden*, 2/5, 287–98.

1935. "Ein neues Europa?" *Volk im Werden*, 3/6, 325–31.

Kymlicka, Will. 1995. *Multicultural Citizenship: A Liberal Theory of Minority Rights.* Oxford: Clarendon Press.

Lange, Friedrich. 1934. "Was gehen uns Volksgruppe an?" *Wille und Macht*, 2/20, 8–12.

Levinas, Emmanuel. 1969. *Totality and Infinity.* Trans. Alphonso Lingis. Pitttsburgh: Duquesne University Press.

1987. "Meaning and Sense." In *Collected Philosophical Papers*, trans. Alphonso Lingis. The Hague: Martinus Nijhoff.

1991. *Humanismus des anderen Menschen*, trans. Ludwig Wenzler, *Mit einem Gespräch zwischen Emmanuel Lévinas und Christoph von Wolzogen.* Hamburg: Felix Meiner.

Mackie, J.L. 1977. *Ethics: Inventing Right and Wrong.* New York: Penguin.

McKie, Robin. 2010. "Chimps with Everything: Jane Goodall's 50 Years in the Jungle." *The Observer*, June 27, https://www.theguardian.com/science/2010/jun/27/jane-goodall-chimps-africa-interview. Accessed February 15, 2016.

Mill, John Stuart. 1984. "A Few Words on Non-Intervention" (1859). *The Collected Works of John Stuart Mill, v. 21: Essays on Law, Equality and Education*, ed. John M. Robson. New York: Routledge.

"Mirror Test." *Wikipedia: The Free Encyclopedia.* Wikimedia Foundation, Inc. https://en.wikipedia.org/wiki/Mirror_test. Accessed February 12, 2016.

Modood, Tariq. 1997. "Difference,' Cultural Racism and Anti-Racism." In *Debating Cultural Hybridity: Multicultural Identities and the Politics of Anti-Racism*, ed. Pnina Werbner & Tariq Modood. London: Zed Books.

Müller, Adam. 1922. *Die Elemente der Staatskunst.* 2 vols. Ed. J. Baxa. Jena: Gustav Fischer.

"Nationalsozialismus als Grundlage des neuen Deutschen Rechts." 1934. *Völkischer Beobachter*, January 26.

Nietzsche, Friedrich. 1967. *The Will to Power.* Trans. Walter Kaufmann & R. J. Hollingdale. New York: Random House.

1983. *Untimely Meditations.* Trans. R. J. Hollingdale. Cambridge: Cambridge University Press.

1989. *The Genealogy of Morals and Ecce Homo.* Trans. Walter Kaufmann & R. J. Hollingdale. New York: Vintage.

Parekh, Bhikhu. 2006. *Rethinking Multiculturalism: Cultural diversity and Political Theory*, 2nd ed. New York: Palgrave.

Pascal, Blaise. 1958. *Pensées.* Trans. W. F. Trotter. New York: E.P. Dutton & Co.

Pfenning, Andreas. 1940. "Zur Soziologie der Volksidee." *Volk im Werden*, 8/1–2, 22–31.

Pinker, Steven. 1994. *The Language Instinct.* New York: W. Morrow & Co.

Rosenberg, Alfred. 1930. *Der Mythos des 20. Jahrhunderts.* Munich: Hoheneichen.

Ruusbroec, Jan van. 1989. *Boecsken der verclaringhe (Little Book of Enlightenment).* Bilingual edition, ed. J. Alaerts, trans. H. Rolfson. Turnhout: Brepols.

Savage-Rumbaugh, Sue, Stuart Shanker & Talbot J. Taylor. 2001. *Apes, Language, and the Human Mind.* Oxford: Oxford University Press.

Schelling, Friedrich. 1856–1861. *Friedrich Wilhelm Joseph vom Schellings sämmtliche Werke*, ed. K. F. A. Schelling. Stuttgart and Augsburg: J.G. Cotta'scher Verlag.

1860. *Philosophische Untersuchungen über das Wesen der menschlichen Freiheit und die damit zusammenhängenden Gegenstände* (1809). *Schellings sämmtliche Werke*, Vol. 7/1, 331–416.

2006. *Philosophical Investigations into the Essence of Human Freedom.* Trans. Jeff Love & Johannes Schmidt. Albany SUNY Press.

Schleiermacher, Friedrich. 1935. *Patriotische Predigten.* Ed. Walther Schotte. Berlin: Reimar Hobbing Gmbh.

Schmitt, Carl. 1976. *The Concept of the Political.* Trans. George Schwab. New Jersey: Rutgers University Press.

1985. *Political Theology.* Trans. Georg Schwab. Cambridge, MA: MIT Press.

1986. *Political Romanticism.* Trans. Guy Oakes. London: MIT Press.

Shumaker, Robert W, K. R. Walker & B. B. Beck. 2011. *Animal Tool Behavior: The Use and Manufacture of Tools by Animals.* Baltimore: Johns Hopkins University Press.

Sikka, Sonia. 2004. " 'Learning to be Indian': Historical Narratives and the 'Choice' of a Cultural Identity," *Dialogue*, 53, 339–54.

2012a. "In What Sense Are Dalits Black?" In *The Philosophy of Race, Vol IV: Intersections and Positions*, ed. Paul C. Taylor. New York: Routledge. Pp. 253–61.

2012b. "Untouchable Cultures: Memory, Power and the Construction of Dalit Selfhood," *Identities*, 19/1, 43–60.

2016. "On Translating Religious Reasons: Rawls, Habermas and the Quest for a Neutral Public Sphere," *Review of Politics*, 78, 91–116.

Singer, Peter. 1975. *Animal Liberation.* New York: Avon Books.

"Der Sinn der Rassegesetzgebung des Dritten Reiches." 1934. *Völkischer Beobachter*, February 17.

Spengler, Oswald. 1919. *Der Untergang des Abendlandes.* 2 vols. Munich: C. H. Bek'sche Verlagsbuchhandlung.

1959. *The Decline of the West*. 2 vols. Trans. Charles Francis Atkinson. London: George Allen & Unwin. Original text: *Der Untergang des Abendlandes* (Munich: D.H. Beck'sche Verlagsbuchhandlung, 1919).

Sprengen, Hans Rolf. 1934. "Landschaft und Volksgemeinschaft." *Volk im Werden* 2/7, 433–34.

Taylor, Charles. 1999. "Two Theories of Modernity." *Public Culture*, 11/1, 153–74.

Tillich, Paul. 1974. *Mysticism and Guilt-Consciousness in Schelling's Philosophical Development*. Trans. Victor Nuovo. London: Associated University Presses.

Wagner, Richard. 1907. *Das Kunstwerk der Zukunft. Gesammelte Schriften und Dichtungen*, Vol. 3. Leipzig: C. I. W. Siegel.

Weber, Max. 1976. *The Protestant Ethic and the Spirit of Capitalism*, 2nd ed., trans. Talcott Parson. London: George Allen and Unwin.

Wong, David. 2006. *Natural Moralities: A Defense of Pluralistic Relativism*. Oxford: Oxford University Press.

Commentaries on Heidegger and Other Authors

Aho, Kevin A. 2007. "Logos and the Poverty of Animals: Rethinking Heidegger's Humanism." *The New Yearbook for Phenomenology and Phenomenological Philosophy*, 7, 1–18.

2009. *Heidegger's Neglect of the Body*. Albany: SUNY Press.

Arendt, Hannah. 1946. "What is Existenz Philosophy?" *Partisan Review*, 18/1, 34–56.

1978 "Martin Heidegger at Eighty." In Murray 1978, 293–303. First published 1971.

Aschheim, Steven E. 1992. *The Nietzsche Legacy in Germany 1890–1990*. Berkeley: University of California Press.

Bambach, Charles. 2003. *Heidegger's Roots: Nietzsche, National Socialism, and the Greeks*. Ithaca, NY: Cornell University Press.

2013. *Thinking the Poetic Measure of Justice*. Albany: SUNY Press.

Barnard, F. M. 2003. *Herder on Nationality, Humanity, and History*. Montreal: McGill-Queen's University Press.

Bäumler, Alfred. 1931. *Nietzsche der Philosoph und Politiker*. Leipzig: Reklam.

Bernasconi, Robert. 1985a. *The Question of Language in Heidegger's History of Being*. Atlantic Highlands, NJ: Humanities Press.

1985b. "The Double Concept of Philosophy and the Place of Ethics in *Being and Time*." *Research in Phenomenology*, 18, 41–57.

1990. "Heidegger's Destruction of *phronesis*." *Southern Journal of Philosophy*, 28/S1, 127–47.

1992. "Who Is My Neighbour? Who Is the Other? Questioning 'The Generosity of Western Thought'." In *Ethics and Responsibility in the Phenomenological Tradition*. Ninth Annual Symposium of the Simon Silverman Phenomenology Center. Pittsburgh, PA: Simon Silverman Phenomenology Center, Duquesne University. Pp. 1–31.

1998. "Hegel at the Court of the Ashanti." In *Hegel after Derrida*, ed. Stuart Barnett. New York: Routledge. Pp. 41–63.

2000. "Heidegger's Alleged Challenge to the Nazi Conceptions of Race." In Faulconer & Wrathall, 50–67.

2001. "Who Invented the Concept of Race? Kant's Role in the Enlightenment Construction of Race." In *Race*, ed. Robert Bernasconi. Malden, MA: Blackwell. Pp. 11–36.

Boer, Karin de. 2000. *Thinking in the Light of Time: Heidegger's Encounter with Hegel.* Albany, NY: SUNY Press.

Borgmann, Albert. 2007. "Technology." In Dreyfus & Wrathall, 420–32.

Bourdieu, Pierre. 1988. *L'ontologie politique de Martin Heidegger*. Paris: Minuit.

1991. *The Political Ontology of Martin Heidegger*. Trans. Peter Collier. Stanford, CA: Stanford University Press.

Braver, Lee. 2007. *A Thing of This World: A History of Continental Anti-Realism.* Evanston, IL: Northwestern University Press.

2014. *Heidegger: Thinking of Being*. Cambridge: Polity Press.

Brogan, Walter. 2005. *Heidegger and Aristotle: The Twofoldness of Being.* Albany: SUNY Press.

Calarco, Matthew. 2008. *The Question of the Animal from Heidegger to Derrida.* New York: Columbia University Press.

Calle-Gruber, Mireille (ed.). 2016. *Heidegger, Philosophy, and Politics: The Heidelberg Conference*. Jacques Derrida, Hans-Georg Gadamer & Philippe Lacoue-Labarthe, trans. Jeff Fort. New York: Fordham University Press.

Carman, Taylor. 2003. *Heidegger's Analytic: Interpretation, Discourse, and Authenticity in Being_and_Time.* Cambridge: Cambridge University Press.

Carson, Cathryn. 2010. "Science as Instrumental Reason: Heidegger, Habermas, Heisenberg." *Continental Philosophy Review*, 42, 48–509.

Cave, George P. 1982. "Animals, Heidegger, and the Right to Life." *Environmental Ethics*, 4, 249–54.

Cooper, John W. 2006. *Panentheism, the Other God of the Philosophers: From Plato to the Present.* Grand Rapids, MI: Baker Academic

Dallmayr, Fred. 1984. "Ontology of Freedom: Heidegger and Political Philosophy." *Political Theory*, 12/2, 204–234.

1994. "Heidegger on Ethics and Justice." In *Transitions in Continental Philosophy*, ed. Arleen B. Dallery & Stephen H. Watson, 189–120. Albany: SUNY Press.

2001. "Heidegger on Macht and Machenschaft." *Continental Philosophy Review*, 34, 247–67.

2004. "The Underside of Modernity: Adorno, Heidegger, and Dussel." *Constellations*, 11/1, 102–120.

Davidson, Arnold. 1989. "Questions Concerning Heidegger: Opening the Debate." *Critical Inquiry*, 15/2, 407–426.

Davis, Thomas. 1992. "Meeting Place." In McWhorter, 77–92.

Denker, Alfred and Zaborowski, Holger. 2009. *Heidegger und der Nationalsozialismus II: Interpretationen*. Freiburg: Karl Alber.

Derrida, Jacques 1987a. *Of Spirit: Heidegger and the Question*, trans. G. Bennington & R. Bowlby. Chicago: University of Chicago Press.

1987b. "*Geschlec*ht II: Heidegger's Hand." In *Deconstruction and Philosophy: The Texts of Jacques Derrida*, ed. John Sallis, 161–196. Chicago: University of Chicago Press.

2008. "The Animal that I Therefore Am." In *The Animal that I Therefore Am*, ed. Marie-Louis Mallet, trans. David Wills, 1–51. New York: Fordham University Press.

Di Cesare, Donatella. 2006. "Heidegger's Metaphysical Anti-Semitism." In Farin & Malpas, 181–94.

Dreyfus, Hubert. 1992. "Heidegger's History of the Being of Equipment." In Dreyfus & Hall 1992, 173–85. Cambridge, MA: MIT Press, 1991.

Dreyfus, Hubert & Hall, Harrison (eds.). 1992. *Heidegger: A Critical Reader*. Oxford: Blackwell.

Dreyfus, Hubert L. & Wrathall, Mark A. (eds.). 2007. *A Companion to Heidegger*. Oxford: Blackwell.

Duff, Alexander. 2015. *Heidegger and Politics: The Ontology of Radical Discontent*. Cambridge: Cambridge University Press.

Duits, Rufus. 2007. "On Tugendhat's Analysis of Heidegger's Concept of Truth." *International Journal of Philosophical Studies*, 15/2, 207–23.

Ehrlich, Leonard. 1994. "Heidegger's Philosophy of Being from the Perspective of His Rectorate." In Olson, 29–48.

Emad, Parvis. 1975. "Heidegger on Schelling's Concept of Freedom." *Man and World*, 8/2, 137–74.

Fagenblatt, Michael. 2016. "'Heidegger' and the Jews." In Farin & Malpas, 145–68.

Farias, Victor. 1987. *Heidegger et le nazisme*. Paris: Verdier. Translated into English as: *Heidegger and Nazism*, ed. Joseph Margolis & Tom Rockmore. Philadelphia: Temple University Press.

1992. "*Foreword to the Spanish Edition, Heidegger and Nazism*." In Rockmore & Margolis, 33–34.

Farin, Ingo. 1998. "Heideger's Critique of Value Philosophy." *Journal of the British Society for Phenomenology*, 29/3, 268–80.

2016. "The *Black Notebooks* in Their Historical and Political Context." In Farin & Malpas, 289–321.

Farin, Ingo & Malpas, Jeff (eds.). 2016. *Reading Heidegger's* Black Notebooks, *1931–1941*. Cambridge, MA: MIT Press.

Faye, Emmanuel. 2005. *Heidegger – l'introduction du nazisme dans la philosophie*. Paris: Albin Michel.

Feenberg, Andrew. 2005. *Heidegger and Marcuse: The Catastrophe and Redemption of History*. New York: Routledge.

Ferry, Luc & Alain Renaut. 1990. *Heidegger and Modernity*. Trans. Franklin Philip. Chicago: University of Chicago Press.

Foltz, Bruce V. 1993. "Heidegger, Ethics, and Animals." *Between the Species*, 9/2, 84–89.

1995. *Inhabiting the Earth: Heidegger, Environmental Ethics, and the Metaphysics of Nature*. Atlantic Highlands, NJ: Humanities Press.

Gadamer, Hans Georg. 1987. *Neuere Philosophie I*. Gesammelte Werke, Vol. 3. Tübingen: Mohr.

1988. "Zurück von Syrakus?" In *Die Heidegger-Kontroverse*, ed. Jürg Altwegg. Frankfurt am Main: Athenäum.

Glendinning, Simon. 1996. "Heidegger and the Question of Animality." *International Journal of Philosophical Studies*, 4, 67–86.

Gonzalez, Francisco. 2009. *Plato and Heidegger: A Question of Dialogue*. University Park: Pennsylvania State University Press.

Guignon, Charles B. (ed.). 2006. *The Cambridge Companion to Heidegger*, 2nd edition. Cambridge: Cambridge University Press.

2011. "Heidegger's Concept of Freedom, 1927–1930." In *Interpreting Heidegger: Critical Essays*, ed. Daniel O. Dahlstrom. Cambridge: Cambridge University Press. Pp. 79–105.

Guyer, Paul. 2000. *Kant on Freedom, Law, and Happiness*. New York: Cambridge University Press.

Habermas, Jürgen. 1993a. "On the Publication of the Lectures of 1935." Trans. William S. Lewis, in Wolin, 186–97.

1993b. *The Philosophical Discourse of Modernity*, trans. Frederick G. Lawrence. Cambridge, MA: MIT Press.

Han-Pile, Béatrice. 2013. "Freedom and the 'Choice to Choose Oneself' in *Being and Time*." In Wrathall, 291–319.

Harries, Karsten. 1978. "*Heidegger as a Political Thinker*." In Murray, 304–28.

2016. "*Nostalgia, Spite and the Truth of Being*." In Farin & Malpas, 207–21.

Härtle, Heinrich. 1937. *Nietzsche und der Nationalsozialismus*. Munich: Zentralverlag der NSDAP.

Hauser, Mark D., Noam Chomsky & W. Tecumseh Fitch. 2002. "The Faculty of Language, What is It, Who Has It, and How Did It Evolve?" *Science*, 298/5598, 1569–79.

Hellmers, Ryan S. 2008. "Reading in *Ereignis*: Schelling's System of Freedom and the *Beiträge*." *Epoché*, 13/1, 133–62.

Hemming, Laurence Paul. 2016. "The Existence of the *Black Notebooks* in the Background." In Farin & Malpas, 109–26.

Hohendahl, Peter U. 1985. "The Dialectic of Enlightenment Revisited: Habermas' Critique of the Frankfurt School." *New German Critique*, 35, 3–26.

Immerwahr, John. 1992. "Hume's Revised Racism." *Journal of the History of Ideas*, 53/3, 481–86.

Jaspers, Karl. 1955. *Schelling: Grösse und Verhängnis*. München: R. Piper & Co.

Jonas, Hans. 1964. "Heidegger and Theology." *Review of Metaphysics*, 18/2, 207–33.

1990. "*Heidegger's Resoluteness and Resolve: An Interview*." In Neske & Kettering, 197–206.

1996. *Mortality and Morality: A Search for the Good after Auschwitz*. Ed. Lawrence Vogel. Evanston, IL: Northwestern University Press, 1996.

Kaßler, Kurt. 1941. *Nietzsche und das Recht*. Munich: Ernst Reinhardt.

Kim, Alan. 2005. "Frameworks and Foundations: Heidegger's Critique of Technology and Natorp's Theory of Science." *Angelaki*, 10/1, 201–18.

Kisiel, Theodore. 1993. *The Genesis of Heidegger's Being and Time*. Berkeley: University of California Press.

2000. "Schelling's Treatise on Freedom and Heidegger's *Sein und Zeit*." In *Schelling: Zwischen Fichte und Hegel*, ed. Christoph Asmuth, Alfred Denker & Michael Vater. Amsterdam/Philadelphia: B.R. Grüner.

Krieck, Ernst. 1934a. "Germanischer Mythos und Heideggersche Philosophie." *Volk im Werden*, 2/5, 247–49.

1934b. "Das rassisch-völkisch-politische Geschichtsbild." *Volk im Werden*, 2/5, 287–98.

Kuperus, Gerard. 1987. "Attunement, Deprivation and Drive: Heidegger on Animality." In *Phenomenology and the Non-Human Animal*, ed. Corinne Painter & Christian Lotz, 13–27. Dordrecht: Springer.

Lacoue-Labarthe, Philippe. 1987. *La fiction du politique: Heidegger, l'art et la politique*. Paris: C. Bourgois. Translated into English as: *Heidegger, Art and Politics*, trans. Chris Turner (Oxford: Basil Blackwell, 1990)

Lagier, Raphael. 2004. *Les races humaines selon Kant*. Paris: Presses Universitaires de France.

Laland, Kevin N. & Bennett G. Galaf. 2009. *The Question of Animal Culture*. Cambridge, MA: Harvard University Press.

Langton, Rae. 1992. "Duty and Desolation." *Philosophy*, 67, 481–505.

Larrimore, Mark. 1999. "Sublime Waste: Kant on the Destiny of the 'Races'." In *Civilization and Oppression*, ed. Catherine Wilson, 99–126. Calgary: University of Calgary Press.

Löwith, Karl. 1984. "Der okkasionelle Dezionismus von Carl Schmitt." In *Heidegger: Denker in dürftiger Zeit*. Stuttgart: J. B. Metzlersche Verlagsbucchandlung. Pp. 32–71.

1986. *Mein Leben in Deutschland vor und nach 1933*. Stuttgart: Metzler.

1988. "My Last Meeting with Heidegger in Rome, 1936." Trans. Richard Wolin. *New German Critique*, 45, 115–116.

1995. *Martin Heidegger and European Nihilism*. Ed. Richard Wolin. Trans. Gary Steiner. New York: Columbia University Press.

Ma, Lin. 2008a. "All the Rest Must be Translated: Lévinas' Notion of Sense." *Journal of Chinese Philosophy*, 35/4, 599–612.

2008b. *Heidegger on East-West Dialogue: Anticipating the Event*. New York: Routledge.

Mack, Michael. 2003. *German Idealism and the Jew: The Inner Anti-Semitism of Philosophy and German Jewish Responses*. Chicago: University of Chicago Press.

Malpas, Jeff. 2012. *Heidegger and the Thinking of Place: Explorations in the Topology of Being*. Cambridge, MA: MIT Press.

Manning, R.J.S. 1993. *Interpreting Otherwise than Heidegger*. Pittsburgh, PA: Duquesne University Press.

Marx, Werner. 1984. *The Philosophy of F.W.J. Schelling*. Trans. Thomas Nenon. Bloomington: Indiana University Press.

1987. *Is There a Measure on Earth? Foundations for a Nonmetaphysical Ethics*. Trans. Thomas J. Nenon & Reginald Lilly. Chicago: University of Chicago Press.

May, Reinhard. 1996. *Heidegger's Hidden Sources: East Asian Influences on His Work*. Trans. Graham Parkes. Honolulu: University of Hawaii Press.

McGettigan, Andrew. 2006. "The Philosopher's Fear of Alterity: Levinas, Europe and Humaities 'without Sacred History.'" *Radical Philosophy*, 140, 15–25.

McWhorter, Ladelle (ed.). 1992. *Heidegger and the Earth: Essays in Environmental Philosophy*. Kirksville, MO: Thomas Jefferson University Press.

McWhorter, Ladelle & Stenstad, Gail (eds.). 2009. *Heidegger and the Earth: Essays in Environmental Philosophy*. Toronto: University of Toronto Press.

Mehta, J.L. 1992. *J. L. Mehta on Heidegger, Hermeneutics and Indian Tradition*. Ed. William J. Jackson. Leiden: E. J. Brill.

Milchman, Alan & Rosenberg, Alan (eds.). 1996. *Martin Heidegger and the Holocaust*. Atlantic Highlands, NJ: Humanities Press.

Müller, Max. 1990. "*Martin Heidegger – A Philosopher and Politics – A Conversation*." In Neske & Kettering 1990, 175–96.

Murray, Michael (ed.). 1978. *Heidegger and Modern Philosophy*. New Haven, CT: Yale University Press.

Nenon, Thomas. 2008. "Confrontations with Modernity." *Indian Council of Philosophical Research*, 25/1, 61–74.

Neske, Günther (ed.). 1977. *Erinnerungen an Martin Heidegger*. Pfullingen: Neske.

Neske, Günther & Kettering, Emil. 1990. *Heidegger and National Socialism*. New York: Paragon House.

Olafson, Frederick. 1998. *Heidegger and the Ground of Ethics: A Study of Mitsein*. Cambridge: Cambridge University Press.

Ott, Hugo. 1987. *Heidegger: Unterwegs zu seiner Biographie*. Frankfurt: Campus Verlag. Translated into English as: *Martin Heidegger: A Political Life*, trans. Allan Blunden (Hammersmith, London: Basic Books, 1993).

Park, Peter. 2013. *Africa, Asia, and the History of Philosophy: Racism in the Formation of the Philosophical Canon, 1780–1830*. Albany: SUNY Press.

Philipse, Herman. 1998. *Heidegger's Philosophy of Being: A Critical Interpretation*. Princeton, NJ: Princeton University Press.

Pöggeler, Otto. 1987. *Martin Heidegger's Path of Thinking*. Trans. Daniel Magurshuk and Sigmund Barber. Atlantic Highlands, NJ: Humanities Press.

1993. "Hölderlin, Schelling und Hegel bei Heidegger." *Hegel-Studien*, 28, 327–72.

Polt, Richard. 2009. "*Jenseits von Kampf und Macht. Heideggers heimlicher Widerstand*." In Denker & Zaborowski 2009, 155–186.

Raffoul, François & David Pettigrew (eds.). 2002. *Heidegger and Practical Philosophy*. Albany: SUNY Press.

Rathje, Arthur. 1934. "Nietzsche und das neue Werden." *Völkischer Beobachter*, January 22.

Richardson, John. 2012. *Heidegger*. New York: Routledge.

Richardson, William J. 1974. *Heidegger: Through Phenomenology to Thought*. Preface by Martin Heidegger. The Hague: Martinus Nijhoff.

Rockmore, Tom. 1992. *On Heidegger's Nazism and Philosophy*. Berkeley: University of California Press.

Rockmore, Tom & Margolis, Joseph. 1992. *The Heidegger Case*. Philadelphia: Temple University Press.

Rouse, Joseph. 2007. "*Heidegger's Philosophy of Science*." In Dreyfus & Wrathall 2007, 173–89.

Safranski, Rüdiger. 1998. *Martin Heidegger: Between Good and Evil*. Cambridge, MA: Harvard University Press.

Schalow, Frank. 1986. *Imagination and Existence: Heidegger's Retrieval of the Kantian Ethic*. Lanham, MD: University Press of America.

1992. *The Renewal of the Heidegger-Kant Dialogue: Action, Thought, and Responsibility*. Albany: SUNY Press.

2001. "At the Crossroads of Freedom: Ethics Without Values." In *A Companion to Heidegger's Introduction to Metaphysics,"* ed. Richard Polt & Gregory Fried, 250–62. New Haven, CT: Yale University Press.

2013. *Departures: At the Crossroads between Heidegger and Kant*. Berlin: De Gruyter.

Schulz, Walter. 1953/54. "Über den philosophie geschichtlichen Ort Martin Heideggers." *Philosophische Rundschau*, 1, 65–93.

1975. *Die Vollendung des Deutschen Idealismus in der Spätphilosophie Schellings*. First edition 1955. Pfullingen: Neske.

Schuman, Rebecca. 2014. "Heidegger's Hitler Problem Is Worse Than We Thought." *Slate*, March 10. www.slate.com/blogs/browbeat/2014/03/10/heidegger_and_the_nazis_the_black_notebooks_suggest_he_was_anti_semitic.html. Accessed April 11, 2014.

Schürmann, Reiner. 1987. *Heidegger on Being and Acting: From Principles to Anarchy*. Bloomington: Indiana University Press.

Schwann, Alexander. 1989. *Politische Philosophie im Denken Heideggers*. Opladen: Westdeutscher Verlag.

Sheehan, Thomas. 2009. *Heidegger: The Man and the Thinker*. New Brunswick, NJ: Transaction Publishers.

Shell, Susan Meld. 2003. "Kant's 'True Economy of Human Nature': Rousseau, Count Verri, and the Problem of Happiness." In *Essays on Kant's Anthropology*, ed. Brian Jacobs & Patrick Kain. Cambridge: Cambridge University Press. Pp. 194–229.

Sherover, Charles M. 1981. "Founding an Existential Ethic." *Human Studies*, 4, 223–36.

Sikka, Sonia. 1997. *Forms of Transcendence: Heidegger and Medieval Mystical Theology*. Albany: SUNY Press.

1998. "Questioning the Sacred: Heidegger and Levinas on the Locus of Divinity." *Modern Theology*, 14, 299–323.

1999. "How Not to Read the Other: 'All the Rest Can Be Translated'." *Philosophy Today*, 43, 195–206.

2006. "Kantian Ethics in *Being and Time*." *Journal of Philosophical Research*, 31, 309–334.

2011. *Herder on Humanity and Cultural Difference*. Cambridge: Cambridge University Press.

2016. "Heidegger's Argument for the Existence of God?" *Sophia*, doi:10.1007/s11841-015-0510-0.

Sluga, Hans. 1993. *Heidegger's Crisis: Philosophy and Politics in Nazi Germany*. Cambridge, MA: Harvard University Press.

Smith, William. 2007. "Why Tugendhat's Critique of Heidegger's Concept of Truth Remains a Problem." *Inquiry*, 50/2, 156–79.

Steiner, George. 1999. "The Magician in Love." *Times Literary Supplement*, Jan 29, 3–4.

Tanzer, Mark Basil. 2001. "Heidegger on Freedom and Practical Judgment." *Journal of Philosophical Research*, 26, 343–57.

2002. *Heidegger: Decisionism and Quietism*. New York: Humanity Books.

Taylor, Charles. 1992. "*Heidegger, Language, and Ecology*." In Dreyfus & Hall, 247–69.

Thiele, Leslie Paul. 1994. "Heidegger on Freedom: Political not Metaphysical." *American Political Science Review*, 88/2, 278–91.

1995a. *Timely Meditations: Martin Heidegger and Postmodern Politics*. Princeton, NJ: Princeton University Press.

1995b. "Nature and Freedom: A Heideggerian Critique of Biocentric and Sociocentric Environmentalism." *Environmental Ethics*, 17/2, 171–90.

Thomson, Iain. 2005. *Heidegger on Ontotheology: Technology and the Politics of Education*. Cambridge: Cambridge University Press.

2011. *Heidegger, Art and Postmodernity*. Cambridge: Cambridge University Press.

2012. "In the Future Philosophy will be neither Continental nor Analytic but Synthetic: Towards a Promiscuous Miscegenation of (All) Philosophical Traditions and Styles." *Southern Journal of Philosophy*, 50/2, 191–205.

Tillette, Xavier. 1970. *Schelling: une philosophie en devenir*. Paris: Librairie Philosophique J. Vrin.

Tillich, Paul. 1974. *Mysticism and Guilt-Consciousness in Schelling's Philosophical Development*. Trans. Victor Nuovo. London: Associated University Presses.

Trawny, Peter. 2014. *Heidegger und der Mythos der jüdischen Weltverschörung*. Frankfurt: Klostermann.

2016. "*Heidegger and the Shoah*." In Farin & Malpas, 169–80.

Tugendhat, Ernst. 1967. *Der Wahrheitsbegriff bei Husserl und Heidegger*. Berlin: de Gruyter.

1993. "*Heidegger's Idea of Truth*." Trans. Richard Wolin. In Wolin 1993, 245–63.

Van Buren, John. 1994. *The Young Heidegger: Rumor of the Hidden King*. Bloomington: Indiana University Press.

Velkley, Richard L. 2011. *Heidegger, Strauss and the Premises of Philosophy: On Original Forgetting*. Chicago: University of Chicago Press.

Villa, Dana R. 1996. *Arendt and Heidegger: The Fate of the Political*. Princeton, NJ: Princeton University Press.

Vogel, Lawrence. 1994. *The Fragile "We": Ethical Implications of Heidegger's Being and Time*. Evanston, IL: Northwestern University Press.

Wisnewski, Jeremy. 2013. *Heidegger: An Introduction*. Lanham, MD: Rowman and Littlefield.

Wolin, Richard. 1990. *The Politics of Being*. New York: Columbia University Press.

1993. *The Heidegger Controversy: A Critical Reader*. Cambridge, MA: MIT Press.

2001. *Heidegger's Children: Hannah Arendt, Karl Löwith, Hans Jonas, Herbert Marcuse*. Princeton, NJ: Princeton University Press.

2004. *The Seduction of Unreason: The Intellectual Romance with Fascism from Nietzsche to Postmodernism*. Princeton, NJ: Princeton University Press.

Wood, Allen. 1990. *Hegel's Ethical Thought*. Cambridge: Cambridge University Press.

1995. "Humanity as End in Itself." In *Proceedings of the Eighth International Kant Congress*. Milwaukee, WI: Marquette University Press. Pp. 301–22.

Wrathall, Mark A. (ed.). 2011. *Truth, Language, and History*. Cambridge: Cambridge University Press.

(ed.). 2013. *The Cambridge Companion to Heidegger's Being and Time*. Cambridge: Cambridge University Press.

Young, Julian. 1997. *Heidegger, Philosophy, Nazism*. Cambridge: Cambridge University Press.

Zaborowski, Holger. 2009. "War Heidegger ein Antisemit? Zu einer kontroversen Frage." In Denker & Zaborowski, 2009.

2010. *"Eine Frage von Irre und Schuld?" Martin Heidegger und der Nationalsozialismus*. Frankfurt: Fischer.

Zimmerman, Michael E. 1990. *Heidegger's Confrontation with Modernity: Technology, Politics, and Art*. Bloomington: Indiana University Press.

1992. "The Search for a Heideggerian Ethics." In *Ethics and Responsibility in the Phenomenological Tradition*. Ninth Annual Symposium of the Simon Silverman Phenomenology Center. Pittsburgh, PA: Simon Silverman Phenomenology Center, Duquesne University. Pp. 57–90.

Index